Prayer, the concept and the practice, exposes our core doubts and desperation for God. Paul Miller captures the promise of prayer as a gift that connects us to the heart of the Father and as a path for transforming the world. Paul's honest struggle with living a life full of prayer and his childlike delight in hearing the heart of God invite us to gratitude and call us to speak boldly to our God. This book will be like having the breath of God at your back. Let it lift you to new hope.

DAN B. ALLENDER, PhD, author of *Bold Love*

A Praying Life is a deeply moving testimony to God's power in prayer. Paul Miller shares his life and biblical wisdom to instill in us, his readers, a "heart that becomes a factory of prayer"—that is, a passion to speak to God honestly and in a way that will change our life and the lives of others for whom we pray.

TREMPER LONGMAN III, PhD, author of *Reading the Bible with Heart and Mind*

If Jesus or Jesus' saving grace is just an abstraction to you, Paul Miller will be a great help in making his love a living reality to your heart.

TIM KELLER, author of *The Reason for God*

Paul Miller refuses to separate the spiritual life from the rest of our daily living. In *A Praying Life*, he shows the difference that constant communication with Christ makes in the everyday experiences of life, especially the life of the family. Reading this book will help you make prayer a more important part of your own life story by integrating prayer into the daily routines of life.

PHILIP RYKEN, author of *The Message of Salvation*

This is as fine a book on prayer as you will ever read, but it is so much more. It is the story of our struggle to actually live like we believe that our heavenly Father really does love us. If we did, nothing could keep us from being committed to the day-by-day hard work of prayer. Paul Miller exegetes our struggle in a way that is convicting, insight giving, and encouraging. This is a book on prayer that actually makes you want to pray!

PAUL DAVID TRIPP, presiden

In my library, I have perhaps twenty different volumes on prayer, but none captured my heart or propelled me into fresh communion with our Father as much as *A Praying Life*. Finally, a book that applies the radical implications of the gospel of God's grace to prayer! With childlike wonder, sage-like wisdom, and heartfelt candor, Paul shows us that to pray is to see Jesus more clearly and meet him more regularly in every single aspect and moment of the day. Thanks, my friend, for calling me back to what really matters.

SCOTTY SMITH, teacher in residence, West End Community Church

The timely word and work of Paul Miller has had a profound effect on me. Now with *A Praying Life*, here he is with another right-on-time delivery! This book reveals that the secret to a prayerful life is an active understanding of the stories you are living. In every story a prayer; in every prayer a story.

CHARLIE PEACOCK, cofounder, Art House America

Like many Christians, I struggle to maintain a meaningful prayer life. Too often my prayers are hurried, shallow, and perfunctory. In his book *A Praying Life*, Paul Miller has provided an inspirational and helpful resource for all of us who want to pray better. Paul uses compelling stories, solid scriptural support, and insightful spiritual principles to first explain the nature of prayer and then to provide practical suggestions on how to pray. You will enjoy reading this book and then, I think, marvel at how much more meaningful your prayer life can become.

BOB RUSSELL, author of *When God Builds a Church*

Charles Spurgeon wrote, "Prayer does not fit us for the greater works; prayer is the greater work." Paul Miller's superb book calls us back to this "greater work," reminding us of the joy we find in our Lord's presence and equipping us with practical insight on how to recapture the intimacy and power of a praying life.

KEN SANDE, founder, Relational Wisdom 360

A
PRAYING LIFE

CONNECTING WITH GOD IN A DISTRACTING WORLD

Paul E. Miller

A NavPress resource published in alliance
with Tyndale House Publishers

NavPress is the publishing ministry of The Navigators, an international Christian organization and leader in personal spiritual development. NavPress is committed to helping people grow spiritually and enjoy lives of meaning and hope through personal and group resources that are biblically rooted, culturally relevant, and highly practical.

For more information, visit NavPress.com.

A Praying Life: Connecting with God in a Distracting World

Copyright © 2009, 2017 by Paul Miller. All rights reserved.

Previous edition published in 2009 under ISBN 978-1-60006-300-8.

A NavPress resource published in alliance with Tyndale House Publishers

NAVPRESS and the NavPress logo are registered trademarks of NavPress, The Navigators, Colorado Springs, CO. *TYNDALE* is a registered trademark of Tyndale House Publishers. Absence of ® in connection with marks of NavPress or other parties does not indicate an absence of registration of those marks.

The Team:
Don Pape, Publisher
David Zimmerman, Acquisitions Editor
Jeff Miller of Faceout Studio, Cover Designer
Beth Sparkman, Interior Designer

Cover photograph of geometric waves copyright © meow_meow/Shutterstock. All rights reserved.

Some of the anecdotal illustrations in this book are true to life and are included with the permission of the persons involved. All other illustrations are composites of real situations, and any resemblance to people living or dead is purely coincidental.

For information about special discounts for bulk purchases, please contact Tyndale House Publishers at csresponse@tyndale.com or call 1-855-277-9400.

Cataloging-in-Publication Data is available.

ISBN 978-1-63146-683-0

Printed in the United States of America

29 28 27 26 25 24
13 12 11 10   9   8

In memory of Benjamin Edward Miller
—March 10, 2009—
our seventh grandchild and heavenly treasure

A special thank you to
Jane Hebden of Chelten Baptist Church, Dresher, Pennsylvania;
The Huston Foundation;
and our friends at Trinity Presbyterian Church in Lakeland, Florida—
including Ron and Kim Avery, Howard and Deanna Bayless,
Jack and Tina Harrell, Tim and Tina Strawbridge, Jim
and Christy Valenti, and Justin and Jen Wilson—
for helping make this book possible.

Contents

Foreword

IT'S HARD TO PRAY. It's hard enough for many of us to make an honest request to a friend we trust for something we truly need. But when the request gets labeled "praying" and the friend is termed "God," things often get very tangled up. You've heard the contorted syntax, formulaic phrases, meaningless repetition, vague nonrequests, pious tones of voice, and air of confusion. If you talked to your friends and family that way, they'd think you'd lost your mind! But you've probably talked that way to God. You've known people who treat prayer like a rabbit's foot for warding off bad luck and bringing goodies. You've known people who feel guilty because their quantity of prayer fails to meet some presumed standard. Maybe you are one of those people.

Prayer—it tends to become a production and a problem.

Life—it's always a production and a problem. You cycle through your to-do list, your anxieties, distractions, pressures, pleasures, and irritants.

God—he's there, somewhere, sometimes.

Somehow those two problematic productions and the Lord of heaven and earth don't all get on the same page very often.

But prayer isn't meant to be a production or a problem. And God is here, now. Prayer is meant to be the conversation where your life and your God meet. Paul Miller understands that. *A Praying Life* aims to help you join him in living out that understanding.

A praying life is an oddly normal way to live. The best our world has to offer is to teach you how to talk to *yourself*. Change what you tell yourself, and your feelings about what happened will change. Change your self-talk, and how you feel about yourself will change. Talk yourself out of getting upset about what you can't change. Do something constructive about what you can change. Those are the world's best efforts. It's a familiar but abnormal way to live.

But Jesus lives and teaches something different. What he does— and helps you do—is unfamiliar but normal. It's human and it's humane: how life's meant to be. He teaches you how to *stop* talking to yourself. He shows how to *stop* making prayer into a production. Jesus teaches you to start talking to your Father—to "my Father and your Father" (John 20:17), as he put it to Mary from Magdala. He shows you how to start talking with the God who rules the world, who has freely chosen to take your best interests to heart.

Talking life over with this on-scene God is the sort of conversation worth calling "prayer." You find several hundred examples in the Bible, and Paul Miller has listened. The Bible's prayers traffic in both daily life and the real God. They bring real troubles and need to a God who really listens. They never seem like a production. They sound and feel real because they *are* real.

Paul offers you a vision for how a working fellowship with God thinks, talks, feels, and acts. He takes you inside his family life and his prayer life. By seeing how life and God weave together, you'll discover the joy of living as God's child, experiencing the adventure of walking closely with your Father and Good Shepherd.

A Praying Life will bring a living, vibrant reality to your prayers. Take it to heart.

DAVID POWLISON, MDiv, PhD
Author of Speaking Truth in Love

Introduction

I NEVER STARTED OUT to write a book on prayer. I simply discovered that I'd learned how to pray. Life's unexpected turns had created a path in my heart to God; God taught me to pray through suffering.

In the late 1990s a pastor asked me to cover his pulpit for a month during the summer. I agreed, and one afternoon I sketched out what I'd learned about prayer. Those notes became the prayer seminar that my friend Bob Allums and I have now given nearly 150 times. The response to the seminar has been almost electric. It has touched a deep nerve in people's lives.

I thought the seminar was enough, that another book on prayer was unnecessary. Plus, I wasn't sure I had time. But my friend David Powlison and my wife, Jill, urged me to write, and my board chairperson, Lynette Hull, suggested I begin my day by writing. So I wrote. I wrote for Christians, for those struggling to do life, who pray badly yet long to connect with their heavenly Father.

The book opens with a chapter on our frustrations with prayer and another that describes where we're headed. Part 1, "Learning to Pray like a Child," examines the basics of relating to our heavenly Father like a little child. In part 2, "Learning to Trust Again," we go deeper and look at some adult habits that can dull our hearts to prayer and keep us from being drawn into the life of the Father. Part 3, "Learning to Ask Your Father," examines barriers to asking that come from the spirit of our age. Part 4, "Living in Your Father's Story," is where it all comes together. When we have a praying life, we become aware of and enter into the story God is weaving in our lives. The final part, "Praying in Real Life," introduces some simple tools and ways of praying that have helped many people learn to pray. As we look at these tools, we'll continue to learn about our hearts and how God weaves stories in our lives.

That's the skeleton. The meat of the book is the family stories I tell. They are not dramatic; they're nitty-gritty tales of surviving and thriving in a world of stress and disappointment. As you watch us, I hope you experience the presence of Jesus.

The apostle Paul said this about how all true ministry works: "For just as the sufferings of Christ flow over into our lives, so also through Christ our comfort overflows" (2 Corinthians 1:5, NIV). I pray that through this book my relatively light suffering will overflow into your life as comfort, freeing you to touch the heart of God.

CHAPTER I

"WHAT GOOD DOES IT DO?"

I WAS CAMPING for the weekend in the Endless Mountains of Pennsylvania with five of our six kids. My wife, Jill, was home with our eight-year-old daughter, Kim. After a disastrous camping experience the summer before, Jill was happy to stay home. She said she was giving up camping for Lent.

I was walking down from our campsite to our Dodge Caravan when I noticed our fourteen-year-old daughter, Ashley, standing in front of the van, tense and upset. When I asked her what was wrong, she said, "I lost my contact lens. It's gone." I looked down with her at the forest floor, covered with leaves and twigs. There were a million little crevices for the lens to fall into and disappear.

I said, "Ashley, don't move. Let's pray." But before I could pray, she burst into tears. "What good does it do? I've prayed for Kim to speak, and she isn't speaking."

Kim struggles with autism and developmental delay. Because of her weak fine motor skills and problems with motor planning, she is also mute. One day after five years of speech therapy, Kim crawled out of the speech therapist's office, crying from frustration. Jill said, "No more," and we stopped speech therapy.

Prayer was no mere formality for Ashley. She had taken God at his word and asked that he would let Kim speak. But nothing happened. Kim's muteness was testimony to a silent God. Prayer, it seemed, doesn't work.

Few of us have Ashley's courage to articulate the quiet cynicism or spiritual weariness that develops in us when heartfelt prayer goes unanswered. We keep our doubts hidden even from ourselves because we don't want to sound like bad Christians. No reason to add shame to our cynicism. So our hearts shut down.

The glib way people talk about prayer often reinforces our cynicism. We end our conversations with "I'll keep you in my prayers." We have a vocabulary of "prayer speak," including "I'll *lift you up* in prayer" and "I'll *remember* you in prayer." Many who use these phrases, including us, never get around to praying. Why? Because we don't think prayer makes much difference.

Cynicism and glibness are just part of the problem. The most common frustration is the activity of praying itself. We last for about fifteen seconds, and then out of nowhere the day's to-do list pops up and our minds are off on a tangent. We catch ourselves and, by sheer force of the will, go back to praying. Before we know it, it has happened again. Instead of praying, we are doing a confused mix of wandering and worrying. Then the guilt sets in. *Something must be wrong with me. Other Christians don't seem to have this trouble praying.* After five minutes we give up, saying, "I am no good at this. I might as well get some work done."

Something *is* wrong with us. Our natural desire to pray comes from Creation. We are made in the image of God. Our inability to pray comes from the Fall. Evil has marred the image. We want to talk to God but can't. The friction of our desire to pray, combined with our badly damaged prayer antennae, leads to constant frustration. It's as if we've had a stroke.

Complicating this is the enormous confusion about what makes for good prayer. We vaguely sense that we should begin by focusing on God, not on ourselves. So when we start to pray, we try to worship. That works for a minute, but it feels contrived; then guilt sets in again. We wonder, *Did I worship enough? Did I really mean it?*

In a burst of spiritual enthusiasm we put together a prayer list, but praying through the list gets dull, and nothing seems to happen. The list gets long and cumbersome; we lose touch with many of the needs. Praying feels like whistling in the wind. When someone is healed or helped, we wonder if it would have happened anyway. Then we misplace the list.

Praying exposes how self-preoccupied we are and uncovers our doubts. It was easier on our faith *not* to pray. After only a few minutes, our prayer is in shambles. Barely out of the starting gate, we collapse on the sidelines—cynical, guilty, and hopeless.

The Hardest Place in the World to Pray
American culture is probably the hardest place in the world to learn to pray. We are so busy that when we slow down to pray, we find it uncomfortable. We prize accomplishments, production. But prayer is nothing but talking to God. It feels useless, as if we are wasting time. Every bone in our bodies screams, "Get to work."

When we aren't working, we are used to being entertained. Television, the Internet, video games, and cell phones make free time as busy as work. When we do slow down, we slip into a stupor. Exhausted by the pace of life, we veg out in front of a screen or with earplugs.

If we try to be quiet, we are assaulted by what C. S. Lewis called "the Kingdom of Noise."[1] Everywhere we go we hear background noise. If the noise isn't provided for us, we can bring our own via iPod.

Even our church services can have that same restless energy. There is little space to be still before God. We want our money's worth, so something should always be happening. We are uncomfortable with silence.

One of the subtlest hindrances to prayer is probably the most pervasive. In the broader culture and in our churches, we prize intellect, competency, and wealth. Because we can do life without God, praying seems nice but unnecessary. Money can do what prayer does, and it is quicker and less time-consuming. Our trust in ourselves and in our talents makes us structurally independent of God. As a result, exhortations to pray don't stick.

The Oddness of Praying

It's worse if we stop and think about how odd prayer is. When we have a phone conversation, we hear a voice and can respond. When we pray, we are talking to air. Only crazy people talk to themselves. How do we talk with a Spirit, with someone who doesn't speak with an audible voice?

And if we believe that God can talk to us in prayer, how do we distinguish our thoughts from his thoughts? Prayer is confusing. We vaguely know that the Holy Spirit is somehow involved, but we are never sure how or when a spirit will show up or what that even means. Some people seem to have a lot of the Spirit. We don't.

Forget about God for a minute. Where do you fit in? Can you pray for what you want? And what's the point of praying if God already knows what you need? Why bore God? It sounds like nagging. Just thinking about prayer ties us all up in knots.

Has this been your experience? If so, know that you have lots of company. Most Christians feel frustrated when it comes to prayer!

A Visit to a Prayer Therapist

Let's imagine that you see a prayer therapist to get your prayer life straightened out. The therapist says, "Let's begin by looking at your relationship with your heavenly Father. God said, 'I will be a father to you, and you shall be sons and daughters to me' (2 Corinthians 6:18). What does it mean that you are a son or daughter of God?"

You reply that it means you have complete access to your heavenly Father through Jesus. You have true intimacy, based not on how good you are but on the goodness of Jesus. Not only that, Jesus is your brother. You are a fellow heir with him.

The therapist smiles and says, "That is right. You've done a wonderful job of describing the *doctrine* of Sonship. Now tell me what it is like for you to *be with* your Father? What is it like to *talk* with him?"

You cautiously tell the therapist how difficult it is to be in your Father's presence, even for a couple of minutes. Your mind wanders. You aren't sure what to say. You wonder, *Does prayer make any difference? Is God even there?* Then you feel guilty for your doubts and just give up.

> I WONDERED, *DOES PRAYER MAKE ANY DIFFERENCE? IS GOD EVEN THERE?*

Your therapist tells you what you already suspect. "Your relationship with your heavenly Father is dysfunctional. You talk as if you have an intimate relationship, but you don't. Theoretically, it is close. Practically, it is distant. You need help."

Ashley's Contact

I needed help when Ashley burst into tears in front of our minivan. I was frozen, caught between her doubts and my own. I had no idea that she'd been praying for Kim to speak. What made Ashley's tears so disturbing was that she was right. God had not answered her prayers. Kim was still mute. I was fearful for my daughter's faith and for my own. I did not know what to do.

Would I make the problem worse by praying? If we prayed and couldn't find the contact, it would just confirm Ashley's growing unbelief. Already, Jill and I were beginning to lose her heart. Her childhood faith in God was being replaced by faith in boys. Ashley was cute, warm, and outgoing. Jill was having trouble keeping track of

Ashley's boyfriends, so she started naming them like ancient kings. Ashley's first boyfriend was Frank, so his successors became Frank the Second, Frank the Third, and so on. Jill and I needed help.

I had little confidence God would do anything, but I prayed silently, *Father, this would be a really good time to come through. You've got to hear this prayer for the sake of Ashley.* Then I prayed aloud with Ashley, "Father, help us to find this contact."

When I finished, we bent down to look through the dirt and twigs. There, sitting on a leaf, was the missing lens.

Prayer made a difference after all.

WHERE WE ARE HEADED

EVEN IF YOU FEEL that you pray badly, we need to know what good prayer looks and feels like in order to develop a praying life. Knowing where we are headed can help us on the journey. So before we get into the nitty-gritty of how to pray, let's get a clearer picture of what we are aiming for.

The Praying Life . . . Feels like Dinner with Good Friends

The highlight of Kim's week is our Saturday evening meal with Mom-Mom, her grandmother, at a local restaurant. On a hot summer day or a bitter winter day, Kim comes in exhausted from her job as a dog walker at a kennel, but she perks up when she sits down to eat with Mom-Mom. We prop up her speech computer in front of her, and she chats away on her 112-key keyboard. We never get tired of hearing her electronic voice, partly because we're never sure what is going to come out next.

Recently, we were in a restaurant, and Kim ordered lasagna with her speech computer by selecting a three-icon sequence that spoke the word *lasagna*.[1] When the waitress told Kim the lasagna was vegetarian, Kim, not being a fan of vegetables and not liking change of

7

any sort, hit the table with her fist, making the silverware and plates dance. The poor waitress about jumped out of her shoes. When she came back with our food, she circled us cautiously, not sure when she was going to get a repeat performance. Our family will be telling that story for years.

Our best times together as a family are at dinner. At home after a meal, we push our dishes aside and linger together over coffee or hot chocolate. We have no particular agenda; we simply enjoy one another. Listening, talking, and laughing. If you experience the same thing with good friends or with family, you know it is a little touch of heaven.

When Jesus describes the intimacy he wants with us, he talks about joining us for dinner. "Behold, I stand at the door and knock. If anyone hears my voice and opens the door, I will come in to him and eat with him, and he with me" (Revelation 3:20).

A praying life feels like our family mealtimes because prayer is all about relationship. It's intimate and hints at eternity. We don't think about *communication* or *words* but about whom we are talking with. Prayer is simply the medium through which we experience and connect to God.

Oddly enough, many people struggle to learn how to pray because they are focusing on praying, not on God. Making prayer the center is like making *conversation* the center of a family mealtime. In prayer, focusing on the conversation is like trying to drive while looking *at* the windshield instead of *through* it. It freezes us, making us unsure of where to go. Conversation is only the vehicle through which we experience one another. Consequently, prayer is not the center of this book. Getting to know a person, God, is the center.

The Praying Life . . . Is Interconnected with All of Life

Because prayer is all about relationship, we can't work on prayer as an isolated part of life. That would be like going to the gym and working out just your left arm. You'd get a strong left arm, but it would look odd. Many people's frustrations with prayer come from working on prayer as a discipline in the abstract.

We don't learn to pray in isolation from the rest of our lives. For example, the more I love our youngest daughter, Emily, the more I pray for her. The reverse is true as well; the more I learn how to pray for her, the more I love her. Nor is faith isolated from prayer. The more my faith grows, the bolder my prayers get for Jill. Then, the more my prayers for her are answered, the more my faith grows. Likewise, if I suffer, I learn how to pray. As I learn how to pray, I learn how to endure suffering. This intertwining applies to every aspect of the Christian life.

Since a praying life is interconnected with every part of our lives, learning to pray is almost identical to maturing over a lifetime. What does it feel like to grow up? It is a thousand feelings on a thousand different days. That is what learning to pray feels like.

So don't hunt for a feeling in prayer. Deep in our psyches we want an experience with God or an experience in prayer. Once we make that our quest, we lose God. *You don't experience God; you get to know him.* You submit to him. You enjoy him. He is, after all, a person.

Consequently, a praying life isn't something you accomplish in a year. It is a journey of a lifetime. The same is true of learning how to love your spouse or a good friend. You never stop learning this side of heaven. There is far too much depth in people to be able to capture love easily. Likewise, there is far too much depth in God to capture prayer easily.

Things such as *growing up* and *learning to love* do have an overall feel, though. They are slow, steady, filled with ups and downs. Not spectacular but nevertheless real. There is not one magic bullet but a thousand pinpricks that draw us into a spiritual journey or pilgrimage. And every spiritual pilgrimage is a story.

The Praying Life . . . Becomes Aware of the Story

If God is sovereign, then he is in control of all the details of my life. If he is loving, then he is going to be shaping the details of my life for my good. If he is all-wise, then he's not going to do everything I want because I don't know what I need. If he is patient, then he is going to take time to do all this. When we put all these things together—God's sovereignty, love, wisdom, and patience—we have a divine story.

People often talk about prayer as if it is disconnected from what God is doing in their lives. But we are actors in his drama, listening for our lines, quieting our hearts so we can hear the voice of the Playwright.

You can't have a good story without tension and conflict, without things going wrong. Unanswered prayers create some of the tensions in the story God is weaving in our lives. When we realize this, we want to know what God is doing. What pattern is God weaving?

The Praying Life . . . Gives Birth to Hope

If God is composing a story with our lives, then our lives are no longer static. We aren't paralyzed by life; we can hope.

Many Christians give in to a quiet cynicism that leaves us unknowingly paralyzed. We see the world as monolithic, frozen. To ask God for change confronts us with our doubt about whether prayer makes any difference. Is change even possible? Doesn't God control everything? If so, what's the point? Because it is uncomfortable to feel our unbelief, to come face-to-face with our cynicism, we dull our souls with the narcotic of activity.

Many Christians haven't stopped believing in God; we have just become functional deists, living with God at a distance. We view the world as a box with clearly defined edges. But as we learn to pray well, we'll discover that this is my Father's world. Because my Father controls everything, I can ask, and he will listen and act. Since I am his child, change is possible—and hope is born.

The Praying Life . . . Becomes Integrated

Many assume that the spiritual person is unruffled by life, unfazed by pressure. This idea that the spiritual person floats above life comes from the ancient world and, in particular, the Greek mind—although we see it strongly in the Eastern mind as well.

But even a cursory glance at Jesus' life reveals a busy life. All the Gospel writers notice Jesus' busyness, although Mark in particular highlights it. At one point Jesus' family tries to stage an intervention because he is so busy. "Then he went home, and the crowd gathered again, so that they could not even eat. And when his family heard it, they went out to seize him, for they were saying, 'He is out of his mind'" (Mark 3:20-21). Given the sacredness in the ancient world of eating together, Jesus' life seems out of balance. But he loves people and has the power to help, so he has one interruption after another. If Jesus was among us today, his cell phone would be ringing constantly.

The quest for a contemplative life can actually be self-absorbed, focused on my quiet and me. If we love people and have the power to help, then we are going to be busy. Learning to pray doesn't offer us a less busy life; it offers us a less busy heart. In the midst of outer busyness we can develop an inner quiet. Because we are less hectic on the inside, we have a greater capacity to love . . . and thus to be busy, which in turn drives us even more into a life of prayer. By spending time with our Father in prayer, we integrate our lives with his, with what he is doing in us. Our lives become more coherent. They feel calmer, more ordered, even in the midst of confusion and pressure.

> LEARNING TO PRAY DOESN'T OFFER YOU A LESS BUSY LIFE; IT OFFERS YOU A LESS BUSY HEART.

The Praying Life . . . Reveals the Heart

Finally, as you get to know your heavenly Father, you'll get to know your own heart as well. As you develop your relationship with him, it will change you. Or more specifically, he will change you. Real change is at the heart level.

We keep forgetting God is a person. We don't learn to love someone without it changing us. That is just the nature of love that reflects the heart of God. Because God's love is unchanging, the second person of the Trinity, Jesus of Nazareth, now has a scarred body. The Trinity is different because of love.

As you develop your relationship with your heavenly Father, you'll change. You'll discover nests of cynicism, pride, and self-will in your heart. You will be unmasked. None of us likes being exposed. We have an allergic reaction to dependency, but this is the state of the heart most necessary for a praying life. A needy heart is a praying heart. Dependency is the heartbeat of prayer.

So when it starts getting uncomfortable, don't pull back from God. He is just starting to work. Be patient.

Let me put these themes together for you with this story.

A Walk to the Train

I was walking to the train station after work, and without realizing it, I began comparing the mission I worked for with another mission. It dawned on me that I was jealous, trying to make a name for myself at the expense of someone else. My jealousy surprised me. It was not the first time I'd been jealous about this, just the first time I'd named it.

As I continued to walk, I thought, *This is ridiculous, being jealous, competing in my heart with other Christians when we are all involved in the same task.* So before I got to the train, I prayed, quietly giving my work to Jesus. I remember thinking he might actually take it.

He did, of course, take it. It happened over several years, beginning with my burnout a few months later. Six years later I was at another train station, waiting to go home, when tears started flowing. It had been a hard day at work, and I realized it was over. I had to leave the work I loved.

How does this story illustrate the praying life? First, it reflects a real relationship. During those six years God drew me tighter and tighter into his heart. It was a feast for my soul. Just as my wife might do, God was nudging my spirit about an area of my life that wasn't right. Second, my prayer was interconnected with every aspect of my life. It affected my attitude toward work—to everything, really. Releasing control of something I loved opened the door to communion with God. Third, my life became a story filled with tension that eventually led to change, to hope, because during those six years I learned to pray. Fourth, my life became integrated. I understood the connections between my prayer and some of the hard things that came my way. My prayer wasn't isolated from my life. And finally, my prayer was inseparable from my repentance, from encountering God. As Anthony Bloom, a Greek Orthodox writer said, "Abandon all, you will receive heaven."[2] When you give God your life, he gives you the gift of himself.

Now let's learn, step by step, how to develop a praying life.

PART I

LEARNING TO PRAY LIKE A CHILD

CHAPTER 3

BECOME LIKE A LITTLE CHILD

ON MORE THAN ONE OCCASION, Jesus tells his disciples to become like little children. The most famous is when the young mothers try to get near Jesus so he can bless their infants. When the disciples block them, Jesus rebukes his disciples sharply. "Let the children come to me; do not hinder them, for to such belongs the kingdom of God. Truly, I say to you, whoever does not receive the kingdom of God like a child shall not enter it" (Mark 10:14-15). Jesus' rebuke would have surprised the disciples. It would have seemed odd. Children in the first century weren't considered cute or innocent. Only since the nineteenth-century Romantic era have we idolized children.[1]

Another incident occurs when the disciples are traveling and begin arguing with one another as to who is the greatest (see Mark 9:33-37). When they get to Peter's house in Capernaum, Jesus asks them what they were talking about on the way. The disciples just look at the ground and shuffle their feet. At first Jesus says nothing. He sits down, takes a little boy, and has him stand in their midst. Then Jesus picks him up and, while holding him, says, "Unless you turn and become like children, you will never enter the kingdom of heaven" (Matthew 18:3). Little children, even in adult form, are important to Jesus.

A lesser-known incident happens when the disciples return all excited from their first missionary journey, saying, "Lord, even the demons submit to us in your name" (Luke 10:17, NIV). Jesus responds with a joyous prayer, "I thank you, Father, Lord of heaven and earth, that you have hidden these things from the wise and understanding and revealed them to little children" (Luke 10:21). Jesus is thrilled his disciples are like little children.

Not surprisingly, the disciples often behave like little children. For instance, what does Peter do with whatever is on his mind? He blurts it out. That's what children do. Once when I preached at an inner-city church, a woman with an operatic voice sang a solo. After the service she kindly came up to Kim and asked her what she thought of her singing. Kim, who because of her autism cringes at loud music, put her fist to her forehead, the sign for "dumb." The woman turned to Jill and asked her what Kim had just signed. Jill gulped. Jill was in sign-language interpreter training, which trains people to interpret exactly what the other person says. So Jill said, "It was dumb."

The disciples, like Kim, just say what is on their minds, seemingly without thinking. After the Last Supper they tell Jesus, "Ah, now you are speaking plainly and not using figurative speech!" (John 16:29). When James and John want to become number one and two in the kingdom, they have their mother go to bat for them (Matthew 20:20-21). Except for Judas, the disciples are without pretense.

Jesus wants us to be without pretense when we come to him in prayer. Instead, we often try to be something we aren't. We begin by concentrating on God, but almost immediately our minds wander off in a dozen different directions. The problems of the day push out our well-intentioned resolve to be spiritual. We give ourselves a spiritual kick in the pants and try again, but life crowds out prayer. We know that prayer isn't supposed to be like this, so we give up in despair. We might as well get something done.

What's the problem? We're trying to be spiritual, to get it right.

We know we don't need to clean up our act in order to become a Christian, but when it comes to praying, we forget that. We, like adults, try to fix ourselves up. In contrast, Jesus wants us to come to him like little children, just as we are.

Come Messy

The difficulty of coming just as we are is that we are messy. And prayer makes it worse. When we slow down to pray, we are immediately confronted with how unspiritual we are, with how difficult it is to concentrate on God. We don't know how bad we are until we try to be good. Nothing exposes our selfishness and spiritual powerlessness like prayer.

In contrast, little children never get frozen by their selfishness. Like the disciples, they come just as they are, totally self-absorbed. They seldom get it right. As parents or friends, we know all that. In fact, we are delighted (most of the time!) to find out what is on their little hearts. We don't scold them for being self-absorbed or fearful. That is just who they are.

That's certainly how Jill and I responded to Kim. We were uncertain whether she would ever be able to walk, so when she took her first step at three years old, we didn't say, "Kim, that was all very well and good, but you *are* two years late. You have a lot of catching up to do, including long-range walking, not to mention running, skipping, and jumping." We didn't critique how messy or late Kim was. What *did* we do? We screamed; we yelled; we jumped up and down. The family came rushing in to find out what had happened. Cameras came out, and Kim repeated her triumph. It was awesome.

This isn't just a random observation about how parents respond to little children. This is the gospel, the welcoming heart of God. God also cheers when we come to him with our wobbling, unsteady prayers. Jesus does not say, "Come to me, all you who have learned how to concentrate in prayer, whose minds no longer wander, and I will give you rest." No, Jesus opens his arms to his needy children and says, "Come to Me, all who are weary and heavy-laden, and I will give you rest" (Matthew 11:28, NASB). The criteria for coming to Jesus is weariness. Come overwhelmed with life. Come with your wandering mind. Come messy.

COME OVERWHELMED WITH LIFE. COME WITH A WANDERING MIND. COME MESSY.

What does it feel like to be weary? You have trouble concentrating. The problems of the day are like claws in your brain. You feel pummeled by life.

What does heavy-laden feel like? Same thing. You have so many problems you don't even know where to start. You can't do life on your own anymore. Jesus wants you to come to him that way! Your weariness drives you to him.

Don't try to get the prayer right; just tell God where you are and what's on your mind. That's what little children do. They come as they are, runny noses and all. Like the disciples, they just say what is on their minds.

We know that to become a Christian we shouldn't try to fix ourselves up, but when it comes to praying we completely forget that. We'll sing the old gospel hymn "Just as I Am," but when it comes to praying, we don't come just as we are. We try, like adults, to fix ourselves up.

Private, personal prayer is one of the last great bastions of legalism. In order to pray like a child, you might need to unlearn the nonpersonal, nonreal praying that you've been taught.

The Real You

Why is it so important to come to God just as you are? If you don't, then you are artificial and unreal, like the Pharisees. Rarely did they tell Jesus directly what they were thinking. Jesus accused them of being hypocrites, of being masked actors with two faces. They weren't real.

Nor did they like little children. The Pharisees were indignant when the little children poured into the temple (after Jesus had cleansed it) and began worshipping him. Jesus replied, quoting Psalm 8, "Out of the mouth of infants and nursing babies you have prepared praise" (Matthew 21:16).

The only way to come to God is by taking off any spiritual mask. The real you has to meet the real God. He is a person.

So, instead of being frozen by your self-preoccupation, talk with God about your worries. Tell him where you are weary. If you don't begin with where you are, then where you are will sneak in the back door. Your mind will wander to where you are weary.

We are often so busy and overwhelmed that when we slow down to pray, we don't know where our hearts are. We don't know what troubles us. So, oddly enough, we might have to worry before we pray. Then our prayers will make sense. They will be about our real lives.

Your heart could be, and often is, askew. That's okay. You have to begin with what is real. Jesus didn't come for the righteous. He came for sinners. All of us qualify. The very things we try to get rid of—our weariness, our distractedness, our messiness—are what get us in the front door! That's how the gospel works. That's how prayer works.

In bringing your real self to Jesus, you give him the opportunity to work on the real you, and you will slowly change. The kingdom will come. You'll end up less selfish.

The kingdom comes when Jesus becomes king of your life. But it has to be *your life*. You can't create a kingdom that doesn't exist, where you try to be better than you really are. Jesus calls that hypocrisy—putting on a mask to cover the real you.

Ironically, many attempts to teach people to pray encourage the creation of a split personality. You're taught to "do it right." Instead of the real, messy you meeting God, you try to re-create yourself by becoming spiritual.

No wonder prayer is so unsatisfying.

So instead of being paralyzed by who you are, begin with who you are. That's how the gospel works. God begins with you. It's a little scary because you are messed up.

Become like the little children Jesus surrounded himself with. When Nathanael first hears about Jesus, he says the first thing that comes to his mind: "Can anything good come out of Nazareth?" (John 1:46). It is the pure, uncensored Nathanael. When Jesus greets Nathanael, you can almost see Jesus smiling when he says, "Behold, an Israelite indeed, in whom there is no deceit!" (1:47). Jesus ignores the fact that Nathanael has judged Jesus' entire family and friends in Nazareth. He simply enjoys that Nathanael is real, without guile, a man who doesn't pretend. Jesus seems to miss the sin and see a person. It is classic Jesus. He loves real people.

God would much rather deal with the real thing. Jesus said that he came for sinners, for messed-up people who keep messing up (see Luke 15:1-2). Come dirty. The point of the gospel is that we are incapable of beginning with God and his kingdom. Many Christians pray mechanically for God's kingdom (for missionaries, the church, and so on), but all the while their lives are wrapped up in their own kingdoms. You can't add God's kingdom as an overlay to your own.

Touching Our Father's Heart

The opening words of the Lord's Prayer are *Our Father*. You are the center of your heavenly Father's affection. That is where you find rest for your soul. If you remove prayer from the welcoming heart of God (as much teaching on the Lord's Prayer does), prayer becomes a legalistic chore. We do the duty but miss touching the heart of God. By coming to God "weary and heavy-laden," we discover his heart; heaven touches earth and his will is done.

We have much more to learn about praying, but by coming like a little child to our Father, we have learned the heart of prayer. I say "we" deliberately because I regularly forget the simplicity of prayer. I become depressed, and after failing to fix my depression, I give up on myself and remain distant from God. I forget the openness of my Father's heart. He wants me to come depressed, just as I am.

If you get this simple truth, then, like Kim, you have taken your first wobbly step. In fact, you might want to take a wobbly step now by pausing to pray like a little child.

LEARN TO TALK WITH YOUR FATHER

How DO WE LEARN to talk with our Father? By asking like a child, believing like a child, and even playing like a child.

Asking like a Child

Let's do a quick analysis on how little children ask.

What do they ask for? Everything and anything. If they hear about Disneyland, they want to go there tomorrow.

How often do little children ask? Repeatedly. Over and over again. They wear us out. Sometimes we give in just to shut them up.

How do little children ask? Without guile. They just say what is on their minds. They have no awareness of what is appropriate or inappropriate.

Jesus tells us to watch little children if we want to learn how to ask in prayer. After introducing the idea of bold asking in the Sermon on the Mount ("Ask, and it will be given to you") he tells us why we can boldly ask. "Which one of you, if his son asks him for bread, will give him a stone? Or if he asks for a fish, will give him a serpent? If you then, who are evil, know how to give good gifts to your children, how much more will your Father who is in heaven give good things to those who ask him!" (Matthew 7:7, 9-11).

When our son John was six months old, he stuck out his hand in the general direction of the butter and said "bubu." We didn't say, "John, you should say 'please.' And it's not 'bubu,' but B-U-T-T-E-R. Furthermore, there is a self-orientation here that if left unchecked will ruin your life." *Bubu* was our son's first word, so we laughed and gave him the butter.

Kim got her first speech computer when she was five years old. We took it down to the Jersey shore for vacation. We explained the keys to her and waited. She leaned over and pressed the key with little McDonald's golden arches on it. The electronic voice came to life and said "McDonald's." It was two o'clock in the afternoon, and we'd just eaten lunch. We dropped everything, leapt into the car with Kim, raced off to McDonald's, and got Kim a hamburger and a soda. We were thrilled. It wasn't long before she was ordering her entire meal at McDonald's. She's particularly happy if Mom isn't around so she can get french fries.

If we earthly parents, with all our brokenness, still give our kids good gifts, won't our heavenly Father do even more? Our kids' requests, no matter how trivial, tug at our hearts. God feels the same.

Believing like a Child

The second thing we must do in learning to pray is believe like a child. Children are supremely confident of their parents' love and power. Instinctively, they trust. They believe their parents want to do them good. If you know your parent loves and protects you, it fills your world with possibility. You just chatter away with what is on your heart.

It works the same in the world of prayer. If you learn to pray, you learn to dream again. I say "again" because every child naturally dreams and hopes. To learn how to pray is to enter the world of a child, where all things are possible. Little children can't imagine that their parents won't eventually say yes. They know if they keep pestering their parents, they'll eventually give in. Childlike faith drives this persistence.

But as we get older, we get less naive and more cynical. Disappointment and broken promises are the norm instead of hoping and dreaming. Our childlike faith dies a thousand little deaths. Jesus encourages us to believe like little children by telling stories about adults who acted like children: the parable of the persistent widow, who won't take no for an answer from an unjust judge (see Luke 18:1-8), and the parable about a man who badgers his neighbor to lend him three loaves for a friend who has come at midnight (see Luke 11:5-8).

On the rare occasion when Jesus encounters an adult who believes like a child, he stands on a soapbox and practically yells, "Pay attention to this person. Look how he or she believes!" He only does that twice; both times the person was a Gentile, from outside the community of faith. The first is a Roman officer, a centurion, who is so confident of Jesus' ability to heal his paralyzed servant that he asks Jesus to heal without even visiting his home. He tells Jesus, "But say the word, and let my servant be healed" (Luke 7:7). Jesus is stunned. He turns to the crowd following him and says, "I tell you, not even in Israel have I found such faith" (7:9). The second is a Canaanite woman whose daughter is possessed by a demon. Even though Jesus rebuffs her, she keeps coming back. Jesus marvels at her faith, giving her his second Great Faith Oscar: "Woman, great is your faith! Be it done for you as you desire" (Matthew 15:28).

In the last chapter we saw that believing the gospel—knowing God's acceptance for us in Jesus—helps us to come to him messy. Now we see that the gospel also frees us to ask for what is on our hearts.

Learning to Play Again

Besides asking and believing like a child, learning to pray involves, surprisingly, learning to play again. How do little children play? If you ask a parent how long a one-year-old stays on task, he or she just smiles. But if you must know, it varies anywhere from three seconds to three minutes. It isn't long, nor is it particularly organized.

How can that teach us to pray? Think for a minute. How do we structure our adult conversations? We don't. Especially when talking with old friends, the conversation bounces from subject to subject. It has a fun, meandering, play-like quality. Why would our prayer time be any different? After all, God is a person.

Even the apostle Paul's prayer in Ephesians has a play-like quality. He starts praying by saying, "I do not cease to give thanks for you, remembering you in my prayers, that the God of our Lord Jesus Christ, the Father of glory, may give you the Spirit of wisdom" (Ephesians 1:16-17). He continues to pray for several verses, but you can't be sure where he stops. He starts praying again at the beginning of chapter 3, "For this reason I, Paul, a prisoner of Christ Jesus on behalf of you Gentiles . . ." but as soon as he mentions Gentiles, he seemingly gets distracted and stops praying. Finally, he picks up his prayer again in 3:14, "For this reason I bow my knees before the Father." Paul's praying is all over the map. It is classic ADD praying. He starts praying, interrupts himself, starts praying again, gets distracted, and then finally finishes his prayer.

Prayer that lacks this play-like quality is almost autistic. When you are autistic, you have trouble picking up social clues from the other person. For instance, Kim calls me around one thirty when she gets home from work. She presses the speaker button on our phone, dials my cell, and tells me on her speech computer how her day went. She never says "hi"; she just jumps into a description of her day and hangs up. No questions. No "good-bye" or "see you later." Just *click*.

When your mind starts wandering in prayer, be like a little child. Don't worry about being organized or staying on task. Paul certainly wasn't! Remember you are in conversation with a person. Instead of beating yourself up, learn to play again. Pray about what your mind is wandering to. Maybe it is something that is important to you. Maybe the Spirit is nudging you to think about something else.

Learn to Babble Again

For the last nine years, Jill has been doing almost-daily speech therapy with Kim. Kim has made remarkable progress, but now she's at the stage when she just needs to get words out, no matter how bad it sounds. Most of the time she's embarrassed by how bad she sounds. Just this morning, I took Kim to get an X-ray on her right knee, which had been bothering her. She lost her temper three times during the morning, the last time because she had to stand still for the X-ray. When we got home, I sat down with her and asked what she thought about the morning. She signed, "Sorry." I said, "Use your voice." So she prayed haltingly, *Please forgive me for getting mad.* It was barely intelligible, but it was from her heart.

When it comes to prayer, we, too, just need to get the words out. Feel free to stop and pray now. It's okay if your mind wanders or your prayers get interrupted. Don't be embarrassed by how needy your heart is and how much it needs to cry out for grace. Just start praying. Remember, the point of Christianity isn't to learn a lot of truths so you don't need God anymore. We don't learn God in the abstract. We are drawn into his life.

> DON'T BE EMBARRASSED BY HOW NEEDY YOUR HEART IS AND HOW MUCH IT NEEDS TO CRY OUT FOR GRACE. JUST START PRAYING.

Become like a little child—ask, believe, and, yes, even play. When you stop trying to be an adult and get it right, prayer will just flow because God has done something remarkable. He's given you a new voice. It is his own. God has replaced your badly damaged prayer antenna with a new one—the Spirit. He is in you praying. Paul told us that the Spirit puts the praying heart of Jesus in you. "God has sent the Spirit of his Son into our hearts, crying, 'Abba! Father!'" (Galatians 4:6). You'll discover your heart meshing with God's.

You'll discover that prayer is a feast. As you get the clutter off your heart and mind, it is easy to be still in God's presence. You'll be able to say with David, "I have calmed and quieted my soul, like a weaned child with its mother" (Psalm 131:2).

CHAPTER 5

SPENDING TIME WITH YOUR FATHER

YOU'D THINK IF JESUS was the Son of God, he wouldn't need to pray. Or at least he wouldn't need a *specific* prayer time because he'd be in such a constant state of prayer. You'd expect him to have a direct line to his heavenly Father, like broadband to heaven. At the least, you'd think Jesus could do a better job of tuning out the noise of the world. But surprisingly, Jesus seemed to need time with God just as much as we do.

On the first day of his public ministry Jesus is teaching in the Capernaum synagogue on the Sabbath (see Mark 1:21-39). While the audience marvels at his authority, a demon-possessed man cries out, "I know who you are—the Holy One of God." Jesus rebukes the demon sharply and effortlessly casts it out. The crowd is stunned.

After the synagogue service, Jesus returns to Peter's house for the Sabbath meal, only to discover that Peter's mother-in-law is in bed with a fever. Jesus takes her by the hand and instantly heals her. She gets up and prepares lunch.

Word of the healing and the exorcism race through the seaside city of Capernaum. But the tradition of the elders doesn't permit healing on the Sabbath unless it is life threatening, so the town waits until evening. Mark tells us that as soon as the sun went down, "the whole city was gathered together at the door"(1:33). It is easy to imagine the street in front of his house illuminated by the soft glow of hundreds of flickering oil lamps. Jesus heals far into the night. That's why he came—there aren't supposed to be mute children, abandoned wives, or thoughtless bosses.

The next morning before sunrise, Jesus wakes up, makes his way out of town to a desolate place, and prays. He is gone long enough that the crowds gather again, prompting the disciples to go searching. When Peter finds him, he tells Jesus, "Everyone is looking for you" (Mark 1:37).

It is a remarkable day—the evening and morning of the first day of a new creation. The new Adam rolls back the curse and cuts through evil. Demons and sickness flee the presence of Life. Aslan is on the move.

Why Jesus Needed to Pray

Why does Jesus pray in the morning, in a desolate place where he can't be interrupted? His life offers three clues.

Clue #1: His Identity

Whenever Jesus starts talking about his relationship with his heavenly Father, Jesus becomes childlike, very dependent. "The Son can do nothing of his own accord" (John 5:19). "I can do nothing on my own" (John 5:30). "I do nothing on my own authority, but speak just as the Father taught me" (John 8:28). "The Father who sent me has himself given me . . . what to say and what to speak" (John 12:49). Only a child will say, "I only do what I see my Father is doing."

When Jesus tells us to become like little children, he isn't telling us to do anything he isn't already doing. Jesus is, without question, the most dependent human being who ever lived. Because he can't do life on his own, he prays. And he prays. And he prays. Luke tells us that Jesus "would withdraw to desolate places and pray" (Luke 5:16).

When Jesus tells us that "apart from me you can do nothing" (John 15:5), he is inviting us into his life of a living dependence on his heavenly Father. When Jesus tells us to believe, he isn't asking us to work up some spiritual energy. He is telling us to realize that, like him, we don't have the resources to do life. When you know that you (like Jesus) can't do life on your own, then prayer makes complete sense.

IF YOU KNOW THAT YOU, LIKE JESUS, CAN'T DO LIFE ON YOUR OWN, THEN PRAYER MAKES COMPLETE SENSE.

But it goes even deeper than that. Jesus defines himself only in relationship with his heavenly Father. Adam and Eve began their quest for self-identity after the Fall. Only after they acted independently of God did they have a sense of a separate self.[1] Because Jesus has no separate sense of self, he has no identity crisis, no angst. Consequently, he doesn't try to "find himself." He knows himself only in relationship with his Father. He can't conceive of himself outside of that relationship.

Imagine asking Jesus how he's doing. He'd say, "My Father and I are doing great. He has given me everything I need today." You respond, "I'm glad your Father is doing well, but let's just focus on you for a minute. Jesus, how are *you* doing?" Jesus would look at you strangely, as if you were speaking a foreign language. The question doesn't make sense. He simply can't answer the question "How are you doing?" without including his heavenly Father. That's why contemplating the terror of the cross at Gethsemane was such an agony for Jesus. He had never experienced a moment when he wasn't in communion with his Father. Jesus' anguish is our normal.

His prayer life is an expression of his relationship with his Father. He wants to be alone with the person he loves.

Clue #2: His One-Person Focus

When Jesus interacts with people, he narrows his focus down to one person. When he encounters a lame man by the pool of Bethesda, he first sees a multitude; then he sees just him. In the midst of "a multitude of invalids—blind, lame, and paralyzed . . . Jesus saw him lying there" (John 5:3, 6). When Jesus is with someone, that person is the only person in the room. Jesus slows down and concentrates on one person at a time. The way he loves people is identical to the way he prays to his Father.

This one-person focus is how love works. Love incarnates by slowing down and focusing on just the beloved. We don't love in general; we love one person at a time. I think of that almost every morning as I kneel in front of Kim and lace up her muddy work boots. It is a daily foot-washing service for my soul.

Clue #3: His Limited Humanity

The implication of Jesus' one-person focus is that the fully human Jesus doesn't multitask well.[2] He needs to be away from people in order to tune in to his heavenly Father.

Theoretically, Jesus could have concentrated on his Father while he healed people. He could have used his deity to protect himself from the slowness and inefficiency of life. When the bleeding woman interrupts him on the way to Jairus's house, Jesus could have healed her without stopping to connect with her as a person (see Luke 8:40-48). But he doesn't. When he rejects Satan's temptation to turn the stone into bread, he rejects efficiency and chooses love (see Matthew 4:1-4). So, as a fully human being, he needs to get away to pray.

When Jesus withdraws from the crowded house in Capernaum to a desolate place in the wilderness, he is following his own advice from the Sermon on the Mount to "go into your room, close the door and pray to your Father" (Matthew 6:6, NIV). From all eternity, he has been in relationship with his Father. He needs to concentrate on his Father. He wants to be with him, so he gets alone to pray.

No Substitute for Spending Time

Jesus' example teaches us that prayer is about relationship. When he prays, he is not performing a duty; he is getting close to his Father.

Any relationship, if it is going to grow, needs private space, time together without an agenda, where you can get to know each other. This creates an environment where closeness can happen, where we can begin to understand each other's hearts.

You don't create intimacy; you make room for it. This is true whether you are talking about your spouse, your friend, or God. You need space to be together. Efficiency, multitasking, and busyness all kill intimacy. In short, you can't get to know God on the fly.

If Jesus has to pull away from people and noise in order to pray, then it makes sense that we need to as well.

Praying like Jesus Prayed

Jesus' pattern of a morning prayer follows the ancient rhythm of the Hebrew writers who bent their hearts to God in the morning. Here's a sampling of psalms that describes this practice:

> O Lord, in the morning you hear my voice; in the morning
> I prepare a sacrifice for you and watch.   PSALM 5:3

> I will sing aloud of your steadfast love in the morning.
> PSALM 59:16

> But I, O Lord, cry to you; in the morning my prayer comes
> before you.   PSALM 88:13

Let me hear in the morning of your steadfast love, for in you
I trust. Make me know the way I should go, for to you I lift
up my soul.   PSALM 143:8

Do we have to pray in the morning? No, Jesus' High Priestly
Prayer in John 17 and his prayer later at Gethsemane were both evening prayers.

The Psalms give us a clue to how the Hebrews prayed. Most
psalms have at least one out-loud cue, such as "I lift my *voice* . . . I
cry to you . . . O LORD, hear my *voice*" (see Psalms 5:2-3; 17:1; 28:2).
We've changed them into metaphors of the soul, but the Hebrews
were literally speaking out loud to God for help.

Jesus follows the custom of praying out loud. We know the content of his High Priestly Prayer because his disciples could hear his
voice. Likewise, we know what he is praying in Gethsemane because
his disciples overhear him as he pours out his heart to his Father. "In
the days of his flesh, Jesus offered up prayers and supplications, with
loud cries and tears, to him who was able to save him from death"
(Hebrews 5:7).

When Jesus tells the parable of the Pharisee and the tax collector,
he describes both men as praying aloud. Jesus goes on to encourage
us to pray in the privacy of our rooms so our out-loud praying doesn't
become a verbal show.

Praying out loud can be helpful because it keeps you from getting
lost in your head. It makes your thoughts concrete. But it is more
than technique; it is also a statement of faith. You are audibly declaring your belief in a God who is alive.

Praying aloud is not a New Testament rule; it is just another way
of being real in prayer. Everyone is different. Personally, I've found it
hard to pray out loud because I'm so in the habit of praying silently.
Still, when I confess a sin aloud, it feels more real. When I hear my
own voice admitting that I've done something wrong, I'm surprised

by how concrete the sin feels. I've even thought, *Oh, I guess that really was wrong.* On my way to a social event, I will sometimes pray aloud in the car that I won't fall into sexual lust or people pleasing. This helps me become much more aware of my need. My prayers become more serious.

Overcoming Objections

No matter when or how we pray, we often find reasons why we can't slow down enough to have a regular prayer time. One objection to a daily prayer time is "I pray all the time." While being "constant in prayer" (Romans 12:12) is an important way of praying that we'll talk about later, this is no substitute for focused times of prayer. For example, a husband and wife who only talk in snippets to one another throughout the day would have a shallow relationship. You'd be business partners, not lovers. You can't build a relationship by sound bites.

Another objection is busyness. When I first heard Martin Luther's comment that he couldn't get by unless he had three or four hours of prayer daily, I scratched my head.[3] Knowing how busy Luther was, you'd think he would want to cut out prayer. Now, years later, it makes perfect sense. In fact, the more pressure, the more I need to pray. I pray in the morning because my life is so pressured.

If you are not praying, then you are quietly confident that time, money, and talent are all you need in life. You'll always be a little too tired, a little too busy. But if, like Jesus, you realize you can't do life on your own, then no matter how busy, no matter how tired you are, you will find the time to pray.

Time in prayer makes you even more dependent on God because you don't have as much time to get things done. Every minute spent in prayer is one less minute where you can be doing something "productive." So the act of praying means that you have to rely more on God.

Take Baby Steps

When it comes to spending time with God, take baby steps. Don't set impossible goals and then collapse. If you can remember a time in your life when you had a great half hour of prayer, don't make that your standard. Start slowly. Take a baby step of five minutes.

There is no one way to do this. Some people pray on their way to work. My one caution is that it is tough to be intimate when you are multitasking. It would weaken a marriage if talking to your spouse in the car was the only time you communicated. It will do the same to your relationship with God.

Here are seven simple suggestions for how you can spend time with your Father in the morning:

- *Get to bed.* What you do in the evening will shape your morning. The Hebrew notion of a day as the evening and morning (see Genesis 1) helps you plan for prayer. If you want to pray in the morning, then plan your evening so you don't stay up too late. The evening and the morning are connected.
- *Get up.* Praying in bed is wonderful. In fact, the more you pray *out of* bed, the more you'll pray *in* bed. But you'll never develop a morning prayer time *in* bed. Some of my richest prayer times are at night. I'll wake up praying. But those prayer times only began to emerge because I got out of bed to pray.
- *Get awake.* Maybe you need to make a pot of coffee first or take a shower.
- *Get a quiet place.* Maybe a room, a chair, or a place with a view. Or maybe you do better going for a walk. Make sure that no one can interrupt you.
- *Get comfortable.* Don't feel like you have to pray on your knees. For years I was hindered from praying because I found it so uncomfortable to pray on my knees.

- *Get going.* Start with just five minutes. Start with a small goal that you can attain rather than something heroic. You'll quickly find that the time will fly.
- *Keep going.* Consistency is more important than length. If you pray five minutes every day, then the length of time will slowly grow. You'll look up and discover that twenty minutes have gone by. You'll enjoy being with God. Jesus is so concerned about hanging in there with prayer that he tells "his disciples a parable to show them that they should always pray and not give up" (Luke 18:1, NIV).

Regardless of how or when you pray, if you give God the space, he will touch your soul. God knows you are exhausted, but at the same time he longs to be part of your life. A feast awaits.

CHAPTER 6

LEARNING TO BE HELPLESS

For some reason Kim has always woken up early, sometimes as early as four thirty. She knows she's not supposed to get up so early, so she'll go out in the hallway, flip on the light, and go back to bed. Five minutes later she'll get up again, turn off the light, and go back to bed, only to repeat the process again and again. When Kim starts pacing on the third floor, Jill or I will tell her to get back in bed. Because we are separated by a floor, our telling sounds more like yelling.

When Jill and I get up to pray, it can really get exciting. Jill prays on the first floor, and I pray on the second floor. Jill is more sensitive to noise than I am, so when she hears Kim pacing upstairs, she asks me to tell her to be quiet. Sometimes I yell at Kim so that Jill won't yell at me to yell at Kim. In Jill's defense, Kim's pacing is so hard it is more like jogging.

In the world of autism, Kim's pacing is called perseverating. It got so bad that we consulted her neurologist, who suggested a drug, which we tried, but Kim just gained weight, so we stopped the drug and went back to yelling!

Jill and I have saturated Kim's life with prayer, but it dawned on me recently that I had never prayed for her or with her that she would stop pacing. Why? Because I already knew the solution: "Kim needs to stop pacing. I will tell her to stop pacing." In other words, I didn't feel helpless. I knew what to do. I call this the idiot approach to life. In other words, "You idiot, if you would just stop . . ."

Little children are good at helplessness. It's what they do best. But as adults, we soon forget how important helplessness is. I, for one, am allergic to helplessness. I don't like it. I want a plan, an idea, or maybe a friend to listen to my problem. This is how I instinctively approach everything because I am confident in my own abilities. This is even true in my work of teaching people about prayer. Even though I lead prayer seminars and wrote a study on prayer, up until a year ago, it never occurred to me to pray systematically and regularly for our prayer ministry. Why not? Because I was not helpless. I could manage our prayer ministry on my own. I never said this or even thought it, but I lived it. Ironically, helplessness is one of the central themes in our prayer seminar. I wasn't helpless about the ministry of teaching helplessness! Such is the human heart. I only started praying regularly about our seminar ministry when it wasn't moving forward—when I became helpless.

Prayer = Helplessness

God wants us to come to him empty-handed, weary, and heavy-laden. Instinctively we want to get rid of our helplessness before we come to God. One participant of our prayer seminars put it this way:

> I am starting to see there is a difference between "saying prayers" and honest praying. Both can sound the same on the outside, but the former is too often motivated by a sense of obligation and guilt; whereas the latter is motivated by a conviction that I am completely helpless to "do life" on my own. Or in the case of praying for others, that I am completely helpless to help others without the grace and power of God.

The Norwegian Lutheran Ole Hallesby articulated the importance of helplessness in his classic book *Prayer*. He described how Mary's request to Jesus at the wedding of Cana—"They have no wine" (John 2:3)—is a perfect description of prayer.[1] Prayer is bringing your helplessness to Jesus. Thomas Merton, the Trappist monk, summarized it beautifully: "Prayer is an expression of who we are. . . . We are a living incompleteness. We are a gap, an emptiness that calls for fulfillment."[2]

Throughout the book of John we see people coming to Jesus because of their helplessness. The Samaritan woman has no water (see John 4). Later in that same chapter, the official's son has no health. The crippled man by the pool of Bethesda has no help to get into the water (see John 5). The crowd has no bread (see John 6). The blind man has no sight (see John 9). And finally, Lazarus has no life (see John 11).

We received Jesus because we were weak, and that's how we follow him. Paul told the Colossians, "Therefore, as you received Christ Jesus the Lord, so walk in him" (Colossians 2:6). We forget that helplessness is how the Christian life works.

Paul was reminded of this when he prayed three times for God to remove his thorn in the flesh. It didn't happen. Instead, God reminded Paul of how the gospel works. "But he said to me, 'My grace is sufficient for you, for my power is made perfect in weakness.' Therefore I will boast all the more gladly of my weaknesses, so that the power of Christ may rest upon me" (2 Corinthians 12:9).

The gospel, God's free gift of grace in Jesus, only works when we realize we don't have it all together. The same is true for prayer. The very thing we are allergic to—our helplessness—is what makes prayer work. It works because we *are* helpless. We can't do life on our own.

Prayer mirrors the gospel. In the gospel, the Father takes us as we are because of Jesus and gives us his gift of salvation. In prayer, the Father receives us as we are because of Jesus and gives us his gift of help. We look at the inadequacy of our praying and give up, thinking something is wrong with us. God looks at the adequacy of his Son and delights in our sloppy, meandering prayers.

A Wrong View of Maturity

We tell ourselves, "Strong Christians pray a lot. If I were a stronger Christian, I'd pray more." Strong Christians do pray more, but they pray more because they realize how weak they are. They don't try to hide it from themselves. Weakness is the channel that allows them to access grace.

I'm not referring to well-known Christians. An interviewer once asked Edith Schaeffer, author and wife of evangelist and philosopher Francis Schaeffer, "Who is the greatest Christian woman alive today?" She replied, "We don't know her name. She is dying of cancer somewhere in a hospital in India." I'm talking about that woman. Underneath her obedient life is a sense of helplessness. It has become part of her very nature . . . almost like breathing. Why? Because she is weak. She can feel her restless heart, her tendency to compare herself with others. She is shocked at how jealousy can well up in her. She notices how easily the world gets its hooks into her. In short, she distrusts herself. When she looks at other people, she sees the same struggles. The world, the flesh, and the Devil are too much for her. The result? Her heart cries out to God in prayer. She needs Jesus.

As we mature as Christians, we see more and more of our sinful natures, but at the same time we see more and more of Jesus. As we see our weaknesses more clearly, we begin to grasp our need for more grace.

The following chart shows how this works in the Christian life. The immature Christian on the left side has a small cross and a small view of her sin. She has little need to pray. The mature Christian on the right side has a large cross and a large view of her sin. The result? She prays more.

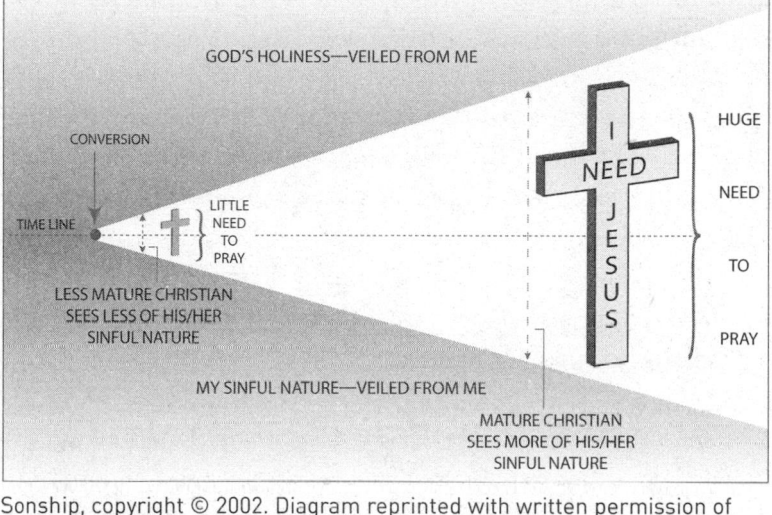

This chart came to me when I was scrubbing the kitchen floor, depressed about the lack of progress in the lives of people I was discipling. As I continued to scrub, I realized I had the same problems, which made me even more depressed. Then it dawned on me that my inability, my minidepression, was my door to God. In fact, God wanted me depressed about myself and encouraged about his Son. The gospel uses my weakness as the door to God's grace. That is how grace works.

Less mature Christians have little need to pray. When they look at their hearts (which they rarely do), they seldom see jealousy. They are barely aware of their impatience. Instead, they are frustrated by all the slow people they keep running into. Less mature Christians are quick to give advice. There is no complexity to their worlds because the answers are simple—"just do what I say, and your life will be easier." I know all this because the "they" I've been talking about is actually "me." That is what I'm naturally like without Jesus.

Surprisingly, mature Christians feel less mature on the inside. When they hear Jesus say, "Apart from me you can do nothing" (John 15:5), they nod in agreement. They reflect on all the things they've done without Jesus, which have become nothing. Mature Christians are keenly aware that they can't raise their kids. It's a no-brainer. Even if they are perfect parents, they still can't get inside their kids' hearts. That's why strong Christians pray more.

John of Landsburg, a sixteenth-century Catholic monk, summarized this well in his classic *A Letter from Jesus Christ*. He imagined Jesus speaking personally to us:

> I know those moods when you sit there utterly alone, pining, eaten up with unhappiness, in a pure state of grief. You don't move towards me but desperately imagine that everything you have ever done has been utterly lost and forgotten. This near-despair and self-pity are actually a form of pride. What you think was a state of absolute security from which you've fallen was really trusting too much in your own strength and ability. . . . What really ails you is that things simply haven't happened as you expected and wanted.
>
> In fact I don't want you to rely on your own strength and abilities and plans, but to distrust them and to distrust yourself, and to trust me and no one and nothing else. As long as you rely entirely on yourself, you are bound to come to grief. You still have a most important lesson to learn: your own strength will no more help you to stand upright than propping yourself on a broken reed. You must not despair of me. You may hope and trust in me absolutely. My mercy is infinite.[3]

Jesus isn't asking us to do anything he isn't already doing. He is inviting us into his life of helpless dependence on his heavenly Father. To become more like Jesus is to feel increasingly unable to do life, increasingly wary of your heart. Paradoxically, you get holier while you are feeling less holy. The very thing you were trying to escape—your inability—opens the door to prayer and then grace.

When our kids were two, five, eight, twelve, fourteen, and sixteen, I wrote this in my prayer journal:

> March 19, 1991. Amazing how when I don't pray in the morning evil just floods into our home. I absolutely must pray! Oh, God, give me the grace to pray.

It took me seventeen years to realize I couldn't parent on my own. It was not a great spiritual insight, just a realistic observation. If I didn't pray deliberately and reflectively for members of my family by name every morning, they'd kill one another. I was incapable of getting inside their hearts. I was desperate. But even more, I couldn't change my self-confident heart. My prayer journal reflects both my inability to change my kids and my inability to change my self-confidence. That's why I need grace even to pray.

God answered my prayer. As I began to pray regularly for the children, he began to work in their hearts. For example, I began to pray for more humility in my eldest son, John. (As Jill says, "The apple didn't fall far from the tree.") About six months later he came to me and said, "Dad, I've been thinking a lot about humility lately and my lack of it." It didn't take me long to realize I did my best parenting by prayer. I began to speak less to the kids and more to God. It was actually quite relaxing.

If we think we can do life on our own, we will not take prayer seriously. Our failure to pray will always feel like something else—a

47

lack of discipline or too many obligations. But when something is important to us, we make room for it. Prayer is simply not important to many Christians because Jesus is already an add-on. That is why, as we'll see later, suffering is so important to the process of learning how to pray. It is God's gift to us to show us what life is really like.

When You Open the Door . . .

Not long ago Kim started pacing again in the early-morning hours. I started to get out of bed, and Jill asked, half-asleep, "Are you going to yell at Kim?" I said, "No, that hasn't worked for ten years, so I thought I'd pray with her." Jill started laughing. "What do you mean ten years? It's been twenty!"

I went up to Kim's bedroom, aware that absolutely nothing I could say would stop her pacing. I went quietly over to her bed, laid my hand on her covers (she was pretending to be asleep), and asked the Holy Spirit to quiet her. God heard our prayer. She fell asleep and didn't go back to her pacing that morning.

As soon as I started praying, a thought came completely from left field: I had underestimated Kim's ability to pray on her own, to connect with God. My view of her had been too narrow. In this area of her life, I'd looked at her as a disabled person and not as a young woman made in the image of God, able to communicate with her heavenly Father. It created a new expectation in my heart for her, a new hope that she can grow spiritually. When she bites her wrist, I can pray with her about it. When I rub oil on her calloused wrist, I can pray with her. Instead of fighting Kim's problems with anger, I can focus on a new vision of her learning to pray.

But Kim continued to pace. About every other time, I'd drag myself out of bed and pray with her. Then four months later, we moved, and her pacing completely stopped. We knew Kim was super-sensitive to noise because of her autism, but we'd not realized how the diesel trucks at the factory across the street from our old house and the road noise itself were waking her up. Our new house is set back from the road and much quieter. God answered my prayer for Kim.

All the themes of good praying are hidden in this story of praying for Kim: helplessness, relationship, repentance, asking, story, and hope. When you open a door to God, you find some amazing treasures inside.

CHAPTER 7

CRYING "ABBA"—CONTINUOUSLY

I WAS LISTENING TO THE DISCUSSION at a staff meeting when our con-
sultant said, "Paul is so quiet. He doesn't seem to be passionate about
anything, except maybe the person of Jesus." I smiled, partly because
it was funny and partly because on the inside I am like Barney Fife,
the nervous deputy on the old *Andy Griffith Show*. My mind churns
with ideas, and my mouth is eager to assist.

So why did I appear so calm? Because I was praying, quietly to
myself, over and over again: *Father, Father, Father*. At other times I
will pray the name of Jesus or the name *Christ*. Sometimes I find
myself praying a short phrase, such as *Come, Spirit*.

This is not a mindless chant I practice in order to reach some
higher spiritual plane. Just the opposite. I realize I'm on a low spiritual
plane, and I am crying out for help like a little child who runs to his
mother saying, "Mommy, Mommy, Mommy." My heart is hunting
for its true home. The psalmist David captured the feel of the praying soul:

> O God, you are my God; earnestly I seek you;
> my soul thirsts for you;

my flesh faints for you,
    as in a dry and weary land where there is no water.
PSALM 63:1

Why am I quietly crying out for help? My tendency to interrupt in staff meetings is a "dry and weary land." When I feel my inner Barney Fife crying out for attention, I pray quietly, *Jesus, Jesus, Jesus.* Like Augustine, my heart is restless, and I need to find my rest in God.[1]

I'm at my worst when I'm passionate about a new idea. I can drift into selling instead of listening and can easily become dominating. My heart is a dry and weary land. But when I begin to pray, the energy of my life is directed into the life of God and not into changing people's minds . . . and I shut up!

When someone shares an idea that was originally mine, I want to mention that I first thought of it. I feel unsettled, as if the universe is out of balance. In short, I want to boast. The only way to quiet my soul's desire for prominence is to begin to pray: *Apart from you I can do nothing.*

Interrupting, selling, and boasting are just a few of the things that draw me into continuous prayer, into continual childlike dependence on my Father. Each of us has our own list. We can let it drive us into a praying life.

Poverty of Spirit, Not Discipline

I didn't learn continuous prayer; I discovered I was already doing it. I found myself in difficult situations I could not control. All I could do was cry out to my heavenly Father. It happened often enough that it became a habit, creating a rut between my soul and God.

Even now I often don't realize that I am praying. Possibly, it isn't even me praying, but the Spirit. Paul said, "God has sent the Spirit of his Son into our hearts, crying, 'Abba! Father!'" (Galatians 4:6). The

Spirit is not assisting us to pray; he is the one who is actually praying. He is the pray-er.

More specifically, it is the Spirit of *his Son* praying. The Spirit is bringing the childlike heart of Jesus into my heart and crying, *Abba, Father.* Jesus' longing for his Father becomes my longing. My spirit meshes with the Spirit, and I, too, begin to cry, *Father.*

When Jesus prayed, most scholars think he regularly addressed his Father as *abba.* It is similar to our word *papa.* Their logic goes like this: We know the word *abba* because it burned itself on the disciples' minds. They were so stunned—no one had ever spoken to God so intimately before—that when they told the Greek Christians about Jesus, they carried over the Aramaic *abba* into the Greek translations of the Bible. This so shocked Paul that he used *abba* in both Romans and Galatians. Translators have continued the pattern set by the early disciples, and no matter what language Scripture is in, they still use *abba.*

This one-word prayer, *Father,* is uniquely Jesus' prayer. His first recorded sentence at age twelve is about his father: "Did you not know that I must be in my Father's house?" (Luke 2:49). *Abba* is the first word the prodigal son utters when he returned home. It is the first word of the Lord's Prayer, and it is the first word Jesus prays in Gethsemane. It is his first word on the cross—"Father, forgive them" (Luke 23:34)—and one of his last—"Father, into your hands I commit my spirit!" (Luke 23:46). *Father* was my first prayer as I began praying continuously, and I find that it is still my most frequent prayer.

I discovered myself praying simple two- and three-word prayers, such as *Teach me* or *Help me, Jesus.* The psalms are filled with this type of short bullet prayer. Praying simple one-word prayers or a verse of Scripture takes the pressure off because we don't have to sort out exactly what we need. Paul tells us, "We do not know what to pray for as we ought, but the Spirit himself intercedes for us with groanings too deep for words" (Romans 8:26). Often we are too weary to figure out what the problem is. We just know that life—including ours—doesn't work. So we pray, *Father, Father, Father.*

This is the exact opposite of Eastern mysticism, which is a psycho-spiritual technique that disengages from relationship and escapes pain by dulling self. Eastern mystics are trying to empty their minds and become one with the nonpersonal "all." But as Christians we realize we can't cure ourselves, so we cry out to our Father, our primary relationship.

I was driving to work one day, thinking about all the options for a new three-year plan at work. The closer I got to the office, the more overwhelmed I became—I didn't have the wisdom to sort through the options. The Scripture "Lead me to the rock that is higher than I" (Psalm 61:2) came to mind, and I turned it into a simple prayer. I needed a rock higher than myself. That momentary poverty of spirit (I became overwhelmed . . . I didn't have the wisdom) was the door to prayer. We don't need self-discipline to pray continuously; we just need to be poor in spirit. Poverty of spirit makes room for his Spirit. It creates a God-shaped hole in our hearts and offers us a new way to relate to others.

A praying spirit transforms how we look at people. As we walk through the mall, our hearts can tempt us to judge, despise, or lust. We see young adults with piercings and tattoos, overweight people, well-dressed women, misbehaving children, security guards, and older people shuffling along. If we are tempted to judge an overweight person, we might instead pray for his or her long-term health. When we see a security guard, we might pray for the challenges of his career. As we pass by, we can pray for the weary mom struggling to manage her children. We can ask God to give the shuffling older couple grace as they age.

Paul the apostle was constantly aware of his helplessness and the helplessness of the churches he loved—and so he prayed constantly.

Paul's Example and Teaching

"Unceasing prayer" is Paul's most frequent description of how he prayed and of how he wanted the church to pray. This was a real experience for Paul and not a formula. In the twelve times he mentions continuous praying, he seldom says it the same way twice (emphasis added).

- *Without ceasing* I mention you always in my prayers. (Romans 1:9-10)
- I give thanks to my God *always* for you. (1 Corinthians 1:4)
- I *do not cease* to give thanks for you, remembering you in my prayers. (Ephesians 1:16)
- Praying *at all times* in the Spirit. (Ephesians 6:18)
- We *have not ceased* to pray for you. (Colossians 1:9)
- *Continue steadfastly* in prayer. (Colossians 4:2)
- *Always* struggling on your behalf in his prayers. (Colossians 4:12)
- *Constantly* mentioning you in our prayers. (1 Thessalonians 1:2)
- We also thank God *constantly* for this. (1 Thessalonians 2:13)
- As we pray most earnestly *night and day*. (1 Thessalonians 3:10)
- We *always* pray for you. (2 Thessalonians 1:11)
- I remember you *constantly* in my prayers *night and day*. (2 Timothy 1:3)

When Paul tells the young churches to pray, he encourages them in this same pattern of "constant in prayer" (emphasis added):

- Be *constant* in prayer. (Romans 12:12)
- Pray *without ceasing*. (1 Thessalonians 5:17)

Given Paul's emphasis, it is not surprising to see examples of continual prayer in the early church.

The Jesus Prayer

The Greek Orthodox Church still uses a simple fifth-century prayer sometimes called the Prayer of Jesus: *Lord Jesus Christ, Son of God, have mercy on me, a sinner.*[2] The Orthodox tradition calls short prayers like this "breath prayers" because they can be spoken in a single breath.

The earliest version of this prayer came from a blind beggar named Bartimaeus, who cried out as Jesus was passing by, "Jesus, Son of David, have mercy on me!" (Luke 18:38). If you add Paul's Philippian hymn, "confess that Jesus Christ is Lord" (Philippians 2:11), you've got the Jesus Prayer. From the beginning, this prayer was used continuously. When the crowd shushed Bartimaeus, "he cried out all the more" (Luke 18:39). He must have been shouting at the top of his lungs because three of the Gospels mention his loud persistence!

Jill has her own version of the Jesus Prayer. When we walk the dogs together on Sunday morning, we pass by an incredibly neat house with a well-manicured lawn. It is especially entertaining in the fall, when both the husband and the wife run around with a shoulder-pack leaf vacuum, chasing individual leaves. With her German heritage, Jill feels the pressure to obsess over neatness. As we walk by this immaculate house, she'll start praying repeatedly, *God, save me from myself. God, save me from myself.*

When our kids were teenagers, Jill asked me, "Do you know what our family needs most?" Lots of things came to mind, including a newer car. Her one-word answer took me completely by surprise: "mercy." We didn't need to get more organized. We didn't need more money. We needed mercy. That mind-set creates a praying heart.

A praying life isn't simply a morning prayer time; it is about slipping into prayer at odd hours of the day, not because we are disciplined but because we are in touch with our own poverty of spirit, realizing that we can't even walk through a mall or our neighborhood without the help of the Spirit of Jesus.

CHAPTER 8

BENDING YOUR HEART TO YOUR FATHER

SEVERAL MONTHS AGO I was on a flight, sitting next to a drug rep for a major pharmaceutical company. I mentioned to her that from listening to people talk, I suspected that one-third of suburban American women were on antidepressants. The drug rep shook her head. "You're wrong. It's at least two-thirds." And it's not just women. The CDC reports that 1 in 7 Americans are on antidepressants.

Most of us simply want to get rid of anxiety. Some hunt for a magic pill that will relieve the stress. Others pursue therapy. While antidepressants and counseling have helped many people, including me, the search for a "happy pill" or "happy thoughts" will not stop our restless anxiety. It runs too deep.

Instead of fighting anxiety, we can use it as a springboard to bending our hearts to God. Instead of trying to suppress anxiety, manage it, or smother it with pleasure, we can turn our anxiety toward God. When we do that, we'll discover that we've slipped into continuous praying.

Here's an example of how anxiety creates an opening for prayer. When I was a kid, I didn't like answering the phone, possibly because I am not quick with words. I can get tongue-tied in new situations, and I used to have a stuttering problem. Jill would joke that she wanted to name one of our kids Lillian because the letter *L* was a particular problem for me. So was *H*. Saying "hello" could really set me back. Sometimes when the phone rings, I still feel a twinge of anxiety. As I reach for the phone, I pray a quick, wordless prayer. I just lean in the direction of God. My anxiety becomes a prayer.

A Brief History of Anxiety and Prayer

The connection between anxiety and continuous praying goes back to Eden, where Adam and Eve were in unbroken fellowship with God and continuous prayer was normal. When they sought independence from God, they stopped walking with God in the cool of the day and their prayer link was broken.

What does an unused prayer link look like? Anxiety. Instead of connecting with God, our spirits fly around like severed power lines, destroying everything they touch. Anxiety wants to be God but lacks God's wisdom, power, or knowledge. A godlike stance without godlike character and ability is pure tension. Because anxiety is self on its own, it tries to get control. It is unable to relax in the face of chaos. Once one problem is solved, the next in line steps up. The new one looms so large, we forget the last deliverance.

ANXIETY IS UNABLE TO RELAX IN THE FACE OF CHAOS; CONTINUOUS PRAYER CLINGS TO THE FATHER IN THE FACE OF CHAOS.

Oddly enough, it took God to show us how not to be godlike. Jesus was the first person who didn't seek independence. He wanted to be in continuous contact with his heavenly Father. In fact, he humbled himself to death on the cross, becoming anxious so we could be free from anxiety. Now the Spirit brings the humility of Jesus into our hearts. No longer do we have to be little gods, controlling everything. Instead, we cling to our Father in the face of chaos by continuously praying. Because we know we don't have control, we cry out for grace. Instead of flailing around, our praying spirits can bless everything we touch.

David captured the connection between a humble heart and a quiet heart.[1]

> O LORD, my heart is not lifted up;
>   my eyes are not raised too high;
> I do not occupy myself with things
>   too great and too marvelous for me.
> But I have calmed and quieted my soul,
>   like a weaned child on its mother;
>   like a weaned child is my soul on me.
>
> PSALM 131:1-2[2]

We become anxious when we take a godlike stance, occupying ourselves with things too great for us. We return to sanity by becoming like little children, resting on our mothers.

One of the unique things about continuous praying is that it is its own answer to prayer. As you pray Psalm 131, your heart becomes quiet. You rest, not because there is magic in the words but because your eyes are no longer raised too high. Charles Hodge gave us this example of continuous prayer from his childhood.

> In my childhood I came nearer to "Pray without ceasing" than in any other period of my life. As far back as I can remember, I had the habit of thanking God for everything I received, and asking him for everything I wanted. If I lost a book, or any of my playthings, I prayed that I might find it. I prayed walking along the streets, in school and out of school, whether playing or studying. I did not do this in obedience to any prescribed rule. It seemed natural. I thought of God as an everywhere-present Being, full of kindness and love, who would not

be offended if children talked to him. I knew he cared for sparrows. I was as cheerful and happy as the birds and acted as they did.[3]

Your heart can become a prayer factory because, like Jesus, you are completely dependent. You needed God ten minutes ago; you need him now. Instead of hunting for the perfect spiritual state to lift you above the chaos, pray *in* the chaos. As your heart or your circumstances generate problems, keep generating prayer. You will find that the chaos lessens. That's why the apostle Paul actually commands us to convert anxiety into prayer.

> Do not be anxious about anything, but in everything by prayer and supplication with thanksgiving let your requests be made known to God. And the peace of God, which surpasses all understanding, will guard your hearts and your minds in Christ Jesus. PHILIPPIANS 4:6-7

Here's the point: Anxiety is relentless. That is, it doesn't rest; it keeps coming back. That's the same dynamic of continuous prayer—it keeps coming back to the Father. Maybe the fears and concerns driving anxiety are real, so why not be realistic with the churning and bring it to your Father, who doesn't tire of hearing your heart? In fact, Jesus' two parables on prayer from Luke describe people (a widow and a host) in anxious situations that lead them to relentlessly badgering someone else!

And finally, just an aside about antidepressants. This is complex, so let me just share two thoughts: First, I had a bout with depression in my late 30s, and antidepressants were immensely helpful to me. Second, just be careful to first give your Father a chance to hear your anxiety. He never ever tires of hearing the same old thing!

Invitations for Prayer

When you pray continuously, moments when you are prone to anxiety can become invitations to drift into prayer. A traffic jam, a slight from a friend, or a pressured deadline can serve as a door to God. You'll find yourself turning off the car radio to be with your Father. You'll wake up at night and discover yourself praying. It will be like breathing.

When you stop trying to control your life and instead allow your anxieties and problems to bring you to God in prayer, you shift from worry to watching. You watch God weave his patterns in the story of your life. Instead of trying to be out front, designing your life, you realize you are inside God's drama. As you wait, you begin to see him work, and your life begins to sparkle with wonder. You are learning to trust again.

PART 2

LEARNING TO TRUST AGAIN

CHAPTER 9

UNDERSTANDING CYNICISM

THE OPPOSITE OF A CHILDLIKE SPIRIT is a cynical spirit. Cynicism is, increasingly, the dominant spirit of our age. Personally, it is my greatest struggle in prayer. If I get an answer to prayer, sometimes I'll think, *It would have happened anyway.* Other times I'll try to pray but wonder if it makes any difference.

Many Christians stand at the edge of cynicism, struggling with a defeated weariness. Their spirits have begun to deaden, but unlike the cynic, they've not lost hope. My friend Bryan summarized it this way: "I think we have built up scar tissue from our frustrations, and we don't want to expose ourselves anymore. Fear constrains us."

Cynicism and defeated weariness have this in common: They both question the active goodness of God on our behalf. Left unchallenged, their low-level doubt opens the door for bigger doubt. They've lost their childlike spirit and thus are unable to move toward their heavenly Father.

When I say that cynicism is the spirit of the age, I mean it is an influence, a tone that permeates our culture, one of the master temptations of our age. By reflecting on cynicism and defeated weariness, we are meditating on the last petition of the Lord's Prayer: "Lead us not into temptation, but deliver us from the evil one" (Matthew 6:13, NIV).

Cynicism is so pervasive that, at times, it feels like a presence. Behind the spirit of the age lies an unseen, personal evil presence, a spirit. If Satan can't stop you from praying, then he will try to rob the fruit of praying by dulling your soul. Satan cannot create, but he can corrupt.

The Feel of Cynicism
Satan's first recorded words are cynical. He tells Adam and Eve, "For God knows that when you eat of it your eyes will be opened, and you will be like God" (Genesis 3:5). Satan is suggesting that God's motives are cynical. In essence, he tells them, "God has not been honest about the tree in the middle of the garden. The command not to eat from the tree isn't for your protection; God wants to protect himself from rivals. He's jealous. He is projecting an image of caring for you, but he really has an agenda to protect himself. God has two faces." Satan seductively gives Adam and Eve the inside track—here is what is *really* going on behind closed doors. Such is the deadly intimacy that gossip offers.

Satan sees evil everywhere, even in God himself. Ironically, it became a self-fulfilling prophecy. Since the Fall, evil feels omnipresent, making cynicism an easy sell. Because cynicism sees what is "really going on," it feels real, authentic. That gives cynicism an elite status since authenticity is one of the last remaining public virtues in our culture.

I shared these reflections on cynicism with Cathie, a friend who was struggling with cynicism. She reflected on her own heart, saying: "Cynicism is taught in our schools, embraced by our culture, and lifted up as ideal. It seems insidious to me. Somehow these dulled, partial truths often feel more real to me than the truths taught by

Scripture. It is easier for me to feel skepticism and nothing than *to feel* deep passion. So cynicism takes root and 'feels' more real to me than truth.

"I know that I am not alone in my struggle with cynicism. But most of us are not aware that it is a problem, or that it is taking hold in our hearts. It just feels like we can't find the joy in things, like we are too aware to trust or hope."

Cathie's insights are on target. Cynicism creates a numbness toward life.

Cynicism begins with the wry assurance that everyone has an angle. Behind every silver lining is a cloud. The cynic is always observing, critiquing, but never engaged, loving, and hoping. R. R. Reno, a Catholic scholar, called cynicism a perverse version of "being in the world but not of the world." We've moved from a Promethean age of great deeds to a listless, detached age.[1] A leading spokesperson for her generation, Cuban blogger Yoani Sánchez, at thirty-two years old, wrote, "Unlike our parents, we never believed in anything. Our defining characteristic is cynicism. But that's a double-edged sword. It protects you from crushing disappointment, but it paralyzes you from doing anything."[2]

> IF I GET AN ANSWER TO PRAYER, SOMETIMES I'LL THINK, IT WOULD HAVE HAPPENED ANYWAY.

To be cynical is to be distant. While offering a false intimacy of being "in the know," cynicism actually destroys intimacy. It leads to a creeping bitterness that can deaden and even destroy the spirit. Cathie is feeling the early edges of that.

A praying life is just the opposite. It engages evil. It doesn't take no for an answer. The psalmist was in God's face, hoping, dreaming, asking. Prayer is feisty. Cynicism, on the other hand, merely critiques. It is passive, cocooning itself from the passions of the great cosmic battle we are engaged in. It is without hope.

If you add an overlay of prayer to a cynical or even weary heart, it feels phony. For the cynic, life is already phony; you feel as if you are just contributing to the mess.

A Journey into Cynicism

Cynicism begins, oddly enough, with too much of the wrong kind of faith, with *naive optimism* or foolish confidence. At first glance, genuine faith and naive optimism appear identical since both foster confidence and hope. But the similarity is only surface deep. Genuine faith comes from knowing my heavenly Father loves, enjoys, and cares for me. Naive optimism is groundless. It is childlike trust without the loving Father.

No culture is more optimistic than ours. America's can-do spirit comes from the Judeo-Christian confidence in the goodness of God acting on our behalf. Knowing that the Good Shepherd is watching and protecting me gives me courage to go through the valley of the shadow of death. Even in the presence of my enemies, I can enjoy a rich feast because God is with me. Faith in God leads to can-do boldness and daring action, the hallmarks of Western civilization.

In the nineteenth century that optimism shifted its foundation from the goodness of God to the goodness of humanity. Faith became an end in itself. President Roosevelt rallied the nation during the Depression by calling people to have faith in faith. In *The Sound of Music* Julie Andrews sang about having confidence in confidence itself. Disneyland, the icon of naive optimism, promises that we'll find Prince Charming and live happily ever after.

Optimism rooted in the goodness of people collapses when it confronts the dark side of life. The discovery of evil for most of us is highly personal. We encounter the cruelty of our friends in junior and senior high. In college the princes turn out to be less than charming. If we have children, we learn they can be demanding and self-centered.

At breakfast recently I asked Kim if she wanted to get married.

She typed out on her speech computer, "No, it is too noisy." At first, I thought she meant the wedding, but then she corrected me. She was talking about the kids. She's right. Children can be self-absorbed, constantly demanding attention. Our modern child-centered homes simply reinforce this. Jesus is acutely aware of this side of children when he calls the Pharisees whining children:

> To what then shall I compare the people of this generation, and what are they like? They are like children sitting in the marketplace and calling to one another, "We played the flute for you, and you did not dance; we sang a dirge, and you did not weep." LUKE 7:31-32

Shattered optimism sets us up for the fall into defeated weariness and, eventually, cynicism. You'd think it would just leave us less optimistic, but we humans don't do neutral well. We go from seeing the bright side of everything to seeing the dark side of everything. We feel betrayed by life.

As my friend Cathie reflected on why this is true in her own life, she observed, "I make the jump from optimism to darkness so quickly because I am not grounded in a deep, abiding faith that God is in the matter, no matter what the matter is. I am looking for pleasant results, not deeper realities."

The movement from naive optimism to cynicism is the new American journey. In naive optimism we don't need to pray because everything is under control, everything is possible. In cynicism we can't pray because everything is out of control, little is possible.

With the Good Shepherd no longer leading us through the valley of the shadow of death, we need something to maintain our sanity. Cynicism's ironic stance is a weak attempt to maintain a lighthearted equilibrium in a world gone mad. These aren't just benign cultural trends; they are your life.

At some point, each of us comes face-to-face with the valley of the shadow of death. We can't ignore it. We can't remain neutral with evil. We either give up and distance ourselves, or we learn to walk with the Shepherd. There is no middle ground.

Without the Good Shepherd, we are alone in a meaningless story. Weariness and fear leave us feeling overwhelmed, unable to move. Cynicism leaves us doubting, unable to dream. The combination shuts down our hearts, and we just show up for life, going through the motions. Some days it's difficult to get out of our pajamas.

The Age of Cynicism

Our personal struggles with cynicism and defeated weariness are reinforced by an increasing tendency toward perfectionism in American culture. Believing you have to have the perfect relationship, the perfect children, or a perfect body sets you up for a critical spirit, the breeding ground for cynicism. In the absence of perfection, we resort to spin—trying to make ourselves look good, unwittingly dividing ourselves into a public and private self. We cease to be real and become the subject of cynicism.

The media's constant Monday-morning quarterbacking ("this shouldn't have happened") shapes our responses to the world, and we find ourselves demanding a pain-free, problem-free life. Our can-do attitude is turning into relentless self-centeredness.

Psychology's tendency to hunt for hidden motives adds a new layer to our ability to judge and thus be cynical about what others are doing. No longer do people commit adultery out of lust—they have unmet longings that need to be fulfilled.

Cynicism is the air we breathe, and it is suffocating our hearts. Unless we become disciples of Jesus, this present evil age will first deaden and then destroy our prayer lives, not to mention our souls. Our only hope is to follow Jesus as he leads us out of cynicism.

CHAPTER 10

FOLLOWING JESUS OUT OF CYNICISM

JESUS OFFERS SIX CURES for cynicism. Let's look at them in turn.

1. Be Warm but Wary

Jesus does not ignore evil. When he sends the disciples on their first missionary journey, he says, "I am sending you out as sheep in the midst of wolves, so be wise as serpents and innocent as doves" (Matthew 10:16). The overwhelming temptation when faced with evil is to become a wolf, to become cynical and lose your sheeplike spirit. Jesus tells us to instead be warm but wary—warm like a dove but wary like a serpent.

Jesus keeps in tension wariness about evil with a robust confidence in the goodness of his Father. He continues, "Beware of men" (10:17); then in the next breath he warms our hearts to our Father's love, saying, "Fear not, therefore; you are of more value than many sparrows" (10:31). Since your Father is intimately involved with the death of even one sparrow, won't he watch over your life? You don't have to distance yourself with an ironic, critical stance. You don't have to shut down your heart in the face of evil. You can engage it.

Instead of naive optimism, Jesus calls us to be wary, yet confident in our heavenly Father. We are to combine a robust trust in the Good Shepherd with a vigilance about the presence of evil in our own hearts and in the hearts of others.

The feel of a praying life is cautious optimism—caution because of the Fall, optimism because of redemption. Cautious optimism allows Jesus to boldly send his disciples into an evil world.

SO THE FEEL OF A PRAYING LIFE IS CAUTIOUS OPTIMISM—CAUTION BECAUSE OF THE FALL, OPTIMISM BECAUSE OF REDEMPTION.

When I was discussing this with my friend Cathie, she responded: "I love it! I am not called to put on rose-colored glasses and see everything in life as pretty and good and uplifting. Rather, I am called to trust that God sees what I see. In fact, he sees beyond what I see. He sees the whole story and is completely trustworthy to be at work on a grand scale, in the minutiae, and even in my own life."

Our confidence in the face of evil comes directly from the spirit of Jesus and animates a praying spirit. Audacious faith is one of the hallmarks of Jesus' followers. As we shall see later, praying is the principal way we enter into this expansion of the rule of Christ.

Jesus isn't just offering practical wisdom. His wisdom works because in his death he himself acted boldly, trusting his Father to help him. While Jesus is hanging on the cross, the religious leaders cynically mock him for his childlike trust. "He saved others; he cannot save himself. . . . He trusts in God; let God deliver him" (Matthew 27:42-43). In effect they are saying, "Look what happens when you act like a child and trust your Father. He abandons you." They accuse Jesus of naiveté, of acting foolishly because he believes in God's goodness.

Jesus does not answer his mockers because his ear is tuned to his Father. Like a wise serpent, he says nothing. Like a harmless dove, he does nothing. Even as his Father turns his back on him, Jesus trusts. Faced with the storm of life, he tightens his grip on his Father.

Jesus' childlike faith delighted his Father, and on Easter morning his Father acted on Jesus' dead body, bringing him to life. *He trusted in God; God delivered him.* Evil did not have the last word. Hope was born.

2. Learn to Hope Again

Cynicism kills hope. The world of the cynic is fixed and immovable; the cynic believes we are swept along by forces greater than we are. Dreaming feels like so much foolishness. Risk becomes intolerable. Prayer feels pointless, as if we are talking to the wind. Why set ourselves and God up for failure?

But Jesus is all about hope. Watch what he says *before* he helps these people. Before he heals a blind man, he tells his disciples that "this happened so that the works of God might be displayed in him" (John 9:3, NIV). Before he raises the widow of Nain's son, he tells her, "Weep not" (Luke 7:13, KJV), reversing the ancient Jewish funeral dirge, "Weep, all that are bitter of heart." When Jairus tells Jesus that his daughter is dead, Jesus says, "Do not fear; only believe" (Luke 8.50). Before Jesus heals a crippled woman, he tells her, "Woman, you are freed from your disability" (Luke 13:12). In each of these accounts, Jesus brings hope before he heals. He is not a healing machine—he touches people's hearts, healing their souls before he heals their bodies.

Hope begins with the heart of God. As you grasp what the Father's heart is like, how he loves to give, then prayer will begin to feel completely natural to you.

Many of us believe in the Christian hope of ultimate redemption, but we breathe the cynical spirit of our age and miss the heart of God. This was brought home to me when I discovered from a widow that her husband's philosophy of life went like this: "Expect nothing. Then if something good happens, be thankful." He had been a dear friend and godly counselor to me, but I was so surprised that I blurted out to his wife a confused mix of Romans 15:13 and Hebrews 13:20—"Sue, that sounds so different from 'May the God of hope, who brought again from the dead our Lord Jesus, fill you with all joy and peace in believing, so that by the power of the Holy Spirit you may abound in hope.'" Paul and the writer of Hebrews were bursting with the goodness of God. It spilled out of their hearts.

Disney is right. Because of the intrusion of a good God into an evil world, there are happy endings. Some of God's last words in the Bible are, "Behold, I make all things new" (Revelation 21:5, KJV). When you pray, you are touching the hopeful heart of God. When you know that, prayer becomes an adventure.

3. Cultivate a Childlike Spirit

I recently had a cynical moment during my morning prayer time. I was reflecting on some answers to the previous day's prayer, and I felt a lingering distaste in my soul. All I'd done was pray, and God had acted. It seemed too easy. Trite. I realized I was hunting for something to doubt. I was also hunting for something to do. At bottom, I didn't like grace. I wanted to be a player in the way God answered my request. In fact, at that moment I didn't like God. I was more comfortable with his distance.

What do I do with this old heart of mine? Exactly what we have been talking about. Cry out for grace like a hungry child. As soon as I begin simply asking for help, I have become like a little child again. I've stopped becoming cynical. Oddly enough, my prayer is answered almost immediately because in the act of praying I've become like a child. The cure for cynicism is to become like a little child again. Instead of critiquing others' stories, watch the story our Father is weaving.

To hear a good story, we need a simple, childlike wonder. Alan Jacobs, in his biography of C. S. Lewis, reflected that "those who will never be fooled can never be delighted, because without self-forgetfulness there can be no delight."[1] Lewis was able to write such captivating children's stories because he never lost his childlike spirit of wonder. The cynic is never fooled, so he is never delighted.

Years ago I went through a time when my life became so difficult I was unable to pray. I couldn't concentrate. So I stopped trying to have a coherent prayer time, and for weeks on end during my morning prayer time, I did nothing but pray through Psalm 23. I was fighting for my life. I didn't realize it at the time, but I was following the habit of divine reading called *lectio divina*, which was developed by the early church. By praying slowly through a portion of Scripture, I was allowing Scripture to shape my prayers.

As I prayed through Psalm 23, I began to reflect on the previous day and to look for the Shepherd's presence, for his touches of love. Even on especially hard days, I began to notice him everywhere, setting a table before me in the presence of my enemies, pursuing me with his love. Both the child and the cynic walk through the valley of the shadow of death. The cynic focuses on the darkness; the child focuses on the Shepherd.

Not long after my conversations with Cathie about cynicism, she went through the valley of the shadow of death and told me: "Cynicism feels more like bondage to me now. Jesus sets me free to love by showing me the dark, self-serving agenda I cling to in my cynicism. I am well aware that the journey is far from over, but I am learning to live in hope. I just need more practice."

The Shepherd's presence in the dark valley is so immediate, so powerful, that cynicism simply vanishes. There is no room for an ironic disengagement when you are fighting for your life. As you cling to the Shepherd, the fog of cynicism lifts.

Because cynicism misses the presence of the Shepherd, it reverses the picture in John 1 of light invading darkness. Like Saruman in *The Lord of the Rings*, cynicism looks too long into the Dark Lord's crystal ball. Its attempt to unmask evil unwittingly enlarges evil. Increasingly, we are returning to the world of pre-Christian paganism, where evil seemingly has the loudest voice and the last word.

Our modern, secular world has removed the Shepherd from Psalm 23. Look what happens to the psalm when you remove the Good Shepherd and everything he does:

> ~~The LORD is~~ my ~~shepherd,~~ I shall ~~not~~ be in want.
>   ~~He makes~~ me ~~lie down in green pastures,~~
> ~~he leads~~ me ~~beside quiet waters,~~
>   ~~he restores~~ my soul.
> ~~He guides~~ me ~~in paths of righteousness~~
>   ~~for his name's sake.~~
> ~~Even though~~ I walk
>   through the valley of the shadow of death,
> I ~~will~~ fear ~~no~~ evil,
>   ~~for you are with~~ me;
> ~~your rod and your staff,~~
>   ~~they comfort~~ me.
> ~~You prepare a table before~~ me
>   in the presence of my enemies.
> ~~You anoint~~ my head ~~with oil,~~
>   my cup ~~overflows.~~
> ~~Surely goodness and love will follow~~ me
>   all the days of my life,
> ~~and~~ I ~~will dwell in the house of the LORD~~
>   ~~forever.~~
>
> PSALM 23:1-6, NIV

We are left obsessing over our wants in the valley of the shadow of death, paralyzed by fear in the presence of our enemies. No wonder so many are so cynical. With the Good Shepherd gone, we are alone in a world of evil.

In contrast, a childlike spirit interprets life through the lens of Psalm 23. Jesus acts out Psalm 23 at the feeding of the five thousand. When he sees that the crowds are "like sheep without a shepherd," he feeds them spiritually by "teach[ing] them many things." Then he has them "sit down . . . on the green grass" and feeds them with so much food that their baskets overflow (Mark 6:34-44).

Jesus meditates on Psalm 22 to prepare for his death. On the cross, overwhelmed by evil, he recites Psalm 22:1: "My God, my God, why have you forsaken me?" In the darkness, Jesus doesn't analyze what he doesn't know. He clings to what he knows.

4. Cultivating a Thankful Spirit

Immersing myself in Psalm 23 became a habit during this period of suffering. Prayer wasn't self-discipline; it was desperation. I began by thanking God for his touches of grace from the previous day. Either I thanked God or I gave into bitterness, the stepchild of cynicism. There was no middle ground.

Now years later, I still begin my prayer times by reflecting on the Shepherd's care. I drift through the previous day and watch God at work. Nothing undercuts cynicism more than a spirit of thankfulness. You begin to realize that your whole life is a gift.

Thankfulness isn't a matter of forcing yourself to see the happy side of life. That would be like returning to naive optimism. Thanking God restores the natural order of our dependence on God. It enables us to see life as it really is.

Not surprisingly, thanklessness is the first sin to emerge from our ancient rebellion against God. Paul writes, "For although they knew God, they did not honor him as God or give thanks to him" (Romans 1:21).

Paul's own life reflects a spirit of thanksgiving. Almost every time he describes how he prayed for people, he mentions thanksgiving.

- First, I thank my God through Jesus Christ for all of you. (Romans 1:8)
- I give thanks to my God always for you. (1 Corinthians 1:4)
- I do not cease to give thanks for you, remembering you in my prayers. (Ephesians 1:16)
- I thank my God in all my remembrance of you, always in every prayer of mine. (Philippians 1:3-4)
- We always thank God, the Father of our Lord Jesus Christ, when we pray for you. (Colossians 1:3)
- We give thanks to God always for all of you, constantly mentioning you in our prayers. (1 Thessalonians 1:2)
- We also thank God constantly. (1 Thessalonians 2:13)
- For what thanksgiving can we return to God for you? (1 Thessalonians 3:9)
- We ought always to give thanks to God for you. (2 Thessalonians 1:3)
- But we ought always to give thanks to God for you. (2 Thessalonians 2:13)
- I thank God . . . as I remember you constantly in my prayers night and day. (2 Timothy 1:3)
- I thank my God always when I remember you in my prayers. (Philemon 1:4)

Paul encourages that same style of praying in the churches:

- In everything by prayer and supplication with thanksgiving let your requests be made known to God. (Philippians 4:6)
- Continue steadfastly in prayer, being watchful in it with thanksgiving. (Colossians 4:2)
- Pray without ceasing, give thanks in all circumstances. (1 Thessalonians 5:17-18)

To become thankful is to be drawn into the fellowship of the Father, the Son, and the Spirit, into their enjoyment of one another, of life, and of people.

Cynicism looks reality in the face, calls it phony, and prides itself on its insight as it pulls back. Thanksgiving looks reality in the face and rejoices at God's care. It replaces a bitter spirit with a generous one.

In the face of Adam and Eve's evil, God takes up needle and thread and patiently sews fine leather clothing for them (see Genesis 3:21). He covers their divided, hiding selves with love. The same God permits his Son to be stripped naked so we could be clothed. God is not cynical in the face of evil. He loves.

5. Cultivating Repentance

Cynics imagine they are disinterested observers on a quest for authenticity. They assume they are humble because they offer nothing. In fact, they feel deeply superior because they think they see through everything.

C. S. Lewis pointed out that if you see through everything, you eventually see nothing.

> You cannot go on "explaining away" forever: you will find that you have explained explanation itself away. You cannot go on "seeing through" things for ever. The whole point of seeing through something is to see something through it. . . . If you see through everything, then everything is transparent. But a wholly transparent world is an invisible world. To "see through" all things is the same as not to see.[2]

Lewis said that what was required was a restoration of the innocent eye, the eye that can see with wonder.[3] That is the eye of a child.

While purporting to "see through" others' façades, cynics lack purity of heart. A significant source of cynicism is the fracture between my heart and my behavior. It goes something like this: My heart gets out of tune with God, but life goes on. So I continue to perform and say Christian things, but they are just words. I talk about Jesus without the presence of Jesus. There is a disconnect between what I present and who I am. My words sound phony, so others' words sound phony too. In short, my empty religious performance leads me to think that everyone is phony. The very thing I am doing, I accuse others of doing. Adding judgment to hypocrisy breeds cynicism.

All sin involves a splitting of the personality—what James calls being "double-minded" (4:8). If we become proud, we have an inflated sense of self that has lost touch with who we really are. If a husband watches porn online and then warmly greets his wife, he has created two people—one public and one hidden. If you talk about friends disparagingly behind their backs, you've created two personalities—the loving friend and the gossiping friend. You try to keep the personalities separate by telling those to whom you gossip, "Please keep this in confidence."

We first see this split immediately after Adam and Eve sin. Their friendly, walking-with-God selves are replaced by hiding, naked selves. God's searching question, "Where are you?" (Genesis 3:9), attempts to expose this fracture of the two selves.

Repentance brings the split personality together and thus restores integrity to the life. The real self is made public. When the proud person is humbled, the elevated self is united with the true self.

In contrast, cynicism focuses on the other person's split personality and need to repent. It lacks the humility that comes from first taking the beam out of its own eye. Jesus says, "You hypocrite, first take the log out of your own eye, and then you will see clearly to take the speck out of your brother's eye" (Matthew 7:5).

You see these dynamics when David arrives at King Saul's camp, bringing food for his older brothers. David is surprised to hear Goliath taunting the Israelites and their God. He is shocked that no one has the courage to challenge Goliath and blurts out, "Who is this uncircumcised Philistine, that he should defy the armies of the living God?" (1 Samuel 17:26). David reacts to the split between Israel's public faith and its battlefield cowardice.

David has been off by himself, separated from the current of unbelief dominating his culture, developing a rich walk with the Shepherd. David's obscurity has protected him from the cynical spirit of the age. His public faith and private practice are in harmony. His *normal* is experiencing God's presence in the valley of the shadow of death, where he has killed both lions and bears with his sling. Goliath just looks like a big bear. The result? Israel's unbelief feels odd, out of place.

When David's older brother Eliab gets wind of David questioning the other soldiers, he mocks David: "Why have you come down? And with whom have you left those few sheep in the wilderness? I know your presumption and the evil of your heart, for you have come down to see the battle" (17:28). Eliab mistakenly believes he sees right through his brother's motivations. He thinks that David, bored with the sheep, is there for adventure, egging the soldiers on so he can see a battle. Eliab's perception of David's motivation is likely his own motivation. He reads his own issues into David, cynically accusing his little brother of having cynical motives. Eliab lacks purity of heart, so he presumes David lacks it as well.

We see the same dynamics in the Garden of Eden. Satan accuses God of cynical motivations, when in fact Satan cynically twists God's commands to his own ends. Cynicism is the seed for Adam and Eve's rebellion against God, and it is the seed for our own personal rebellions. While attempting to unmask evil, the cynic creates it.

Eliab also sees himself incorrectly. He has a false, elevated view of himself. He mocks David's lowly job as a shepherd: "With whom have you left those few sheep in the wilderness?" Eliab the Mighty Warrior mocks his little brother's sheep tending while the real Eliab is cowering in his tent with the rest of the Israelites.

David brushes aside Eliab's cynicism and ends up with Saul's blessing and armor. He quickly realizes that he can't fight in Saul's armor. He can't be something he is not. He is a shepherd, not a warrior. His inner and outer lives need to match. He is authentic.

David reaches for his staff, gathers five smooth stones from the creek, and moves toward Goliath. Goliath, enraged by the insult of the Israelites sending only a boy, misses the sling and sees only the staff. "Am I a dog, that you come to me with sticks?" (17:43).

David's reply evokes the spirit of prayer: "The LORD saves not with sword and spear. For the battle is the LORD's, and he will give you into our hand" (17:47). David quickens his pace. The closer he is, the greater the stone's velocity and the more accurate the placement. Goliath never even sees it coming.

Like David, the pure in heart begin with seeing through themselves. Having confronted their own bears and lions in the valley of the shadow of death, they see clearly the abnormality of Goliath cursing the living God. By cultivating a lifestyle of repentance, the pure in heart develop integrity, and their own fractures are healed. By beginning with their own impurity, they avoid the critical, negative stance of cynicism.

The good news is that by following Jesus we don't have to be captured by the spirit of the age. We don't have to be defined by our culture. Like Paul in Philippi, we can sing in jail (see Acts 16:25). Like David, we can calmly pick up five smooth stones when faced with overwhelming odds.

I've saved the sixth cure for cynicism for the next chapter.

DEVELOPING AN EYE FOR JESUS

JILL AND I MANAGE a part-time, seasonal tax business. Several years ago I arrived at the office at eight in the morning for a quick visit before customers arrived. I was depressed, struggling with cynicism and even bouts of unbelief. I noticed the computer's hard drive was almost full, so I decided to delete an old program. Without thinking, I clicked "yes" to "Delete all shared files?" and I got the blue screen of death. The computer was dead.

I glanced at the appointment book and saw our first appointment wasn't due until eleven thirty. The next several hours were a frenzy of activity, calling help desks and hunting for backup disks. But the problem still wasn't fixed when our customer walked in. I asked our preparer to tell her that we'd be ready "any minute now."

I needed to go home to get a disk, so I slunk past our "eleven thirty," avoiding eye contact. It was close to noon when I slipped by her again to get a backup computer. I stole a glance at her and noticed that she was sitting quietly, without a hint of impatience. When I came back at one, she was still waiting serenely. Her calm demeanor was unchanged when we finally did her tax return at three o'clock.

I am not kidding—this woman sat in our office for three-and-a-half hours without a single question or complaint. And this is Philadelphia! She'd taken the bus, so I offered to drive her home. Depressed and frustrated, I blurted out, "Does Jesus make a difference in your life?" (I thought she might be Catholic.) Please understand, I was not witnessing—I wanted to be witnessed to. She replied, "Jesus is everything to me. I talk to him all the time."

I was floored, partly by the freshness and simplicity of her faith but mainly by the unusual patience that displayed her faith. My frantic busyness was a sharp contrast to her quiet waiting in prayer. She reflected the spirit of prayer. I reflected the spirit of human self-sufficiency.

I'd begun the day depressed, partly struggling with the relevance of Jesus. Now I was overwhelmed by the irony of my unbelief. Jesus had been sitting in our waiting room, right in front of me, as obvious as the daylight. I had walked by him all day. I had wondered if Jesus was around, and he had been silently waiting all day, saying nothing. It was a stunning display of patience.

JESUS HAD BEEN SITTING IN OUR WAITING ROOM, RIGHT IN FRONT OF ME, AS OBVIOUS AS THE DAYLIGHT.

Cynicism looks in the wrong direction. It looks for the cracks in Christianity instead of looking for the presence of Jesus. It is an orientation of the heart. The sixth cure for cynicism, then, is this: develop an eye for Jesus.

I knew from my study of the Gospels where to look for Jesus. For the most part, his earthly life was hidden, like a seed in the field. If you were to look at a photo album of his life, you would not see him with the best and the brightest but with the low and the slow. The only photo of him with a famous person would be with Pilate at his trial, but then Jesus was in bad shape. The seed was beginning to die.

A principal source of cynicism comes from looking up at Christian leaders who have gotten Jesus' kingdom mixed up with their own. Ministry itself can create a mask of performance, the projection of success. Everyone wants to be a winner. In contrast, Jesus never used his power to show off. He used his power for love. So he wasn't immediately noticeable. Humility makes you disappear, which is why we avoid it.

In order to see Jesus, I would have to look lower. I would have to look at people simply, as a child does. I began to ask myself, "Where did I see Jesus today?" I hunted for the difference between what others would normally be like and what they had become through the presence of Jesus. The presence of Jesus, the only truly authentic person who ever lived, would reveal itself in the restoration of authenticity in people. I'd see Christians whose inner and outer lives matched.

Spotting Jesus in Cleveland

When we look for Jesus we can find him, even in seemingly mundane encounters, as I did one morning in Cleveland, just a month later.

My friend Jim picked me up at six fifteen in the morning and drove me to a men's breakfast Bible study. Afterward, I returned my rental car to the airport and, while taking the rental car bus to the airport, talked to my wife. A little later I talked with my mom.

When Jim picked me up for breakfast, the first thing he did was apologize for not praying for Kim the previous evening. He and I had talked about her over dinner and briefly prayed together. Rarely will someone apologize over such a seemingly small matter, or even make that kind of inquiry in the first place. His apology had the smell of Jesus about it.

At breakfast the men were reading a seventeenth-century Puritan book on a godly perspective of work. These men were taking seriously Jesus' exhortation to build their lives on the rock of obedience to his words. Not exactly edge-of-the-seat reading, but imagine if politicians or corporate executives caught in the latest scandal studied a book by Puritans on work!

When I returned the rental car, the attendant greeted me cheerfully. When he saw my name on the receipt, he said, "You have a name from the Bible." He was partly witnessing, partly fishing for a fellow Christian, and partly just in love with the Bible. His cheerfulness and exuberant faith didn't reflect the seeming lowliness of his job. Once again, I saw the presence of Jesus.

While I was on the rental bus to the terminal, Jill phoned. She was laughing so hard I had trouble hearing her. Earlier that week, the school bus manager had called us. He was concerned that Kim, who was still in high school, wasn't waiting for the bus to stop before she started crossing the street. As soon as the bus began slowing down, Kim would head across the busy street. Her autism made it difficult for her to wait.

So Jill drew a chalk box on our driveway and told Kim she had to stand in the box until the bus driver turned on the red light. When she called me that morning, Jill was standing in the pouring rain in the chalk box with Kim, laughing at the ridiculousness of her situation. It was the laughter of faith, rejoicing in tribulation because the tribulation was so funny. Again, the presence of Jesus.

Then my mom called while I was walking through the airport. She briefly described a situation where she'd been falsely accused and had realized she needed to unilaterally forgive without the possibility of reconciliation. No mention of the gory details, just a quiet reflection on her own heart.

Jesus was everywhere, transforming that mundane morning—caring and apologizing (Jim), studying and obeying (the men), witnessing and befriending (the attendant), suffering and laughing (Jill), forgiving and not gossiping (Mom). Each of these people was living out his or her faith without a mask. With a little conscious reflection, it is easy to see the beauty of Jesus.

Instead of focusing on other people's lack of integrity, on their split personalities, we need to focus on how Jesus is reshaping the church to be more like himself. We need to view the body of Christ with grace.

Paul delights in the influence of Jesus on people's lives. It is at the heart of his praying. He doesn't have a generalized spirit of thanksgiving; he is thankful for "you." Even with the messed-up Corinthian church, Paul is thankful: "I give thanks to my God always for you" (1 Corinthians 1:4). Then he addresses their permitting of incest, suing one another in court, and getting drunk at the Lord's Supper! Because he keeps his eye on the present work of Jesus, Paul is not overcome by evil but overcomes evil with good. Goodness infests Paul's prayer life. He is living out the gospel. Even as God has extended grace to Paul, so Paul extends grace to the Corinthians. He looks at the church through rose-colored glasses, tinted with the blood of his Savior.

Obviously, Christians are not better than non-Christians. In fact, Paul says in 1 Corinthians 1 that the raw material of believers is worse than that of unbelievers. The Corinthians themselves prove that! Christians aren't superior, but our Savior is. He makes the difference. He is alive and well in his church.

Looking Ahead

So far in the book, we've examined the basics of a praying life and learned what it means to become like a little child. The very thing we are afraid of, our brokenness, is the door to our Father's heart. A grace-saturated vision enables us to defeat cynicism and talk with our Father, restoring a childlike simplicity and wonder.

Our vision has been largely interior, looking at our hearts and at heart barriers, such as cynicism, that distance us from the Father. Now in part 3 we shift to a more exterior vision and focus on asking. We shift from *being* to *doing*, from *my* needs to *your* needs. A praying life needs both visions for balance. We'll also continue to see how cynicism has taken root in our larger culture and dulled our hearts to the possibility of a praying life.

LEARNING TO ASK YOUR FATHER

CHAPTER 12

WHY ASKING IS SO HARD

For her seventh-grade science project, our youngest daughter, Emily, decided to measure bacteria levels along the bank of a local stream. I was doing the project with her, and at our first stop, we waded into the creek, got a water sample, and carefully tested it. We were both nervous about following the precise steps of our little bacteria-testing kit, so before we started we prayed.

Our family's record with science projects was not stellar. The previous year Emily barely got a passing grade for her experiment on training fish to eat in response to a flashlight. (There was a reason that Pavlov used dogs and not fish.) The year before that, Jill, thinking it was a bag of trash, took our son Andrew's experiment to the thrift store the day before it was due. She spent the rest of the day going through the thrift-store dumpsters in a vain attempt to retrieve it. We definitely needed to pray.

After we finished our first test, Emily took out her logbook to record each step. She asked me what we'd done first, and I told her we'd prayed.

She said, "I can't write that."

"Why not? We prayed."

"That isn't how it works, Dad. They don't want us to say that."

Emily had gone to Christian schools her whole life, starting with nursery school. She regularly attended church and Sunday school and went to a Christian camp in the summer. All her friends were Christians, along with her brothers and sisters, aunts and uncles. Frankly, she lived in a Christian ghetto. Yet this mysterious "they" trumped this massive Christian influence in her life.

Western culture (North America and Europe), along with public cultures created by the West through communism (such as Russia and China), is the most publicly atheistic culture that has ever existed. Among the thousands of cultures in the history of humanity, our culture is the only one not to have any regular public acknowledgment of a spiritual world. In view of the sweep of human history, our culture is odd.

Reflecting on the ancient world, N. T. Wright, a respected scholar, wrote, "Religion was woven tightly into the whole social fabric of the world, as it has been at almost all times and almost all places in human history, with only the last two centuries in certain parts of the Western world being exceptions."[1] Purely from the standpoint of anthropology, it is odd that our newscasters don't open the news with prayer.[2]

How did this happen? If you go back far enough, "they" is the eighteenth-century Enlightenment. During this period in history, the leading thinkers decided they didn't need God anymore. As illustrated by the following chart, thinkers such as Kant divided the world into *feelings*, things that are true only for me, and *facts*, things that are true for everyone. Kant lumped prayer and religion together with other things we can't be certain of, such as love or right and wrong.[3] They belong to the feeling world of personal opinion reflected by the top half of this chart. In the bottom half of the chart are things we are certain of, such as trees and cars. They are public and real—true for everyone.

Author Nancy Pearcey summarized this split between facts and

HOW MOST PEOPLE VIEW THE WORLD

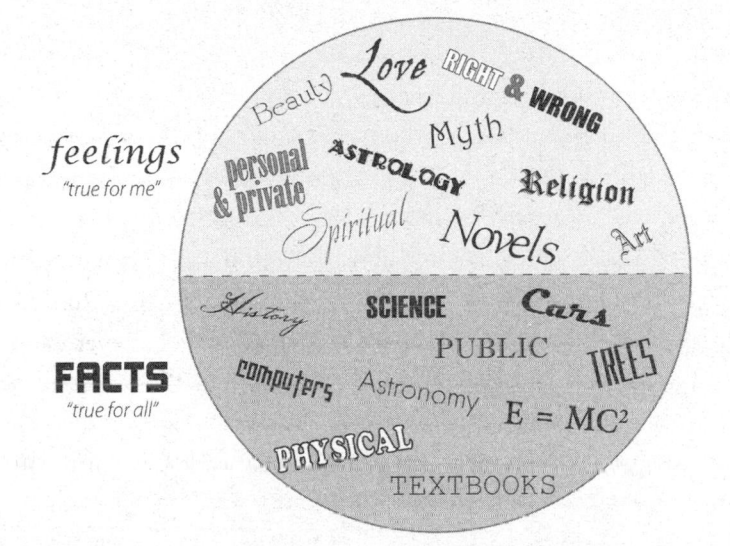

feelings, saying, "The lower story became the realm of publicly veri-fiable *facts* while the upper story became the realm of socially con-structed *values*."[4] This way of viewing the world is called secularism. When you lump God together with feelings and subjective opinion, then God is marginalized. Prayer feels odd.

It used to be that only university professors believed in secularism, but with the advent of television and the rise of popular culture, the Enlightenment has made its way into the living room. It has captured the West, obscuring our view of what the world is really like. Now, we see a flat, two-dimensional world that relegates God to the sidelines as a feel-good cheerleader. Prayer is private and personal, not public and real. If it makes you feel good, then pray for sick people or commune with God, but don't take it seriously or make it public.

C. S. Lewis was referring to the Enlightenment worldview when he said, "Nearly all that I loved [top of the chart] I believed to be imaginary; nearly all that I believed to be real [bottom of the chart] I thought grim and meaningless."[5] When his good friend J. R. R.

Tolkien told him that Christianity was a "true myth," it merged Lewis's two great quests for beauty and truth.[6]

The Power of the Enlightenment

Before the Enlightenment, early scientists in the West wrote in their notes that they prayed. Johannes Kepler, the Danish astronomer who discovered the laws of interplanetary motion, wrote that he was "thinking God's thoughts after him."[7] Newton and others regularly gave glory to God in their writings.

Ironically, modern science is possible because Christianity taught that God created a world separate from himself. If the world is separate, we can investigate it.

Ancient cultures were unable to seriously investigate the world because their gods were inseparable from the world. For instance, the Canaanite god Baal is the god of thunder and storm. When it thunders, you are hearing Baal. If thunder equals Baal, then there is nothing to investigate. Your god is enmeshed in the world.

Even the ancient Greeks, who seemed to get closer than anyone to science, couldn't become real scientists because of their suspicion that physical matter was chaos. They lacked the Judeo-Christian view, which believes that God created a world separate from himself, with wisdom as his companion (see Proverbs 8:12, 22-31).

Secularism is a religious belief that grew out of the pride of human achievement, particularly scientific achievement. It masquerades as science or reality, opposed to religion, which it calls opinion. Secularism claims to have given us the gift of science when, in fact, Christianity gave us the gift of science.

Let me briefly demonstrate the power of the Enlightenment. Almost all the Ivy League colleges, along with hundreds of other American universities, began as Christian universities, but under the influence of secularism they jettisoned their Christian faith. The same thing happened with Jewish-Orthodox faith. It survived attempts to exterminate it by Pharaoh (Moses), the Philistines (David), the Syrians (Elijah), the Babylonians (Daniel), the Persians (Esther), and the Samaritans (Ezra). It survived the Greeks during the time of the Maccabees, the Roman destruction of Jerusalem in AD 70, and the forced evacuation from Palestine in AD 135. It survived Islam, the Crusades, the Spanish Inquisition, the Russian tsars, and Hitler's Final Solution. But Orthodox Judaism has barely survived the Enlightenment. It is but a shadow of its past, claiming only 10 to 15 percent of Judaism.

The Enlightenment mind-set marginalizes prayer because it doesn't permit God to connect with this world. You are allowed a personal, local deity as long as you keep him out of your science notes and don't take him seriously.

Peter Jennings, ABC's former anchorman, used to tell reporters, "When you ask someone, 'What got you through this crisis?' and they say, 'God,' don't say, 'No, what really got you through?'"[8] Jennings was aware that the fog of the Enlightenment tempted our cultural elites to dismiss the value of prayer, of God at work.

Charles Malik, a Greek Orthodox philosopher, theologian, and diplomat, perceptively described the spirit of the Enlightenment:

> Nothing can be farther from and more foreign to the whole temper of modern man than the anguished cry of David: "From the end of the earth will I cry unto thee, when my heart is overwhelmed: lead me to the rock that is higher than I." Modern man recognizes no such rock, and that is the source of all estrangement and all tragedy.[9]

The Modern Roots of Cynicism

The Enlightenment doesn't *say* that religion is not real. It *defines* it as not real. Once you've defined religion as not real, then it isn't even an item for discussion. Add to the secular model of reality our inability to follow Jesus, and you've got phoniness. First, prayer is defined as phony, and then it feels phony.

When our children encounter the pull of the world in their teen-age years, it is easy for them to say that God-talk is phony because it has been relegated to the not-real world. So twelve-year-old Emily instinctively felt that she lived in two worlds: a God world and a real world. When those worlds touched, she tried to keep them separate. She has been breathing the air of the culture.

FIRST, PRAYER IS DEFINED AS PHONY, AND THEN IT FEELS PHONY.

Secularism is a cynical view of reality. For example, because *love* is not quantifiable, it gets relegated to the upper half, which is *feelings*. When Robertson McQuilkin resigned his semi-nary presidency to take care of his ailing wife, he attended a workshop where the expert said that McQuilkin's dedication to his wife was really guilt.[10] The expert had no category for love. It is a perfect example of the limitation of the Enlightenment's view of real-ity. *Love*, this thing that everyone is pursuing, is a noncategory among social scientists. Something is seriously wrong with a view of the world that can't explain the most basic components of life.

A Child Prays in a Secular World

In an article in the *New York Times Magazine*, Dana Tierney described how both she and her husband John, a writer for the *New York Times*, rejected their childhood faith. They had their son Luke baptized to placate their families, but that was it. When her husband went to Iraq as an imbedded reporter, Dana was understandably fearful. She was surprised at how calm four-year-old Luke was. She assumed that it was just youthful naiveté, until one day when they were watching television together they happened to see the wedding of a solider who had returned from Iraq. Thinking it wouldn't cause any undue fears in Luke, she figured it was okay for them to watch it together. But then the soldier described his fear of returning to Iraq. For just an instant, Dana saw Luke form his hands to pray. When she asked him about it, Luke at first denied it, but after he did it a second time, he confessed that he had been praying.

Dana was stunned, partly by Luke's faith, and partly by how his faith allowed him to be calm and her lack of faith caused her to be fearful. She was also embarrassed that her four-year-old son instinctively knew that praying for his dad was socially inappropriate.

Because Luke was created for communion with God, he naturally drifted into prayer. He was unaware that two hundred years ago Kant divided knowledge into public and private, thus marginalizing prayer. Because Luke had become aware of his own culture, he also knew he had to hide his praying from his mother.

Under the influence of the Enlightenment, our modern culture has ruled out prayer and religion from the discussion. So Emily doesn't report in her science notes that she prayed, and Luke folds his hands secretly in his mother's presence.

However, that Dana even wrote this article is indicative of the postmodern winds blowing through our culture. Science is beginning to lose its godlike status.

Dana asked Luke when he first began to believe in God. "I don't know. I've always known he exists." Unlike many of our intellectual gatekeepers, Dana does not patronize believers. In the article she described how many of her nonreligious friends feel freed from religion as if they've been liberated from superstition. Not Dana. She feels like she is missing out. When she watches her religious friends, she notices that they "have an expansiveness of spirit. When they walk along a stream, they don't just see water falling over rocks; the sight fills them with ecstasy. They see a realm of hope beyond this world. I just see a babbling brook. I don't get the message."[11]

What Dana observed about believers—their wonder over the creation—is at the heart of why we even have science. If the stream is a result of accidental natural forces, then you just see water, rocks, and dirt. If God equals the stream, then you worship the stream god, not the creator of the stream. But if God created the stream, then wonder and curiosity naturally flow into study.

In his critique of the Enlightenment worldview, Charles Malik, the Greek Orthodox "C. S. Lewis," said the secret to seeing God behind all things is to become a child again—like little Luke.

> We could see Him beyond all His creation only if we become "babes and sucklings." Just as the children, not the chief priests and the scribes, when they saw him in human form in the temple cried, "Hosanna to the Son of David," so we, if we are born again and become like them, children ourselves—intuitive, pure, simple, direct, receptive, open—could pass from His creation to Himself. . . . I mean the heart is absolutely sure that beyond all this show . . . there is One who created and continues to uphold it. The "strength" that the babes and sucklings of faith show, by their simple and direct and unhesitating affirmation, puts to shame all the strength of the clever and the strong.[12]

Wonder over the universe was at the heart of Einstein's science. He was out of step with the secular spirit of our age when he wrote, "A spirit is manifest in the laws of the universe—a spirit vastly superior to that of man, and one in the face of which we with our modest powers must feel humble."[13]

Because it is my Father's world, then as Emily and I kneel by a stream to do a science experiment, we should pray and ask for his help. It is a complete unity of thinking and feeling, physical and spiritual, public and personal. It is my Father's world.

By the way, Luke's daddy returned safely from Iraq, and Emily's experiment went on to earn first place in the regional science fair and finally our state.

CHAPTER 13

WHY WE CAN ASK

A FEW YEARS AGO I was in London to do a prayer seminar at a church made up of former Hindus, Muslims, and Sikhs. The Sunday morning after the seminar, just as the church service was beginning, a former Hindu woman, Asha, approached me in the vestibule and asked if I'd pray for her twelve-year-old granddaughter, who was having a hard time living with her parents and wanted to live with Asha. I said, "Yes, I'll pray for her." Asha slipped into the service, got her granddaughter, and motioned for me to come into a side room where I prayed for her. We then returned to the service. The entire interaction didn't take more than a couple of minutes.

It would never occur to an American Christian to approach a guest speaker whom you had just met and ask him or her to pray for your granddaughter, right there on the spot. It would feel intrusive, selfish, inappropriate. Our definition of prayer as private and personal makes us hesitant to buttonhole a speaker.

We might approach the speaker to ask his or her advice. We readily admit our lack of knowledge, but it would never occur to us that the speaker might have access to divine power. We don't think it would make any difference. We are confident in science but not

God. The issue of power—the ability to make a difference, to change something—is at the heart of asking.

Asha's culture has not told her that prayer is private and personal, so publicly and shamelessly she asked for God's power to change a situation where she felt trapped. Untouched by the Enlightenment, aware that "this is my Father's world," she didn't hesitate.

Asha had another non-Western idea firmly in mind. She believes that some people are more powerful with God. Any Asian will tell you that is true. Africans would agree, as would Latin Americans. The only people out of touch are Westerners. We know this is true in other realms. For instance, we know that some financial advisers and doctors are better than others. In our egalitarian world, it doesn't occur to us that this would also be true in the spiritual world.

LEARNED DESPERATION IS AT THE HEART OF A PRAYING LIFE.

But unlike these other kinds of experts, power in prayer comes from being in touch with your weakness. To teach us how to pray, Jesus told stories of weak people who knew they couldn't do life on their own. The persistent widow and the friend at midnight get access, not because they are strong but because they are desperate. Learned desperation is at the heart of a praying life.

An Infinite-Personal God

Asha believes that an infinite God is personally involved in the details of her life. An infinite-personal God is such an astounding idea that we struggle to grasp it. Our modern world is okay with an infinite God, as long as he doesn't get too personal, as long as he stays out of science notes. Non-Western cultures have no trouble thinking that God is personal, but they doubt he is infinite. Thus ancient battles between nations were often seen as power struggles between different gods.

The Syrians thought they'd lost the battle with Israel in the hills because they'd been in the wrong place, away from their god's power center. They told their king, "Their gods are gods of the hills, and so they were stronger than we. But let us fight against them in the plain, and surely we shall be stronger than they" (1 Kings 20:23). So they moved the battle to the plain, where their god was stronger. They had no doubt that the Israelite God was real and personal. They just doubted he was infinite. But no one told the Israelite God. He won the battle on the plain as well as the hills. The Syrians had stumbled across the infinite-personal God.

David captures the infinite-personal God with the first sentence of Psalm 23, "The LORD [infinite] is my shepherd [personal]." In the ancient Near East nothing else came close to this picture of intimacy. Occasionally an ancient king would be described as a shepherd of his people, but the gods were never interested in "little old me." The words *me* or *my*, which sound like "ee" in Hebrew, ring thirteen times through the psalm. The infinite God is interested in me.

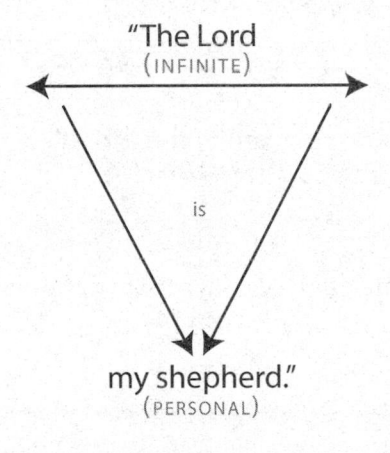

"The Lord
(INFINITE)

is

my shepherd."
(PERSONAL)

Likewise, we can feel Solomon's wonder in his prayer of dedication for the temple as he contemplates the infinite God dwelling personally with us. "Will God indeed dwell with man on the earth?

Behold, heaven and the highest heaven cannot contain you, how much less this house that I have built!" (2 Chronicles 6:18). Because God is both infinite and personal, he will "[listen] to the cry and to the prayer that your servant prays" (6:19).

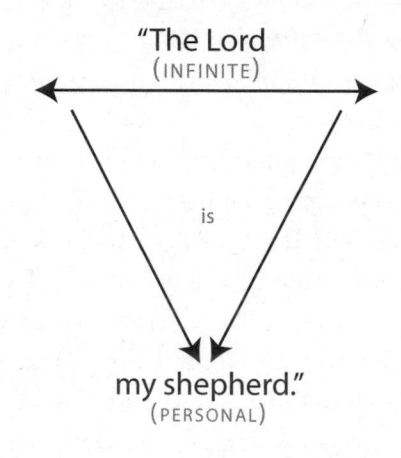

Isaiah is also in awe that God "[dwells] in the high and holy place [infinite], and also with him who is of a contrite and lowly spirit [personal]" (Isaiah 57:15).

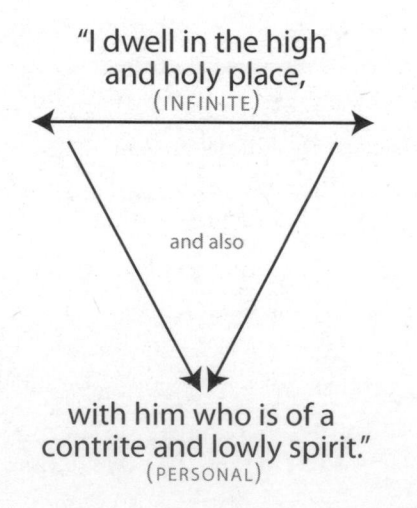

Majesty and humility are such an odd fit. This is one reason we struggle with prayer. We just don't think God could be concerned with the puny details of our lives. We either believe he's too big or that we're not that important. No wonder Jesus told us to be like little children! Little children are not daunted by the size of their parents. They come, regardless.

Einstein struggled with the oddness of a universe that reflects an infinite-personal God. On the one hand, he consistently articulated an Enlightenment view of God as depersonalized and distant. A sixth-grade girl from a Sunday school in New York once asked him, "Do scientists pray?" Einstein replied, "A scientist will hardly be inclined to believe that events could be influenced by a prayer."[1] Yet he frequently referred to God personally. When debating Niels Bohr on quantum theory, Einstein said, "God doesn't play with dice." In his biography of Einstein, Walter Isaacson said that Einstein's frequent references to a personal God were genuine. "It was not Einstein's style to speak disingenuously in order to appear to conform. . . . We should do him the honor of taking him at his word."[2] In fact, Einstein said his science was driven by a belief in a "God who reveals *himself* in the harmony of all that exists" (emphasis added).[3]

We don't like God too close, especially if God is a deity we can't control. We have a primal fear of walking with God in the garden, naked, without clothing. We desperately want intimacy, but when it comes, we pull back, fearful of a God who is too personal, too pure. We're much more comfortable with God at a distance.

A praying life opens itself to an infinite, searching God. As we shall see, we can't do that without releasing control, without constantly surrendering our will to God. "Your will be done, on earth as it is in heaven" (Matthew 6:10) is actually scary.

CHAPTER 14

HOW PERSONAL IS GOD?

I RECENTLY READ an otherwise excellent book on prayer in which the author implied we shouldn't pray for trivial things such as parking places. The author said such requests seem selfish. When I read this, I couldn't wait to tell my mom, Rose Marie Miller.

She was back in Philadelphia for a wedding of one of her twenty-four grandchildren. Mom, now eighty-two, works full time as a missionary in London. After raising five children on a meager pastor's salary, she and my dad went on to share the gospel in the slums of Uganda and the streets of Dublin. Now in addition to discipling South Asian women, Mom is building friendships with South Asian cab drivers in London.

We met for breakfast, and when I told her what this author thought about prayers for parking spaces, she looked a little incredulous, cocked her head, started laughing, and said, "How else would you find a parking place? When I am driving with the grandchildren in London, they always say, 'Grandma, would you pray that we'd find a parking spot?'" Mom's response reminded me of Sarah laughing at the goodness of God when he surprised her with a son. God's gift turned Sarah's cynical laughter of the previous year into pure joy.

Recently, Mom found a letter she'd written from Kampala, Uganda, in December 1979, not long after Idi Amin had fled the country. Mom and Dad were in Uganda, living on the eighth floor of a rundown hotel, sharing the gospel, and doing what they could to help. Trash collection had completely stopped in the city. So along with several Ugandans, they found a trash truck and started sharing the love of God while they collected people's trash. In the letter, she described her typical day:

> Words simply fail to express the almost total chaos of a country after eight years of a brutal civil war. When we use the bathroom, if we are fortunate, the toilet will flush—if not you get the fire hose from the end of the hall—if you are too late, then you find others have used it before you—*so you learn to pray for water*. If it comes on in the middle of the night, you fill the tub so you can wash in the morning. . . .
>
> You pass a building bombed out. You pass through dirty streets *praying as you go* that no one will take your wallet. . . .
>
> You meet some Asians in the hotel. They are very interested in our weaving project so they say, "We will help with the material, but we don't have transportation," *so again you pray*. . . .
>
> The temptation to be aware of self and its utter limitations is strong. There are times *when I pray*, "Lord, I can't go through this day." (emphasis added)

This is a woman who prays for parking spots. How else would you find one?

A View Disconnected from Real Life

Some theologians think we shouldn't pray for parking places because it means that someone else doesn't get one. One spiritual writer said, "If a person hears a fire truck coming down the street and prays, 'God, may it not be my house,' that person is uttering an immoral prayer because he or she is willing it to be someone else's house. It would be better to pray, 'God, may it be my house, but may no one be hurt.'"[1]

When I told Jill what this writer said, she laughed. Exciting things can happen when Kim is home alone, so every time Jill hears a siren, she prays the vehicle isn't headed to our house. A couple of years ago in the middle of winter, an aide wandered off and didn't tell Kim when she would be back. Kim panicked and began wandering up and down the street, crying and looking for the aide. After a neighbor called, I rushed home. When I turned the corner to our street, I was greeted by two police cars blocking off both ends of our street with flares. Kim was in the middle of it all, without a jacket or shoes, almost hysterical.

When Jill prays that our house won't burn down, she is being simple, like a child. She's being honest with God about what is on her heart. That is the point of asking.

Will God reverse a problem at our home? I don't know. What would happen if our house burned down? I don't know. Figuratively speaking, our house did burn down when Kim was born. We soon realized "the house burning down" was a gift. God had a better house for us. The old one needed to go. Jill and I pray because we are helpless against the onslaught of life. When I pray over a problem, that problem begins to sparkle with the energy of God. Strange things happen.

This spiritual writer who said we shouldn't pray that God will spare our house from a fire has made prayer into a zero-sum game. The appearance of a fire truck doesn't necessarily mean a house is on fire. There are other options. Maybe a cat is up in a tree. Maybe someone is hurt. The root problem is that this writer is overspiritualizing prayer. He submits so quickly to God that he as a person can't emerge. When Jesus prays at Gethsemane "take this cup from me," he is being real; Christians rush to "not my will, but yours be done" without first expressing their hearts (Luke 22:42, NIV). They submit so quickly that they disappear. Overspiritualizing prayer suppresses our natural desire that our house not be burning. When we stop being ourselves with God, we are no longer in real conversation with God.

This writer's thinking has its roots in Neoplatonism, the ancient Greek philosophy that de-emphasized the physical world. Greek Stoics prided themselves on their ability to be unruffled by life; Socrates calmly took the cup of poison given him by his executioners. Neoplatonism seeped into the church, equating spirituality with a suppression of desire and emotion. That's why Jesus comes across in so many films as a bit strange and effeminate. He walks slowly, talks slowly, and moves slowly. You want to put a pin in him.

Augustine, one of the greatest church fathers, was influenced by this philosophy. He wrote, "Ask nothing of God, save God himself."[2] Augustine was half right. Jonathan Edwards and his disciple John Piper have reminded us that the best gift God can give us is himself. But "ask nothing of God" is disconnected from life. Let me explain.

Imagine a husband who really loves his wife. He is attentive to her needs. He listens to her heart. He is her best earthly gift. How would she react if he said to her, "Don't ask me for anything. I'm your best gift." When I've said this at our prayer seminars, everyone bursts into laughter. The husband's love for his wife is not disengaged from responding thoughtfully and generously to her requests. If we separate our mundane needs (doing) from God's best gift, his loving presence (being), then we are overspiritualizing prayer.

If we ask nothing of God, we are left adrift in an evil world. Such a position may feel spiritual because it seems unselfish, but it is unbiblical because it separates the real world of our desires from God's world. The kingdom can't come because it is floating.

By discounting the spiritual and physical worlds, Neoplatonism did exactly what the Enlightenment did. The only difference was Neoplatonism valued the spiritual while the Enlightenment valued the physical. So the church is influenced by Neoplatonism (the physical isn't important), and the world is shaped by the Enlightenment (the spiritual isn't important). Both perspectives stifled honest, person-to-person praying in the church.

The church's tendency toward unnatural spirituality has been further influenced in recent years by our culture's embrace of Buddhist spirituality. In Buddhism you become enlightened and reach nirvana when you stop desiring. Thus Buddhist monks repeat "om" mindlessly to themselves in an attempt to become one with the all. The goal is the suppression of desire.

Jesus could not be more different. Read the Gospels and you'll discover a passionate, feeling man. Thank God we have a Savior who is in touch with the real world, who prays that he will not drink the cup of his Father's wrath, who cries out on a rough wooden cross, "My God, my God, why have you forsaken me" (Matthew 27:46). Jesus neither suppresses his feelings nor lets them master him. He is real.

It is perfectly natural to pray, *God, please help whoever's house is on fire. Keep them safe, and help it not to be our house.* You are honest with your desire and loving at the same time. If you are sinking on the *Titanic*, you pray, *God, get me a place on a lifeboat*, and then you put all your energy into helping other people get on. Desire and surrender are the perfect balance to praying.

Pajamas and Milk

My first experience of answered prayer was prompted by my mom when I was nine years old and didn't have any pajamas. We'd just moved from California's Central Valley to San Francisco, where Dad had taken a job as a writer for a foundation. Even in 1963 the cost of housing had surprised us, so our family of seven had squeezed into a two-bedroom cottage south of San Francisco. Because of space problems, I slept on a cot on a deck that looked out over a steep hillside. I was thrilled since I spent most of my childhood wanting to be a forest ranger. The only problem was, the deck didn't have a roof. My sisters locked the door at night, and when it rained, they didn't always hear me when I knocked on the door. I figured out I could sleep in the rain by lying on the side of the cot with the water pooling in the middle of my sleeping bag. I just had to be careful not to roll into the middle. In the winter, I moved indoors and slept in a small space inside the crawlspace just below the hallway skylight. Pajamas were critical.

When I told my mom I didn't have any pajamas, she suggested that I pray for some. So I did. Within a week, a pair of bright red pajamas came in a care package from friends. Within two weeks, a second pair arrived. I am not kidding. I don't recall before or since getting a gift of pajamas. The answer to my prayer was so clear, so quick, I couldn't miss it. God is concerned about pajamas.

He's also concerned about milk. Every day at breakfast, I pray quietly as Kim pours milk for her cereal. Her monocular vision leaves her without depth perception, so aiming is tough. Her weakness in motor planning makes it hard for her to stop pouring once she has started, and her dislike of advice means she doesn't listen when I tell her to stop. The result can be exciting. In fact, Jill usually leaves the kitchen when the milk carton comes out. God is concerned about pouring milk. He's that involved in our lives.

Does that mean we should all pray when we pour milk? Of course not. I hope you've learned how to pour milk by now! It is not a need in your life. But it is for Kim. So we pray. It doesn't make us more spiritual; it is just one of the little prayer journeys Kim and I are on.

A Moment of Incarnation

The wonder of the infinite-personal God is displayed, more than anywhere else, in the Incarnation. Nothing can prepare us for the birth of God: a six-pound, four-ounce Jewish boy with dark brown curly hair born in the fall or winter of 5 BC in a shepherd's cave on the side of a hill in the city of Bethlehem in the Roman province of Judea in western Asia. It is so particular it staggers the imagination. God found a parking spot, a specific place and time where his love would touch our world.

Prayer is a moment of incarnation—God with us. God involved in the details of my life. Another author of an otherwise excellent book on prayer said that prayer was mainly about us being with God and not about God answering our prayers. As an example he mentioned that "mothers in the days of high infant mortality used to pray desperately that their children would not die in infancy. Modern medical techniques have put an end to those prayers in the West."[3] Maybe. Or maybe modern medical techniques were developed in the West because young mothers in the West were praying for the lives of their children.

It is striking how many spiritual writers react to the specificity of real prayer. It runs deeper than Greek Neoplatonism and the influence of Buddhist spirituality. Frankly, God makes us nervous when he gets too close. We don't want a physical dependence on him. It feels hokey, like we are controlling God. Deep down we just don't like grace. We don't want to risk our prayer not being answered. We prefer the safety of isolation to engaging the living God. To embrace the Father and thus prayer is to accept what one pastor called "the sting of particularity."[4]

Our dislike of asking is rooted in our desire for independence. Reinhold Niebuhr, a leading post–World War II theologian, put his finger on the problem: "The human ego assumes its self-sufficiency and self-mastery and imagines itself secure. . . . It does not recognize the contingent and dependent character of its life and believes itself to be the author of its own existence."[5] We don't like being contingent, completely dependent on another. The little child that Jesus urged us to become is completely dependent on his parents for everything.

What do I lose when I have a praying life? Control. Independence. What do I gain? Friendship with God. A quiet heart. The living work of God in the hearts of those I love. The ability to roll back the tide of evil. Essentially, I lose my kingdom and get his. I move from being an independent player to a dependent lover. I move from being an orphan to a child of God.

Every day I experience my Father's caring presence. Last Saturday, for example, I was at an electronics store buying some chargers for an intercom we were setting up for Kim's apartment and received a panicky call from Jill, who had just talked with Kim's aide who assists her at her job walking dogs at a kennel. During her lunch break, Kim had ordered food at McDonald's, but she couldn't find her credit card, so McDonald's had taken the food back. Kim was freaking out. I tried calling the aide, but the aide's cell phone was working intermittently.

How did I see my Father's care? Because I was at the electronics store, I was only ten minutes from Kim. When I finally got through to the aide, he unwittingly gave me directions to the wrong McDonald's. While waiting at a traffic light, I noticed a McDonald's across the street. At that moment, I remembered there was something odd about his directions. I drove into the parking lot, and there was Kim. Ten minutes after I received Jill's call, I was with Kim. God's love for her was so particular.

The stress of that ten minutes was a reminder of my dependence and drew me into a greater dependence. Suffering is God's gift to make us aware of our contingent existence. It creates an environment where we see the true nature of our existence—dependent on the living God. And yet *how* God actually works in prayer is largely a mystery.

The Mystery of Prayer

Something mysterious happens in the hidden contours of life when we pray. If we try to figure out the mystery, it will elude us. The mystery is real.

Like an autistic child, we can only look sideways at how prayer works. When Kim greets people, she does not look at them directly but out of the corner of her eye. Some experts theorize that it is too overwhelming for those with autism to look directly at others.

Many things in life can't be observed directly. In quantum physics, you can't observe a particle's speed and mass at the same time. Sexual love in marriage is beautiful; sexual love observed is pornography. The act of observing changes sexual intimacy. Some things just disappear when you try to capture or observe them.

Studies that try to prove that prayer works don't understand the nature of prayer. They are as odd as trying to prove one's own existence or to measure love. God is a person, and his universe reflects his personhood. The closer something is to the character of God, the more it reflects him and the less it can be measured. Things such as integrity, beauty, hope, and love are all in the same category as prayer. You can tell their presence and even describe them, but you can't define them, simply because they are too close to God's image.

The assumption that we can figure out how everything works comes from the Enlightenment mind-set that says everything is just matter and energy. This definition of "everything" leaves out all the important things of life, such as love, beauty, and people. The most precious things in life can't be proven or observed directly, but we know them as surely as we know that the sun and moon exist.

In 1983 we started to pray that Kim be able to speak. She was about one-and-a-half. Unknown to us, engineers at a computer company in Ohio were designing the first easily accessible speech computer. Four years later, when Kim was five, she spoke her first electronic word, *McDonald's*. She is now on the third generation of speech computer called a Pathfinder.

Some might object, saying, "Speech computers would have been invented anyway." It is often true with answers to prayer that when you look back, everything looks seamless, as if it would have all happened anyway. But looking back is actually a godlike stance, presuming to know how everything works. The child says, "O Lord, my heart is not lifted up; my eyes are not raised too high; I do not occupy myself with things too great and too marvelous for me" (Psalm 131:1).

Prayer is strikingly intimate. As soon as you take a specific answer to prayer and try to figure out what caused it, you lose God. We simply cannot see the causal connections between our prayers and what happens. But don't forget this isn't just true of prayer. All the best things in life have no visible connections. For example, selfless love, love that gets no credit or payback, is completely irrational to our intellectual elites because there is no visible connection between what love gives and what it gets. Yet our world "worships at the feet of love."[6] When Mother Teresa spoke to our intellectual elites at Harvard, she got a thunderous standing ovation.[7] Love, like prayer, makes perfect sense when you realize it is a reflection of the divine image.

> IF YOU ARE GOING TO ENTER THIS DIVINE DANCE WE CALL PRAYER, YOU HAVE TO SURRENDER YOUR DESIRE TO BE IN CONTROL, TO FIGURE OUT HOW PRAYER WORKS.

The inability to see the connection between cause and effect is intrinsic to the nature of prayer because it is the direct activity of God. Trying to dissect how prayer works is like using a magnifying glass to try to figure out why a woman is beautiful. If you turn God into an object, he has a way of disappearing. We do the same thing when a spouse or a friend consistently treats us like an object. We pull back.

Often answers to prayer start prior to the actual prayer. (Kim's speech computer company was founded fourteen years before Kim was born.) The only way to know how prayer works is to have complete knowledge *and control* of the past, present, and future. In other words, you can figure out how prayer works if you are God.

If you are going to enter this divine dance we call prayer, you have to surrender your desire to be in control, to figure out how prayer works. You've got to let God take the lead. You have to trust. Then God will delight you, not only with the gift of himself but also with parking places, pajamas, poured milk, and Pathfinders. No one works like him!

CHAPTER 15

WHAT DO WE DO WITH JESUS' EXTRAVAGANT PROMISES ABOUT PRAYER?

JESUS HAS A WAY of making us nervous, especially when he talks about prayer. After the Last Supper he says some astounding things. While he and the disciples are still sitting around the table, he tells them, "Whatever you ask in my name, this I will do, that the Father may be glorified in the Son." Then in his next breath, he underlines his point: "If you ask me anything in my name, I will do it" (John 14:13-14). Later that night as Jesus and his disciples head to Gethsemane, they walk through the darkened streets of Jerusalem. Possibly as they pass the gate of the temple with its golden vine, he tells his followers that he is the true vine, the source of life. "If you abide in me, and my words abide in you, ask whatever you wish, and it will be done for you" (John 15:7). Our fruit bearing will express itself in answered prayer—"so that whatever you ask the Father in my name, he may give it to you" (John 15:16). As Jesus comes to the end of his final teaching with his disciples, he drives home his point: "Truly, truly, I say to you, whatever you ask of the Father in my name, he will give it to you. . . . Ask, and you will receive, that your joy may be full" (John 16:23-24). Six different times Jesus says, "Ask and I will give it to you."

When I ask people at our prayer seminars to react honestly to Jesus' seeming blank check in this Last Supper conversation, everyone is uncomfortable. One person asked, "Is he exaggerating?" Another said, "I don't like to fail. If I pray and it doesn't work, is my faith real? What is wrong with me? What is wrong with God?" Still another said, "It's just not my experience." Person after person said, "I've prayed, and it didn't happen." Those who paid close attention to Jesus' fine print ("If you abide in me . . ." or "ask in my name") were depressed because they don't remain in him.

What do we do with Jesus' extravagant promises about prayer?

Scholars to the Rescue
Scholars try to get Jesus off the hook. One said:

> A cursory reading of John 14:13-14 may give people the indica-
> tion that Jesus will give a person anything he wants. . . . Satan
> would love to get us to believe the lie that God answers our
> prayers according to our will. . . . Once we discover that God is
> not answering our requests for riches, fame and glory . . . we chalk
> Christianity up to being a sham and accuse Jesus of breaking his
> promises. . . .
>
> Jesus is really saying, "Ask me to do anything for you in the
> area of my work and I will do it." . . . If we intend to be effective
> witnesses, we must employ God's assistance through prayer,
> asking only that His will be done, not ours. Only then do we
> have answered prayer.[1]

To paraphrase this scholar, what Jesus *really* means is if we are going on a missions trip, God will help us, but even then we have to say, "Your will be done." This writer limited the extravagance of Jesus' promise to overtly religious activity such as witnessing. Without realizing it, he bought into the Enlightenment model and relegated prayer to our private world. He solved the problem of Jesus' extravagant claims by explaining them away. He's kept God infinite but lost his closeness.

This scholar is correct that prayer is not magic or an attempt to control God. Hophni and Phinehas brought the Ark of the Covenant into their battle with the Philistines as a magic trick to help them defeat the enemy. They had been sexually assaulting women who came to the temple, but now with the Philistines breathing down their necks they wanted God around. The Philistines won the battle, killed Hophni and Phinehas, and captured the Ark (see 1 Samuel 4:1-11).

In other words, don't mess with God. He is not your toy or your personal vending machine. You've got to be in the vine. But still, what about Jesus' extravagant claims?

James to the Rescue

Jesus' brother James comes to the rescue and balances out Jesus' extravagant promises. James describes two dangers in asking. The first danger, on the left side of the following chart, is Not Asking. James writes, "You do not have, because you do not ask." The second danger is Asking Selfishly: "You ask and do not receive, because you ask wrongly, to spend it on your passions" (James 4:2-3). We can fall off either cliff.

Jesus' prayer at Gethsemane demonstrates perfect balance. He avoids the Not Asking cliff, saying, "Abba, Father, all things are possible for you. Remove this cup from me" (Mark 14:36). Those who err on the Not Asking side surrender to God before they are real with him. Sometimes we try so hard to be good that we aren't real. The result is functional deism, where we are separated from God. The real you doesn't encounter the real God.

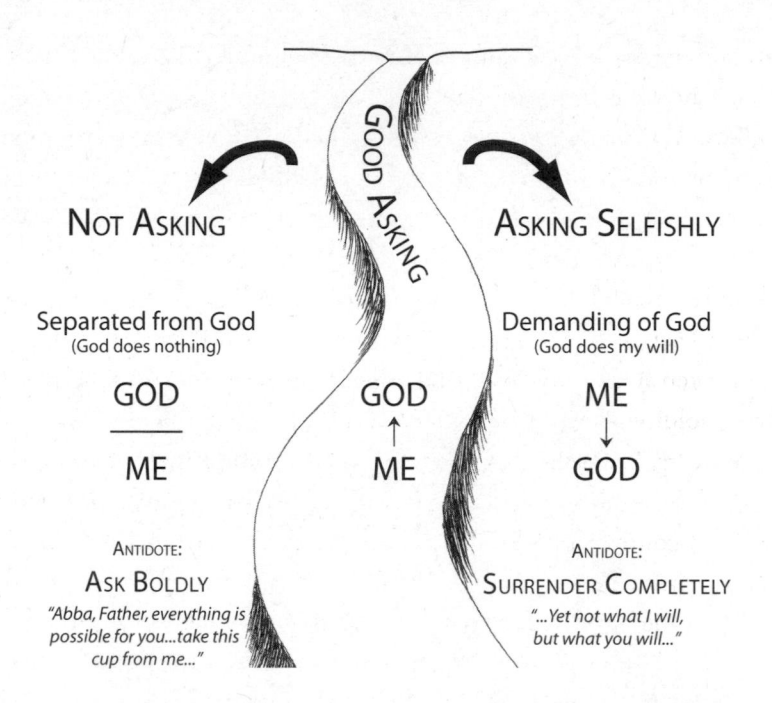

Not Asking

Separated from God
(God does nothing)

GOD
———
ME

ANTIDOTE:
Ask Boldly
*"Abba, Father, everything is
possible for you...take this
cup from me..."*

Good Asking

GOD
↑
ME

Asking Selfishly

Demanding of God
(God does my will)

ME
↓
GOD

ANTIDOTE:
Surrender Completely
*"...Yet not what I will,
but what you will..."*

In the next breath, Jesus avoids the Asking Selfishly cliff by surrendering completely: "Yet not what I will, but what you will" (14:36). Jesus is real about his feelings, but they don't control him, nor does he try to control God with them. He doesn't use his ability to communicate with his Father as a means of doing his own will. He submits to the story that his Father is weaving in his life.

If you try to understand Jesus' prayer purely on a rational level, it seems crazy. Why would Jesus ask his Father for something he knows he wouldn't do? But reason is only part of who we are as image bearers of God. Desire, feelings, and passion are also part of who we are. If we remember that Jesus is a person and not a robot, then it makes perfect sense.

An analogy may help. On 9/11 the intense heat of the fire in the World Trade Center made it impossible for those trapped by the flames to descend but also impossible to stay where they were. People responded with their only alternative—jumping to their deaths, many holding hands as they leaped. What's the point of holding hands? They knew they were going to die, whether or not they were holding hands. But life is more than logic. As humans, we reflect the complexity of God. Part of divine beauty is that we were made for community, so when we leap to our death, we hold hands with a friend. When Jesus asks his Father to "remove this cup from me," he knows that the divine community he shares with his Father is going to be broken at the cross. In asking and surrendering, just for a moment, he is holding hands with his Father.

Shadrach, Meshach, and Abednego are in a similar situation when they face the heat of a blazing furnace. They respond to Nebuchadnezzar's command to bow before him with the identical balance of Jesus. They tell the king, "Our God whom we serve is able to deliver us from the burning fiery furnace, and he will deliver us out of your hand, O king" (Daniel 3:17). They avoid the cliff of Not Asking by boldly declaring that God would rescue them. Then, in the next breath, they say, "But if not, be it known to you, O king, that we will not serve your gods" (3:18). While this sounds like a contradiction, these men are asking boldly and surrendering completely. They avoid functional deism or separation from God by their bold statement of God's deliverance; then they avoid living selfishly by their complete surrender to the story God has placed them in.

Back to Jesus

We now understand one of the critical structures of prayer, but we're still left with Jesus' promise—"Ask whatever you wish." Why didn't he bring balance to that statement if that is what he meant? I think the answer is that *we* are not balanced. Instinctively, we are either confident in ourselves or despairing in ourselves. In both cases we are paralyzed, not moving toward God. Like a parent whose toddler is about to wander off, Jesus is yelling, "My Father has a big heart. He loves the details of your life. Tell him what you need and he will do it for you." Jesus wants us to tap into the generous heart of his Father. He wants us to lose all confidence in ourselves because "apart from [Jesus] you can do nothing"; he wants us to have complete confidence in him because "whoever abides in me and I in him, he it is that bears much fruit" (John 15:5).

All of Jesus' teaching on prayer in the Gospels can be summarized with one word: *ask*. His greatest concern is that our failure or reluctance to ask keeps us distant from God. But that is not the only reason he tells us to ask anything. God wants to give us good gifts. He loves to give.

In the parable of the persistent widow (see Luke 18:1-8), Jesus describes an unjust judge turning a cold shoulder to a helpless widow. When she keeps pestering him, he finally relents, not out of concern for her but because he takes a realistic look at his own self-interest.[2] If he doesn't solve her problem, she will make his life miserable. If an unjust judge will help a widow, won't your Father help you?

In the parable of the friend at midnight (see Luke 11:5-8), the host bangs on his neighbor's door at midnight to borrow three loaves of bread because a friend has come. The neighbor yells at the host to stop bothering him because he is in bed. Finally, he realizes that since he can't sleep with the host pounding on his door, he might as well give him the three loaves just to shut him up. Like the unjust judge, he may not be generous, but he isn't stupid.

Why three loaves? One loaf is for the friend at midnight. A second loaf is for himself, so his friend doesn't eat alone. Then when his friend finishes eating, the host will offer him the third loaf to show his generosity. The host doesn't want to look cheap. His reputation and the reputation of the community are at stake. In summary, the first loaf is for his friend's physical need. The second is for his relational need, for community. The third loaf is for his heart need, to be loved. We have a three-loaf God. He loves to give.

Praying in Jesus' Name

Deep down, we just don't believe God is as generous as he keeps saying he is. That's why Jesus added the fine print—"ask in my name." Let me explain what that means.

Imagine that your prayer is a poorly dressed beggar reeking of alcohol and body odor, stumbling toward the palace of the great king. You have become your prayer. As you shuffle toward the barred gate, the guards stiffen. Your smell has preceded you. You stammer out a message for the great king: "I want to see the king." Your words are barely intelligible, but you whisper one final word, "Jesus. I come in the name of Jesus." At the name of Jesus, as if by magic, the palace comes alive. The guards snap to attention, bowing low in front of you. Lights come on, and the door flies open. You are ushered into the palace and down a long hallway into the throne room of the great king, who comes running to you and wraps you in his arms.

> "ASKING IN JESUS' NAME" ISN'T ANOTHER THING I HAVE TO GET RIGHT SO MY PRAYERS ARE PERFECT. IT IS ONE MORE GIFT OF GOD BECAUSE MY PRAYERS ARE SO IMPERFECT.

The name of Jesus gives my prayers royal access. They get through. Jesus isn't just the Savior of my soul. He's also the Savior of my prayers. My prayers come before the throne of God as the prayers of Jesus. "Asking in Jesus' name" isn't another thing I have to get right so my prayers are perfect. It is one more gift of God because my prayers are so imperfect.

Jesus' seal not only guarantees that my package gets through, but it also transforms the package. Paul says in Romans 8:26, "The Spirit helps us in our weakness. For we do not know what to pray for as we ought, but the Spirit himself intercedes for us with groanings too deep for words."

Answered Prayers

As I look back on my life, Jesus' statement "If you ask me anything in my name, I will do it" makes perfect sense (John 14:14). Let me explain by giving you a quick tour of my prayer cards. (Later I'll explain why I use prayer cards instead of a list.) On my son John's prayer card, I have five prayer requests. Four of the five have clear answers to prayer. I have a separate prayer card for his work. Several months after I began praying, God dramatically answered my requests for John. Emily's prayer card has six requests on it. God has answered five of them. On another card I have seven prayer requests for her. God has answered all of them. I'm puzzling over how to pray for Courtney because God has answered four of my prayer requests for her, and I'm not sure what to pray for now.

At one of our prayer seminars, a man who was struggling with typical garden-variety Christian cynicism challenged me whether this wasn't just the law of averages. That is, lots of things will happen naturally over the course of time. Maybe I was giving God credit for what would have happened anyway. Excellent question. I was thankful for his courage to share what many of us think.

I didn't want to debate theory with him, so I opened up my life and started describing all the ways God has answered prayer. I said, "How do you explain all my answered prayers for my children? It is not just averages." During the break he came up to me and renewed the challenge. When I started to show him one of the prayer cards for one of my children so he could see a concrete example, he asked if he could pick out one of my prayer cards at random. He suspected that I might control the evidence by picking out a "good" prayer card. I said, "Sure." So without looking he opened my stack of prayer cards and put his finger on a one-year-old prayer request. He could not have picked a more dramatically answered prayer. I told him the story of what God had done in response to that prayer. Included in that answer to prayer was an unsolicited gift of $50,000 to help us launch a full-time prayer ministry. He walked away sobered. Maybe God is alive.

Just yesterday I had five clear answers to prayer. That count is high for a typical day, but it is not unusual. Three of them involved people for whom I had been praying for some aspect of Christ's character in their lives. One was a prayer for healing for our bookkeeper, who has been struggling with severe chronic fatigue for sixteen months. No massive healing, just a better diagnosis. The last one was this chapter. I'd been struggling to write it for several months, and it finally came together yesterday.

I find that the closer my prayers are to the heart of God, the more powerfully and quickly they are answered. The three answers to my prayers for others regarding Christlikeness were particularly striking. Two involved phone calls from my children. One shared how God had broken a pattern of idolatry; the other told of being convicted of self-will. I had not spoken with either child about these issues. All my words had been to God. He was dealing with a tendency to harshness in the third person. He had permitted suffering in all three lives, which exposed their hearts, allowing them to see their sin. The Father delights in taking his children into the life of his Son—his life, death, and resurrection. He wants us to abide in the vine. It is his way.

When you are inside your prayers, you can clearly see the weaving of God, but it is often difficult to explain to an outsider. Sometimes you can't explain because it would shame someone needlessly. Some times it is hard because you have to be inside the story to see it. It must remain hidden for the Spirit to work.

Jesus said that even the act of praying should be hidden (see Matthew 6:5-6). He told us that the kingdom is a treasure hidden in a field or a seed hidden in the ground. His earthly life from his birth to his death had this same hidden quality. And yet, purely from a secular point of view, his life was the most influential life in the history of the world. No one else has even come close. Even now Jesus' presence on the earth has that same quality. It is down low, concealed in the lives of his followers.

Learning to Abide

The praying life is the abiding life. Many Christians hit a wall when they connect abiding with asking. They freeze, thinking, *If I were abiding, then I would get my prayers answered.* Abiding feels elusive, like a spiritual pipe dream. Abiding is anything but disconnected from life. It is the way life should be done, in partnership with God.

One of the best ways to learn how to abide is to ask anything. Jesus added the qualifier "abide in me" only once in the six times he told us to "ask anything." His primary concern was to get us into the game. Start asking. Don't just ask for spiritual things or "good" things. Tell God what you want. Before you can abide, the real you has to meet the real God. Ask anything.

If you are going to take Jesus' offer of "ask anything" seriously, what is the first thing you have to do? Any child will tell you. You have to ask, and in order to ask, you have to reflect on what you want. Now it starts getting complicated. Do you want a million dollars? I broke out into a sweat when one of my kids was considering a career that would make him wealthy. There is absolutely nothing wrong with earning a lot of money; I'm just keenly aware of what wealth can do to your soul. Thomas Merton, a Trappist monk, wrote, "Why do we have to spend our lives striving to be something that we would never want to be, if we only knew what we wanted? Why do we waste our time doing things which . . . are just the opposite of what we were made for?"[3]

It takes reflection to answer the question "What do I want?" It doesn't take long before you are looking carefully at Jesus' fine print—"If you abide in me, and my words abide in you, ask whatever you wish, and it will be done for you" (John 15:7). My three prayer requests all came out of me abiding. But they started with me thinking about what I wanted God to do.

My experience is that most people do not put God to the test. They don't ask him for what they want. I say this cautiously because many Christians have experienced unanswered prayers that are still unprocessed. We will talk about that fairly extensively in part 4. Nevertheless, most people consistently fall off the left side of the Not Asking/Asking Selfishly chart. They don't ask.

In the next two chapters we'll look at a few areas where we don't ask God, where we've kept him at a distance.

CHAPTER 16

WHAT WE DON'T ASK FOR

"Our Daily Bread"

IN THE CHURCH, most prayer requests are limited to sickness, joblessness, kids in crisis, and maybe an occasional missionary. Yet Jesus' prayer for daily bread was an invitation to bring all our needs to him. In the Greek, "Give us this day our daily bread" (Matthew 6:11) is an obscure expression that literally means "give us tomorrow's bread today."[1] It hints at the abundance God wants to bring into our lives. I suspect that your refrigerator or your checking account has "tomorrow's bread" already there.

Just once in our life Jill and I didn't have tomorrow's bread today. I was going to college full time and supporting our small family (our first daughter, Courtney, was a year old) with a part-time painting business. It was New Year's Day 1975, and we had run out of food, money, and work. We'd sold our books, our jewelry, and our high-school rings. So we sat down at our kitchen table and prayed for food. The minute we finished praying, the phone rang. It was a painting customer. Could I come the next day? The next day I not only told the customer about how she was an answer to prayer, but I asked her for an advance. No sense getting too spiritual.

I was so struck by how immediately God answered our prayer

that as I went to bed, I asked him for something bigger: *God, would you change me?* I wasn't even sure I was a Christian; at the very least, Christianity wasn't working in my life. I struggled with intellectual doubts. The Bible felt stale. It wasn't just a low point—my whole life had been that way. The next morning I woke up with a song in my heart and a hunger for his Word that has never left. He changed me.

Often our need for daily bread opens doors to deeper heart needs for real food. The day after Jesus fed the five thousand, the crowds met him on the beach at Capernaum hungry for breakfast. Jesus told them he had better food for them: "The bread of God is he who comes down from heaven and gives life to the world" (John 6:33).

What other kinds of daily bread might we not ask for? How might our needs for daily bread show us our need for bread from heaven?

Material Things—Too Selfish, Too Vulnerable

We've already seen how we don't like to ask for mundane things such as pajamas, but there are whole other categories, particularly material things, where it doesn't occur to us to ask God. For example, we balk at praying, *God, I want a vacation home. Would you get me one?* We don't mind *acting* selfishly, but *talking* selfishly is embarrassing. After all, we aren't little children anymore. A vacation home is so beyond the purview of daily bread that it feels presumptuous to ask God for one.

So what do we do instead of asking God for a vacation home? We look at our finances, talk to a realtor, and go buy one—all without seriously praying about the decision. Don't get me wrong. I'm not saying buying a vacation house is inherently sinful. God delights in giving his children good gifts, including vacation homes. But he wants to be part of all the decisions we make. He wants our material needs to draw us into our soul needs. This is what it means to abide—to include him in every aspect of our lives.

Abiding is a perfect way to describe a praying life. For example, many Christians who are thinking of buying a vacation home might even pray, asking God practical questions, such as "Can we afford it?" "Will it be too much work?" "Should we make an offer on this house?" These are good questions. But we seldom ask God heart questions such as "Will a second home elevate us above people?" "Will it isolate us?" In the first set of questions, God is your financial adviser. In the second set, he has become your Lord. You are abiding. You are feeding your soul with food that lasts.

We can do the same thing with a promotion. It feels selfish to pray for one, so instead we'll work for one! We end up separating a big part of our lives from God because we are trying to feel good about ourselves. As we have seen, we create two selves—a spiritual self and a material self.

We also shy away from prayers like these because they invite God to rule our lives. They make us vulnerable. Like the crowds at Capernaum, we want breakfast, not soul food. Left to ourselves, we want God to be a genie, not a person. Scholars have pointed out that Jesus' references to the kingdom are a subtle way of introducing himself as king. When we pray the first petition of the Lord's Prayer, "Your kingdom come," we are saying, "King Jesus, rule my life." The heart is one of God's biggest mission fields.

WE SHY AWAY FROM PRAYERS THAT INVITE GOD TO RULE OUR LIVES. THEY MAKE US VULNERABLE.

Oddly enough, we can also use prayer to keep God distant. We do that by only talking to God and not to mature believers. I can demonstrate that easily. Which is easier, confessing impure thoughts to a mature friend or to God? The friend is tougher. That feels real. We need to ask the body of Christ, Jesus' physical presence on earth, the same questions we ask God.

If you isolate praying from the rule of Jesus by not involving other Christians, you'll end up doing your own will. Many Christians isolate their decision making from the body of Christ, then further isolate themselves in their vacation homes. They say something like this: "Well, my husband and I prayed about it, and the Lord seemed to confirm it." Possibly God did confirm it. It is also possible that you used prayer as a spiritual cover for "doing your own thing." We can mask our desires even from ourselves.

Look at how Scripture and a listening heart are woven together in this hypothetical conversation with a mature friend.

> Bob, my wife and I would love to get a vacation home. You know how pressured life has been for us, and it would be great to get away to a quiet place where we can unwind. We've found this beautiful place up on a lake that the whole family could enjoy. At the same time, we're concerned with what it might do to our hearts. We want to be followers of Jesus, and he warns against building bigger and better barns. Is this a bigger and better barn? Will it elevate us above people? Will it isolate us from people? Is it a wise use of our resources? Will we be limiting what we can give others? At the same time, we think we could use our house to give vacations to people who can't afford them. Tell me what you think.

Along with those questions, give your friend enough data to make an intelligent decision. Be open about how much it will cost, what your income is, and how it will impact your giving and your savings.

One reason we don't ask a mature friend these questions is Western individualism. Individualism goes back to the Judeo-Christian heritage, all the way back to Psalm 23 and God's tender care for *me*. When the Good Shepherd loves *me*, I have dignity and worth. I have value as an individual. But modern secularism has taken the Shepherd out of Psalm 23, leaving just *me* trying to create my own dignity and worth. It is my money; I earned it. I need a break. So it never occurs to me to include God or anyone else in my decision to buy a vacation home.

Wisdom—Too Unexpected

When we need advice, we find a wise person, ask him or her a question, and listen to the answer. It seldom occurs to us to do this with God. For starters, we don't know how God will answer. We don't hear an audible voice, so we dismiss the possibility of God speaking into our lives. In effect we are saying, "I must know how this will work ahead of time. I must be in control." We forget that in most of life we don't have control. When it comes to people, we often don't know how things will work out ahead of time. We forget we are embodied spirits, designed to hear from God.

Without realizing it, we are operating out of an Enlightenment mind-set that denies the possibility of an infinite God speaking personally into our lives. That's why I prefer the biblical term *wisdom* to our more common term *guidance*. Guidance means I'm driving the car and asking God which way to go. Wisdom is richer, more personal. I don't just need help with my plans; I need help with my questions and even my own heart.

Here's an example of how I ask God for wisdom. Below is a page from my prayer notebook in the late '90s. (In part 5 I will talk more about how to use a prayer journal.) I was thinking about how to plan

> *Father, show me how to plan my next two years. I don't know how to do it—I sense that I should first do the curriculum and then do the book.*
>
> *Do I go ahead with forty lessons?*
> *How do I focus my time?*
> *Do I even try to get the ball rolling?*
>
> *Book = house, nice, but you can live in a tent.*

the next couple of years. I was going to seminary, and at the same time I wanted to write both a book and a Bible study on the person of Jesus. I wasn't sure which to write first or whether I should even try.

Even as I was writing, God began to answer my prayer for wisdom. As I wrote those questions, a Scripture came to mind—"Prepare your work outside; get everything ready for yourself in the field, and after that build your house" (Proverbs 24:27). I realized that writing a book was like building a house. Then I wrote "Book = house." A book is like a house—nice but not necessary. We could always rent. So I postponed writing the book. A year later, one of my professors let me do an independent study course, where I wrote the first eight chapters of a book on Jesus.

At the heart of this journal entry is weakness. I was not just asking God for advice—that would have left me in control. I was keenly aware that I didn't have the resources to face the next two years of my life. I wasn't even asking God to be my partner. I was bowing as I asked. I was abiding. Such dependence is not natural for me. A number of years ago Jill wanted to get me a T-shirt that said, "Often Wrong, but Never in Doubt."

Writing those questions in my prayer notebook was a form of surrender. I was at odds with the spirit of our age and its quest for unlimited freedom and self-expression. Instead, I wanted to be in harmony with my Creator. As Einstein observed: "Human beings, vegetables or cosmic dust, we all dance to a mysterious tune, intoned in the distance by an invisible player."[2] I wanted to keep in step with my Father's music. I wanted my true bread to come from heaven.

WHAT WE DON'T ASK FOR

"Your Kingdom Come"

CHRISTIANS HAVE DONE some confusing things with "your kingdom come" that keep the rule of Jesus at a distance. We've spiritualized the kingdom, thinking it only has to do with religious things. Or we've identified the kingdom with Christian institutions. The kingdom is there, but that is only one expression of the kingdom.

Below is a partial list of kingdom prayers that we seldom ask, followed by a more in-depth discussion.

- Change in others (too controlling, too hopeless)
- Change in me (too scary)
- Change in things I don't like in our culture (too impossible)

Change in Others—Too Controlling, Too Hopeless

Seldom do we pray seriously and thoughtfully for those we love as they deal with their besetting sins. I'm going to pick on husbands for a minute because most men don't pray thoughtfully for their wives; they just whine or withdraw. When they do pray, they often simply want their own lives to be pain free. Men will work at making money, keeping the yard neat, or helping the kids in sports, but many don't work at or think about things that last.

For example, a husband will rarely ask God for his wife to become more like Jesus. Let's say she is critical of him. When he tries to talk to her about it, she says, "I wouldn't be so critical of you if you didn't have so many problems." By raising the issue, he just got more criticism, so his heart quietly shuts down. He just doesn't care anymore. She is who she is. So he moves on with life and flips on the television.

Without realizing it, he has become cynical about the possibility of real change in his wife. A childlike spirit seems naive, like a distant memory. He is wise as a serpent, but he's not harmless as a dove. He is surrounded by idiots, and his only choice, like the Greek Stoics, is to tough it out. Low-level evil has worn him down.

To engage God in prayer about his wife's attitude feels like opening up an old wound. Just telling this to God is frustrating because it feels so hopeless, the spiritual version of banging your head against the wall. It is simply easier not even to think about it. Mixed in with his frustration is guilt. Some of what she says is true. He isn't sure where her sin ends and his begins.

The husband also hesitates to pray because he's been told that he shouldn't try to control his wife. But the point of prayer is shifting control from you to God. Moreover, doesn't the Father want all of us to become more like his Son?

Where should the husband begin? Like a little child, he should ask God for what he wants. It might help to write down in a prayer notebook or on a card what he wants changed in his wife and to find a Scripture that describes Christ in her. Then he could start praying that Scripture for her every day and also invite God to work in his own heart.

This prayer request will become a twenty-year adventure. The adventure begins with asking God, *Do I have a critical spirit too? Do I respond to my wife's critical spirit with my own critical spirit?* Usually, what bugs us the most about other people is true of us as well. By first taking the beam out of his own eye (see Matthew 7:1-5), the husband releases in his wife's life the unseen energy of the Spirit. The kingdom is beginning to come.

The husband can let God use his wife's criticism to make him more like Jesus. Instead of fighting what she says, if at all possible he can do it. We can't do battle with evil without letting God destroy the evil in us as well. The world is far too intertwined.

Deep down, we instinctively know that God works this way, and we pull back from prayer. Like Jonah outside the city of Nineveh complaining about God's mercy, we say, "God, I knew you would do that. As soon as I started praying for her, you started working on me."

By taking his wife's criticism seriously, the husband might feel he is losing his identity, becoming a Christian codependent, mindlessly trying to be good. He is not. He is simply following his Master, who "rose from supper . . . laid aside his outer garments, and taking a towel, tied it around his waist. Then he poured water into a basin and began to wash the disciples' feet and to wipe them with the towel that was wrapped around him" (John 13:4-5). Jesus' love is so physical. Our love must be as physical as his.

The husband is not "under his wife's thumb"; he is entering into Jesus' life. The husband can't believe the gospel unless he is also becoming the gospel. In other words, once you've learned that God loves you, you need to extend his love to others. Otherwise, the love of God sours. By extending grace to his wife, the husband is being drawn into the life of the Son. He will become Christlike.

The husband can't leave a vacuum in his heart either. He must replace his critical spirit with a thankful spirit. One of the best ways of doing that is writing out on a card or in a prayer notebook short phrases of how he is thankful for her. By thanking God daily for specific things about his wife, he will begin to see her for who she is—a gift.

At first glance this feels like the husband is whitewashing reality. Life feels uneven, unfair. After all, the wife is the one with the critical spirit; not only is he putting energy into reflecting on his tendency to be critical (which isn't half as bad as hers), but he's also working at being thankful for her. The only thing he has going for him is his pitiful little prayer.

A thankful heart is constantly extending grace because it has received grace. Love and grace are uneven. God poured out on his own Son the criticism I deserve. Now he invites me to pour out undeserving grace on someone who has hurt me. Grace begets grace. This husband is taking a journey into the heart of God.

Welcome to the life of God! That's what a life of grace feels like, especially in the beginning. That pitiful little prayer is tapping into the power center of the universe. If the husband hangs in there, he will be amazed at the creative energy of God. Grace will win the day.

WHEN YOU START "ASKING ANYTHING," YOU'LL BE SURPRISED WITH HOW YOUR LIFE BEGINS TO SPARKLE WITH THE PRESENCE OF GOD.

Praying steadily for his wife will help him to become more aware of her as a person. Peter challenges husbands to treat their wives with "honor . . . since they are heirs with you of the grace of life, so that your prayers may not be hindered" (1 Peter 3:7). You can't separate prayer from love.

Watch what happens over time. By getting his ego out of the way, the husband makes room for the Spirit to work in his wife's life. God will start doing things far more effectively than the husband ever could. No one teaches like God.

Over time the husband might discover that his courage and wisdom are growing. He'll find the best phrasing, the best timing to be gently honest with his wife. He'll move from trying to win a battle to loving a friend. The kingdom is coming!

Character Change in Me—Too Scary

What about change in me? Almost every Christian is confident God will answer a prayer for change in us, and it scares us to death. For example, what happens if you pray for patience? God permits suffering in your life. What happens if you pray for humility? God humbles you. We're scared of such prayers because we want to remain in control of our lives. We don't trust God.

We also don't pray for change in ourselves because we don't want to admit that we need to change. Look at how difficult this prayer is—*Lord, this morning I feel irritable. Would you help me to be kind?* In order to pray this, I have to stop being irritable long enough to admit my grumpiness to myself. It is difficult to see my attitude because the problem isn't me; it's all those other idiots.

The fatalism inherent in so much modern psychology immobilizes us as well. Emotional states are sacred. If I'm grumpy, I have a right to feel that way and to express my feelings. Everyone around me simply has to "get over it." One of the worst sins, according to pop psychology, is to suppress your emotions. So to pray that I won't be angry feels unauthentic, as if I am suppressing the real me.

One day Claire, our granddaughter, said to Jill, "I'm not having a good day, Grammy." Jill was aware that Claire wasn't having a good day, but she still said to her gently, "Claire, because of Jesus you can start any day over again." In our modern world, such a response is almost heretical. Now that we have discovered our feelings, we are trapped by them.

Oddly enough, idolizing our emotions doesn't free us to be ourselves but instead results in us being ruled by the ever-changing wind of feelings. We become a thousand selves or, to use Jesus' words, "a reed shaken by the wind" (Matthew 11:7).

But if you take Jesus' words seriously—"Whatever you ask in my name, this I will do" (John 14:13)—it opens the door to the possibility of real change and hope. No longer are you captured by the mind of the culture. You've been invited into coregency with the Ruler of the universe. The King has come.

Change in Things I Don't Like in Our Culture—Too Impossible

Most of the time we just whine about things in our culture that we don't like. It never occurs to us to pray that culture itself will change. In 2000 I was bothered by our culture's lack of an awareness of evil. Secularism denies the existence of a spiritual world, making evil a social construct, a figment of our imaginations. That bugged me. So I wrote down a simple prayer that "Americans would be more aware of evil." A year later, after 9/11, Americans began talking about evil again.

When I told this to my son John, he looked at me with a smirk on his face and said a little slowly and a little loudly, "So you caused 9/11?!" John, of course, was making fun of any possible pretension in my life to have affected world events. (My family's mission in life is to keep me humble.)

I do not understand prayer. Prayer is deeply personal and deeply mysterious. Adults try to figure out causation. Little children don't. They just ask.

If you slow down and reflect, you'll begin to see whole areas of your life where you've been prayerless.

SURRENDER COMPLETELY

"Your Will Be Done"

EMILY CALLED ME over to the computer to help her with the modem (this was before broadband). She was a freshman in high school and needed to go online, but the modem wouldn't work. After doing a quick check, I realized I needed to reload the modem software. Fortunately, Dell provided the original disk. I reached up into the box of disks that came with our computer but couldn't find the disk. It was gone.

My blood immediately went to a low boil. I knew my son had taken the disk and not returned it. I called upstairs, "Andrew, come down right now." He came out of the upstairs bathroom down to where we were in the living room. I could tell he was irritated by my abruptness, but I didn't care. I was tired of him not putting stuff away. It was just selfish.

Andrew rummaged around, found the disk, and went back upstairs. Feeling the tension between us, I wondered if I had been too harsh. Repentance usually starts with a question, a slight uneasiness. Unlike Jesus, who says, "The Son can do nothing of his own accord" (John 5:19), I had reacted on my own. I didn't ask God for any help on how to deal with my son. I knew he'd taken the disk and not put it back. Case closed. Self-will closed the door to a spirit of prayer.

Until we see how strong our own will is, we can't understand the second petition of the Lord's Prayer—"your will be done" (Matthew 6:10). Not only was I prayerless with that incident, I was also prayerless about this area of Andrew's life. It had never occurred to me to pray that Andrew would put his things away because the solution was obvious: "Andrew, put your things away." There was absolutely no moral ambiguity about what needed to happen.

Consequently, I did the same things Andrew had done. He'd been thoughtless in not putting the disk back, and I'd been thoughtless in angrily demanding that he come down immediately. Andrew had been selfish, and I'd been selfish.

Sin is complicated. We are never a passive observer, dispensing wisdom and justice. We are part of the mess. My solution to the problem made it more complex. That's why we can't afford to do anything on our own.

Because I acted on my own, independent of my heavenly Father, my words by themselves had to do all the work. Because I had not asked God to work inside Andrew's heart, I felt it was up to me to deal with him about his irresponsibility, and this increased my intensity.

Now imagine if I were like Jesus, dependent on my heavenly Father for wisdom, grace, and courage—wisdom to know how to interact with my son, grace to do it without a demanding spirit, and the courage to actually do it. I've just reached into the box to find it empty. Instead of insisting that Andrew come down, I stop and pray. *Lord, I think Andrew did this, and I'm really irritated. Help me to ask him without a demanding spirit. You know how quick I can be to judge.* Then I could call upstairs, "Andrew, Emily and I can't find the disk for fixing the modem. Would you mind coming down and helping us? She can't get online."

Then I'd wait with Emily by the computer. That would mean

hearing Emily get even more and more exasperated as she waited for her brother. While sitting there, I could quietly pray for Emily. I could pray for Andrew. I could pray for grace to wait. My restless spirit wants to get going, but when I accept the place that God has given me—in traffic, a checkout line, or with a whining child—I open a small door from my soul to God.

After my son eventually comes downstairs and finds the modem, I could wait while he fixed it, thank him, and then ask, "Do you have a minute to talk with me about this disk?" If he says no, I could say, "Do you have time later on tonight?" When we finally got together, he might say, "Dad, I already know what you are going to say." I'd let him say it, and then I'd fill in the missing pieces with some questions. "Did you forget to put the disk back? Has that happened before? Do you have a tendency not to put things away? Do you see how that affected both Emily and me? Do you see how that was selfish?"

Notice the lack of self-will in this gentle pursuit of Andrew. Notice also that this is a hypothetical situation. I apologized to my son for the real one!

If I had been in touch with my self-will, then it would have opened up the door to prayer, to abiding. The great struggle of my life is not trying to discern God's will; it is trying to discern and then disown my own. Once I see that, then prayer flows. I have to be praying because I'm no longer in charge. Either I see all of life as a gift, or I demand that life have a certain look to it.

Getting in Touch with Our Self-Will

Jesus' Sermon on the Mount in Matthew 5–7 is a blueprint for getting in touch with your self-will and letting God take control. Jesus introduces us to what it means to be a child of our heavenly Father. To understand the sermon, think of your life as a room filled with open doors called money, sex, power, and fame.

Jesus begins the sermon by telling you he is going to go through your life and close all the doors to human power and glory. In the Beatitudes he says, "Blessed are the meek, for they shall inherit the earth" (Matthew 5:5). In other words, he is saying, "Give up power in relationships, and I will show you an entirely different way to do life. Don't be afraid of being a codependent, of disappearing. I will take care of you."

In the rest of chapter 5 Jesus closes one door after the other. He tells you to empower your enemies, those who abuse you, to think of their needs (5:43-47). If you suspect that someone is irritated with you, don't wait for that person to come to you; go to him or her even if it isn't your fault (5:23-24). Jesus closes the door to revenge, even emotional revenge through distance (5:38-42). And when you are selling something, don't try to get power over people by using oaths or by promising more than you can deliver (5:33-37). He closes the door to a secret life of sexual pleasure by telling you to remove your eye if it is looking at women to use them (5:27-30). If you do what Jesus says in chapter 5, you start to feel spiritual.

In Matthew 6, Jesus deals with wanting to look spiritual. He tells you to keep your prayer life hidden so you don't use it to make yourself look good. If you pray, do it in private (6:5-8). If you fast, pretend you don't (6:16-18). If you give, don't tell anyone (6:1-4). Don't use spirituality as a means for getting power and glory. Jesus closes the door to getting your identity from your own righteousness.

Then Jesus closes the door to getting your security from money. Instead, he says, give your money away (6:19-24). Now that you've lost the security of money, you begin to panic and say, "Who's going to take care of me?" Jesus says, "Your Father will. Look at the lilies of the field. Seek my Father's kingdom first." So not only do you have to give up money, but you have to give up worrying about money (6:25-34). Two more doors close to human power and glory.

As you begin Matthew 7, you have a new view of the world. You've learned how to put God at the center. Everywhere you look, people are so caught up with stuff. Now Jesus taps you on the shoulder and says, "Stop judging. When you see someone else's sin, instead of using that information to correct them, use that information to humble yourself by first finding the beam in your own eye." Instead of using your insights into other people's issues as a spiritual hammer, Jesus wants you to take these insights and deepen your own repentance (7:1-5). Argh! How do I do life?

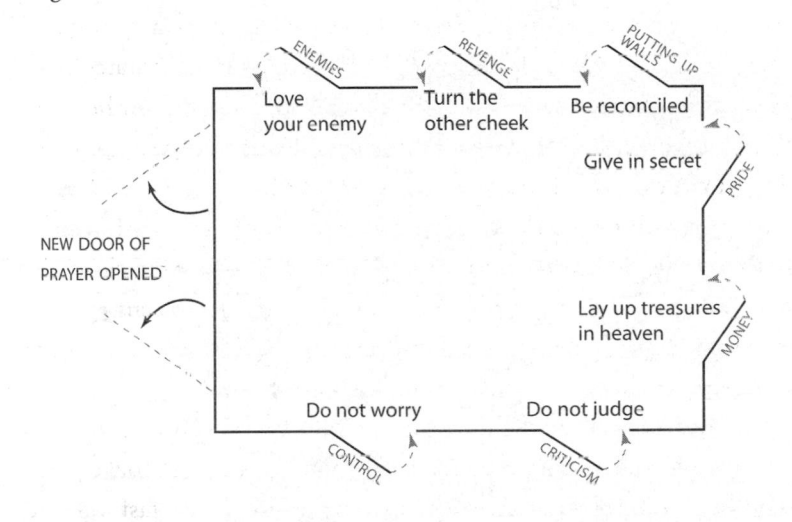

Having closed all your doors, Jesus opens the door to prayer and tells you how he gets things done (7:7). He asks for help from his Father. He talks to his Father and tells him what he wants. Prayer is the positive side of the surrendered will. As you stop doing your own will and wait for God, you enter into his mind. You begin to remain in him . . . to abide. This is the praying life.

Who Will Take Out the Trash?

Let's look at another example of how getting in touch with our self-will is a door to prayer. Imagine that Sue's husband, Joe, takes out the trash every Tuesday. It's his job. Last week he forgot to take it out, and then again this week. He's usually good about taking out the trash, but Sue tells him, "Honey, you forgot to take the trash out again." She says *again* with emphasis and more than a little irritation.

What's behind her irritation? Why does she feel compelled to add a twist to the word *again*? Because it is a hassle to take out the trash. It made her late for work. If she doesn't say *again*, then her husband will keep forgetting. If he doesn't see that this is becoming a pattern, she'll be taking out the trash for the rest of her life.

Notice Sue's underlying assumption: "It all depends on me. If I don't show him, no one else will." God is absent from her thinking; consequently she believes it's up to her to make her husband hear her words. If he doesn't, she fears she'll be swallowed up by his forgetfulness.

Sue speaks on her own, using the word *again* to control her husband. In contrast, Jesus says, "For I have not spoken on my own authority, but the Father who sent me has himself given me a commandment—what to say and what to speak" (John 12:49). Sue is using her words to do her own will. She refuses to accept the possibility of endlessly taking the trash out on Tuesdays. It is unacceptable.

Sue is in charge of her life, determined to make her kingdom pain free. Even if she prayed, prayer would just be another weapon in her arsenal of control. God would likely disappoint her, and she'd end up bitter at both her husband and God. Ironically, self-will often becomes a self-defeating prophecy. The berated spouse pulls back; he not only stops taking out the trash, but he also stops opening up his heart.

Self-will and prayer are both ways of getting things done. At the center of self-will is me, carving a world in my image, but at the center of prayer is God, carving me in his Son's image.

It never occurs to Sue that God might want her to take out the trash for the rest of her life, because to do so would mean she is letting her husband take advantage of her. But isn't Jesus endlessly taking out the church's trash? Isn't this action another way of loving an enemy?

What would happen if Sue puts off self-will? *She doesn't know.* How will God intervene in her husband's life? What does God want to do in her life? What beams will she discover in her own eye? Forgiving her husband would mean losing control.

If Sue surrenders her self-will, she will join Abraham walking up Mount Moriah with Isaac. She will join David as he puts down his knife when Saul is within his reach in the cave. Sue is abiding. She has lost control of the story.

> AT THE CENTER OF SELF-WILL IS ME, CARVING A WORLD IN MY IMAGE. AT THE CENTER OF PRAYER IS GOD, CARVING ME IN HIS SON'S IMAGE.

During a particularly hard time in my life, I remember realizing God is my fortress doesn't mean that God is giving me a fortress. It means he is the fortress (see Psalm 62:2). Except for God, I am completely alone. I wasn't sure I liked that.

When Sue shifts from self-will to a prayer fellowship, it feels scary, as if she is jumping over air. In fact, she is leaving the unstable foundation of her own self-will and entering the stability of God. She is living out the prayer, *Your kingdom come, your will be done.* Instead of trying to create her own story, Sue will be content to let God write his story. If her husband's forgetfulness turns into a habit, she'll be drawn into a deeper prayer fellowship. The trash is likely the tip of the iceberg in his life. He might have issues of self-will, laziness, or just plain selfishness. Sue will have fewer words for her husband and more words for God. She'll also reflect on her own heart. Are there any areas of her life where she does the same thing? She'll discover Jesus on the other side of the trash can.

We can't pray effectively until we get in touch with our inner brat. When we see our own self-will, it opens the door to doing things through God. Instead of singing Frank Sinatra's song "My Way," we enter into God's story and watch him do it his way. No one works like him.

PART 4

LIVING IN YOUR FATHER'S STORY

CHAPTER 19

WATCHING A STORY UNFOLD

WHEN EMILY WAS BORN in 1987, we had a serious space problem in our car. As it was, her five older siblings barely fit into our compact Chevy Cavalier station wagon—the two boys scrunched in the back without seatbelts. After ten years in the inner city, I was the associate director of a struggling overseas mission. Money was tight, so we decided to get a loan and purchase a used '85 Dodge Caravan. With six kids and two adults, we were still a seat short, but Andrew (age three) and Kim (age six) were small enough to squeeze into one seatbelt.

Emily spent most of the first year of her life strapped in her car seat. Jill was in the car almost nonstop, taking Kim to speech therapy, physical therapy, and doctors. We were concerned that the back of Emily's head would become flat—like Indian babies in papooses!

We didn't realize how much Emily liked the minivan until the transmission went out several years later, and we sold the minivan to our mechanic. We replaced it with an older station wagon. More than once, Emily (now six years old) wistfully mentioned the old Dodge minivan, enough that Jill and I commented to one another that this was a side of Emily we'd not seen before. A few years later, I began to pray for Emily almost every day, using this three-by-five card, that she would "not love the world or the things in the world" (1 John 2:15).

Emily

1 John 4:18 "There is no fear in love, but perfect love casts out fear."

1 John 2:15-16 "Do not love the world or anything in the world. If anyone loves the world, the love of the Father is not in him. For everything in the world—the cravings of sinful man, the lust of his eyes and the boasting of what he has and does—comes not from the Father but from the world."

Love of material things was not an all-consuming sin in Emily's life. It was just a slight bent to her heart. If a ship is off a few degrees, it is imperceptible at first, but over time it becomes a vast distance. I was praying to prevent the distance of a heart gone astray. I prayed for little Emily because I couldn't get inside her heart.

Our Prayers Shape Us

God wants to do something bigger than simply answer my prayers. The act of praying draws God into my life and begins to change me, the pray-er, in subtle ways.

One of the first things I noticed as I prayed for Emily was that I became more aware of her as a person. It also took the steam out of my tendency to fix her with quick comments. Because I was speaking to my heavenly Father about the potential drift of her heart, I could relax in the face of sin. Prayer softened me.

Praying regularly and thoughtfully about Emily's bent also influenced what cars Jill and I purchased. In 2003, our '93 Nissan Maxima's transmission gave out as it was approaching 160,000 miles. Again, we sold the car to our mechanic. This time our three older kids were out of the house, so money wasn't as tight. We thought about getting our first-ever new car and visited a Honda showroom. Jill liked the Honda Civic; I liked the Honda CRV. While discussing this over dinner, we noticed that Emily (now fifteen) brightened up at the thought of a new car. Her stock would go up ever so slightly with her friends. Jill and I glanced at one another, and after dinner we compared notes.

Emily attended a school where many of the kids were well-to-do, and the pressure to appear wealthy was beginning to take its toll on her. Driving up in a new car would elevate her social status. We didn't want to contribute to a false identity in her life, and we wanted to avoid a car loan. So we bought a '96 Toyota Avalon, which Jill and our older kids promptly dubbed "an old man's car." I continued to pray for Emily that she would not love the world or the things in the world.

Jill's and my love for Emily was informing our prayers, and our prayers were in turn shaping how we loved Emily. Our prayers didn't sit in isolation from the larger story God was weaving in her life and in ours. The act of praying was alerting us and shaping our decisions. Here's an example of what this looked like.

A year after we bought the Avalon, Emily saved a thousand dollars from a summer job at McDonald's. She wanted to use the money to purchase her older sister's '90 Toyota Corolla. However, Emily wouldn't be able to do that until her older sister and her husband left for Bangladesh in the winter. The fall social calendar took its toll on Emily's finances, so by Christmas she only had five hundred dollars of the original one thousand. She approached Jill and me for an interest-free loan to be repaid "in just a couple of months." But our family rules were clear. We provide the basics, and kids pay for the extras, such as cars and cell phones. So we said no.

Several weeks later, Jill overheard Emily praying for a car, pouring out her heart to God. Her prayer touched us, partly because it showed that Emily's heart was bending toward God instead of toward things—so we loaned her the money.

My prayers for Emily exposed my own heart. I began to see that I, too, loved the world and the things in the world. Even my frugality was a form of the love of money. The obsession of saving small amounts of money isn't that different from the obsession of gaining large amounts of it. In both, money is the center. I also began to notice that I tended to be extra polite with a donor to our ministry. That, too, is a form of the love of money.

I often find that when God doesn't answer a prayer, he wants to expose something in me. Our prayers don't exist in a world of their own. We are in dialogue with a personal, divine Spirit who wants to shape us as much as he wants to hear us. For God to act unthinkingly with our prayers would be paganism, which says the gods do our will in response to our prayers.

When someone's prayers aren't answered, I want to know the backstory. How long did that individual pray? What did God do in that person's heart when he or she prayed? What was God doing in the situation? Most of us isolate prayer from the rest of what God is doing in our lives, but God doesn't work that way. Prayer doesn't exist in some rarified spiritual world; it is part of the warp and woof of our lives. Praying itself becomes a story.

Parenting and Prayer

It is surprising how seldom books on parenting talk about prayer. We instinctively believe that if we have the right biblical principles and apply them consistently, our kids will turn out right. But that didn't work for God in the Garden of Eden. Perfect environment. Perfect relationships. And still God's two children went bad.

Many parents, including myself, are initially confident we can change our child. We don't surrender to our child's will (which is good), but we try to dominate the child with our own (which is bad). Without realizing it, we become demanding. We are driven by the hope of real change, but the change occurs because we make the right moves.

Until we become convinced we can't change our child's heart, we will not take prayer seriously. Consequently, repentance is often missing. When we see, for example, our son's self-will, we usually don't ask, *How am I self-willed?* or *How am I angry?* We want God's help so we can dominate our son. We forget that God is not a genie but a person who wants to shape us in the image of his Son as much as he wants to answer our prayers.

Increasingly, parents in our culture are moving to the opposite extreme and becoming passive. Parents say things like "My son has always been angry" or "Even when he was a kid, he was throwing temper tantrums." This passivity is reinforced by pop psychology's tendency to make descriptions of childhood stages into rules. For instance, if a two-year-old is bad, the mom may shrug her shoulders and say, "She's going through the terrible twos." This mom is trapped by psychological descriptions. Her passivity is further reinforced because she's talked to her little girl and even disciplined her, but nothing worked. This mom pushed against reality, but it didn't budge. She tried praying, but nothing much happened. She ran into the power of another person's self-will and surrendered. She has passively accepted the world as it is. Like the ancient Greeks, she is trapped by the Fates. When we do this, life takes on a fixed, given quality. Prayer becomes pointless.

> UNTIL YOU ARE CONVINCED THAT YOU CAN'T CHANGE YOUR CHILD'S HEART, YOU WILL NOT TAKE PRAYER SERIOUSLY.

The following chart summarizes the two attitudes that keep us from entering into the story that God is weaving in the lives of our children (or any person). Often we begin by being demanding, and then as we encounter human self-will, we drift into despair.

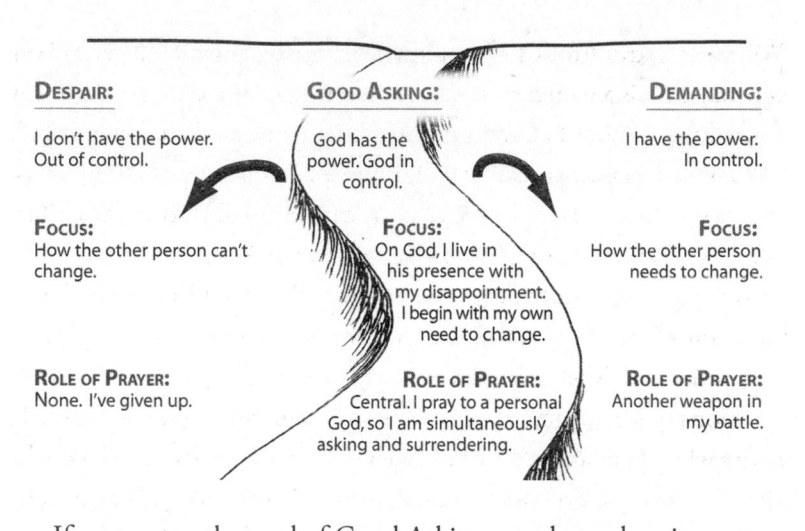

DESPAIR:
I don't have the power.
Out of control.

FOCUS:
How the other person can't change.

ROLE OF PRAYER:
None. I've given up.

GOOD ASKING:
God has the power. God in control.

FOCUS:
On God, I live in his presence with my disappointment. I begin with my own need to change.

ROLE OF PRAYER:
Central. I pray to a personal God, so I am simultaneously asking and surrendering.

DEMANDING:
I have the power.
In control.

FOCUS:
How the other person needs to change.

ROLE OF PRAYER:
Another weapon in my battle.

If you are on the road of Good Asking, you have also given up—but in a good way. You've given up on your ability to change other people. Instead, you cling to God and watch him weave his story. Frankly, Jill and I do our best parenting by prayer.

Field Hockey and Faith

One word summarizes our prayers for Emily: *faith*. We wanted the energy of her life to be coming from God and not from the people or things around her. We wanted her to abide. Here's a story that unfolded out of this prayer.

Emily loves field hockey, which is like ice hockey except it's gentler and requires eleven players on a grass field. Her school had a superb, well-coached program. Their team usually won its division and was frequently in the running for the state championship. The coach was excellent, although Emily thought the coach played favorites. That year she and her friend were not the favorites, and occasionally Emily sat out the entire game.

Another parent heard about the bench warming and, while chatting with me at the local gym, said, "Isn't that unbelievable what the coach is doing? Doesn't that make you mad?" I replied, "Actually, no.

We are thankful Emily has this low-level suffering while she is still on our watch. It is a wonderful opportunity for her to grow in faith. She'll learn far more about God on the bench than out on the playing field."

The other parent expected Jill and me to be angry about what was happening to Emily. Her goal for her child was tied to the child's accomplishments. Our goal was tied to Emily's faith. Because of that, we saw sports as just another venue where she could learn to sink her roots into God. I saw the bench warming as an answer to my daily prayer that Emily would not love the world or the things in the world.

Don't misunderstand. I wanted my daughter to play more. It stung when I glanced over from the bleachers to see her on the bench. But the disappointment was muted by the knowledge that having to sit on the bench was great preparation for life. Life is more about bench sitting than about being a star.

I asked Emily if she wanted me to approach the coach on her behalf, and she said she wanted to work it out for herself. She ended up talking with her coach several times. Not much came of it, but I was thrilled to see her speak honestly with an adult about a perceived injustice. Talking to a superior who might be doing you an injustice *increases* the chances that you'll get even *more* rejection. It was another opportunity for Emily not to get her life from this world. Another answer to prayer.

The following summer Emily was a counselor at a Christian camp, and her faith grew by leaps and bounds. She even missed summer hockey camp. When she came back in the fall, she didn't know how good her playing would be. Best of all, she didn't care what her coach or friends thought. The result? Her play during her senior year was her best ever. I asked her why, and she said, "I don't care as much about what other people think. I can just be myself."

Because we were praying thoughtfully for Emily, we could see God's larger picture weaving in and through her disappointments. God permitted mild pain in her life in order to grow her soul into his. No one works like him.

A FATHER'S LOVE

ALL WAS NOT RIGHT IN MY RELATIONSHIP WITH EMILY. There was distance between us. Most of the time, she was critical of me. In 2002 I jotted a note on her prayer card, *Help me to move toward her.* My note was just above my prayer that the love of the world not displace the love of the Father in her life. I didn't know how closely Emily's view of her earthly father and heavenly Father were connected.

I put feet on my prayers by asking Emily if she wanted to go with me on a couple of speaking trips to San Diego. We had a great time together, but still there was distance. In 2006 I jotted another note on her prayer card, that we would be closer. I couldn't bridge the gap with my daughter. So I prayed.

Guatemala

In September 2007, Emily and I were walking across the yard of a children's home in Guatemala, where she was spending the next nine months. As the sun was setting, I could still make out the razor wire atop the nine-foot walls of the compound. Emily had decided to postpone college and work with forty-five homeless children in Villa Nueva, Guatemala. The home was located in a slum area, surrounded by gangs.

We had encouraged Emily to go, not only because the orphanage needed help but also to free her from the high-school idols of sports, guys, looks, and friends. More than anything, we wanted faith to grow in her life. We wanted her to abide. Emily's willingness to go to Guatemala was another answer to our prayer that she would not love the world, but still, the prayer was largely unanswered.

As the two of us were walking, Emily suddenly made a sharp comment to me about not letting her have a cell phone at home. She'd just gotten one for Guatemala, and it must have triggered her irritation about not having one at home. We'd actually told her she could have a cell phone, but she couldn't afford it along with her car expenses. I knew she was afraid of being alone in a foreign country, away from family, friends, and the familiar, so I said nothing.

At least I said nothing to Emily. I knew that the common thread connecting Emily's fear, her distance from me, and her desire for a cell phone was faith. She was walking a little ahead of me, so I slowed down and prayed, *God, you have got to give Emily faith this year. You have no choice.* I was keenly aware of my inability to grow faith in her heart. God just had to do it. He didn't have a choice. He was bound by his own covenant.

Was this a name-it-and-claim-it power prayer? No, it was actually a powerless prayer. I prayed because I was weak. I wasn't trying to control God. I certainly wasn't in control of Emily. I was simply praying God's own heart back to him. I couldn't imagine him not answering such a prayer.

The next nine months were the hardest in Emily's life. She was thrown in with forty-five Hispanic orphans, and she had only taken a smattering of high-school Spanish. God used her isolation and the challenge of befriending moody teenagers to repeatedly break her and draw her to himself. She came back home a different person.

A year later, she was in college and asked me to proof the following paper for one of her classes. It tells the story of one of the threads God used in her life that year.

Every Thursday morning during high school I had jazz band practice. One of these mornings I was running late. I had to be out of the house by 7:15 and the clock read 7:21. My dad was sitting in the car waiting for me, so I grabbed my mascara and ran out the door swinging my backpack onto my shoulder. I sat in the front seat and complained the whole way, saying that I didn't want to be in band, even though it was my idea. I flipped down the cover of the mirror on the visor, in order to put on my mascara. But the flap kept popping back up, concealing the mirror. After about three times of it popping back up, I pushed the flap down so hard, it broke. My dad began to talk to me about my attitude. As we pulled up to the two glass doors of school, I got out of the car in a huff and shut the door, without a good-bye or a thank you.

I could try to justify my ways, but the real issue was my heart. I was bitter that my sister Kim, who has autism, seemed to receive more attention than me. I was insecure at school. I didn't have the right clothes; I didn't have the right hair; and I was tired of not fitting in. Maybe it was my insecurities that drove me to disrespect my dad by critiquing him day in and day out. But the main reason was I did not have the love of Jesus in me.

I decided at the end of my senior year to take a year off between high school and college and work in an orphanage in Guatemala. During that year, God showed me areas of my life where I had put up walls, places where I didn't want God.

One day, I was sitting in the guest dining room of the orphanage, talking with a volunteer who had come down for a few weeks. I decided to show her pictures of my family. My dad has a blog on his work website, and I knew that he had pictures there. As I scrolled through his past blogs, I came upon pictures of me at my junior year prom [June 2005]. As I read the comments below the pictures, written by my dad, I became so overwhelmed with the love of my father. The person next to me must have thought I was crazy as tears streaked down my face. I remembered all the times I yelled at him for his loud chewing, the times I told him that he didn't love me, the times I would stomp out of a room, not only that year, but through most of my teenage years. As I read the words and saw the pictures, I felt so undeserving of his love, with all the attention, patience, and gentleness he showed me.

As I sat at the table, gazing at the computer screen in front of me, my thoughts came to God. How my dad loved me was an example of God's love for me. My thoughts raced to all the times I had ignored God, in my relationships with other people, in sports, in music, all areas of my life. When times were good, I ignored God, but when times were hard, I blamed God. But nothing that I did separated me from the love of Christ. "But God demonstrates his own love for us in this: While we were still sinners, Christ died for us" (Romans 5:8, NIV). I, completely undeserving, received the greatest gift of all, eternal life, because of God's love and his grace upon me.

I have the love of a father. My earthly father showed me through a simple web page that it isn't what I do that makes him love me. He loves me because I am his daughter. My disrespect didn't push his love away from me. For me, this was a small picture of the love that my heavenly Father has for me. I will never fully comprehend how I can be loved so much, when my heart is often so ugly and unlovable. But I guess that's what makes grace so amazing.

My two prayer requests—for her relationships with her earthly father and her heavenly Father—were closely connected. A breakthrough in one led to a breakthrough in the other. As I watch God's stories unfold, I watch for his little design touches, his poetry.

I was also struck by the wisdom of God's five-year delay to our prayers for Emily. As her heart began to soften while befriending and caring for the orphans, her life goals began to change. She switched both colleges and careers. The whole direction of her life changed. God waited to remove the blinders from her eyes until he had Emily where he wanted her.

When I prayed that Emily would not love the things of this world, it seemed as if she was standing alone in the middle of a field dominated by the icons of modern American teenage life: boyfriends, friends, appearance, sports, and clothes. Jesus was a fading childhood memory. My prayer for her seemed so weak, so powerless. Now the words whispered softly over her heart have swept away the once-powerful images. The quest for popularity has been replaced by love, by a desire to be with those who have nothing to offer her. Prayer has won the day. Like the apostle Paul I can testify that "God chose what is weak in the world to shame the strong; God chose what is low and despised in the world, even things that are not, to bring to nothing things that are" (1 Corinthians 1:27-28).

> SHE WAS STANDING ALONE IN THE MIDDLE OF A FIELD DOMINATED BY THE ICONS OF MODERN AMERICAN TEENAGE LIFE: BOYFRIENDS, FRIENDS, APPEARANCE, SPORTS, AND CLOTHES. JESUS WAS A FADING CHILDHOOD MEMORY. MY PRAYER FOR HER SEEMED SO WEAK, SO POWERLESS.

Broken Images of God

But what if your human father failed you? Some cringe when they hear the word *father*. How can you see God as your father if your father was distant, absent, or harsh?

Because we live in a fallen world, God has to use broken images of himself, such as fathers. In fact, all the images God gives us of himself in Scripture are flawed. Think of king or lord. How many good politicians do you know? The early church's experience of Caesar was not pleasant, yet they took Caesar's title, "Lord," and applied it to Jesus, calling him "Lord Jesus."

The good news is that our heavenly Father trumps the failures of our earthly fathers. The fact that we know our king or father is flawed means we know what a good father should do. Because we are created in the image of the triune God, we have an instinctive knowledge of how a father should love. If we didn't know what a good father was, we couldn't critique our own.[1] Modern psychology can unwittingly trap us in our past. It is just another form of fatalism that kills our ability to see the story God is weaving in our lives.

Emily can still give you a list of my failings as a father. At the top of the list is chewing too loudly! One of her standing requests is for me not to eat carrots or any chips in the same room as her. God uses the weak things of this world—including fathers—to weave his stories.

UNANSWERED PRAYER

Understanding the Patterns of Story

When Jill was pregnant with Kim, she prayed using Psalm 121, asking God to keep her baby from all harm. Next to the psalm Jill wrote the date (August 1981) she started praying this prayer.

When Kim was born, everything went wrong. The doctor gave Jill too much Pitocin, a drug to induce labor, and then left her unattended. I'd seen my wife go through three natural childbirths, but this was different. She was in agony. The doctor never came back to the delivery room. Then, Kim was born blue and her first Apgar score was low. She looked different to me. I called Jill's parents from a pay phone at the hospital. "Something's wrong with the baby," I said and burst into tears.

We had no clear diagnosis of what was wrong—we wouldn't until Kim was nineteen years old—so we, like most parents of disabled children, were operating in the dark. We didn't know if Kim was hurt from birth or if she had some kind of disorder. I talked to the HMO manager about the doctor's behavior. He said, "Yes, he's not a good doctor." I talked to the doctor about his behavior, and he threatened to sue us if we did anything. We were young, confused, and afraid.

In time Jill began to hate the dreaded charts that described what your child should be doing at what age. Some doctors encouraged us, saying Kim was fine. Others didn't. One neurologist at a major medical center wondered if Jill had beaten Kim.

We were overwhelmed with the number of problems Kim had. And new ones just kept coming. Her muscle tone was floppy. Her eyes didn't focus. She had pneumonia. She had trouble breathing, especially in the winter, becoming listless when we turned on the heat. Her breathing problem was so pronounced that we used the last of our savings to convert to electric baseboard heat. For the next twenty years we lived paycheck to paycheck.

It was agony, especially for Jill. She had prayed that God would keep Kim from harm, but we were holding a harmed child. At one point I told Jill, "Why don't you just give Kim to God?" She told me, "Paul, every day I take Kim up in my arms, walk her up to the foot of the cross, and then turn my back and come down again." It would have been easier for us if Jill had not prayed that Kim would be kept from harm. The promise of God actually made it worse. It hurt to hope.

The following chart describes our world. The hope line represents our desire for a normal child, reinforced by our prayers from Psalm 121. The bottom line is the reality of a harmed child. We

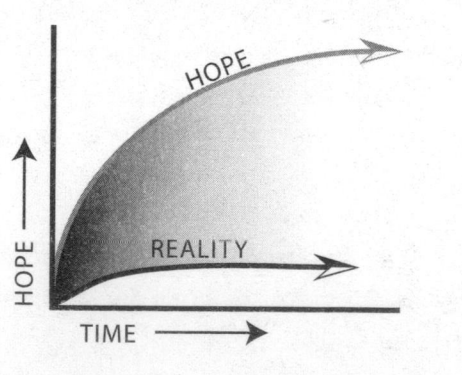

lived in the middle, in the desert, holding on to hope that Kim could somehow be normal yet facing the reality of her disabilities. It is a difficult world in which to live.

Every part of your being wants to close the gap between hope and reality. We will do anything not to live in the desert. Initially, Jill found it difficult to face Kim's disabilities—partly because we had no diagnosis of the cause of her problems, partly because it hurt to face reality.

The next chart describes the denial approach to suffering. It is filled with hope but doesn't face reality. For instance, some Christians try to sidestep suffering by insisting God has healed them, but then they die of cancer.

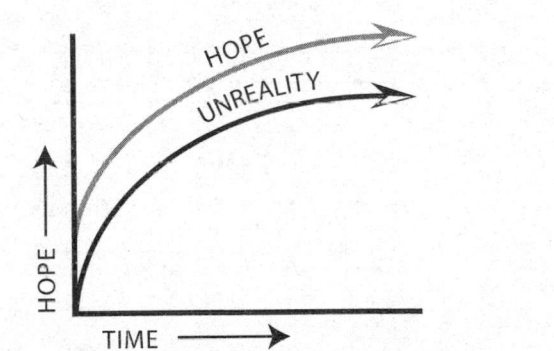

After you've gotten over the initial shock of suffering, a determination often sets in to fix whatever is causing the pain. You have faced enormous obstacles before and overcome them, and you are going to do the same with this. You leave no stone unturned. Money means nothing to you. You are convinced someone somewhere knows how to fix this. By the sheer force of your will, by mobilizing prayer, you are going to make this happen.

The following chart illustrates different attempts to close the gap between hope and reality. Often this determination simply adds another layer of suffering to what you are already facing.

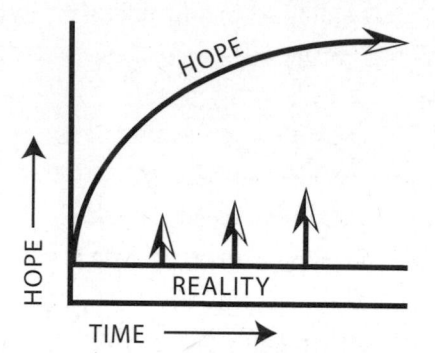

It's a short trip from determination to despair, where you realize that you aren't going to change the situation, no matter what you do. It hurts to hope in the face of continued failure, so you try to stop hurting by giving up on hope. Jill struggled with denial; I wrestled with hope. I thought we just had to face reality. But Jill's hope, her love for Kim, drove her to try new things. Jill took to calling me an unbeliever. It took almost fifteen years before I became a believer in Kim.

In the next chart, despair removes the tension between hope and reality. Despair, in its own strange way, can be comforting, but it and its cousin, cynicism, can kill the soul.

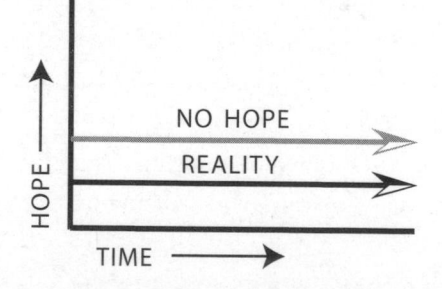

In contrast, people of faith live in the desert. Like Abraham, they are aware of the reality of their circumstances but are fixed on hope. Paul describes how "in hope [Abraham] believed against hope" (Romans 4:18). In the face of Sarah's barrenness and old age, Abraham still had hope.

> He did not weaken in faith when he considered his own body, which was as good as dead (since he was about a hundred years old), or when he considered the barrenness of Sarah's womb. No unbelief made him waver concerning the promise of God, but he grew strong in his faith as he gave glory to God. ROMANS 4:19-20

Abraham stakes his life on the hope line, but he never takes his eye off the reality line. He does have his moments though. He tries to get out of the desert by suggesting to God that his steward Eliezer become his adopted son (see Genesis 15). Sarah tries to close the hope–reality gap by asking Abraham to sleep with her servant Hagar (see Genesis 16). Finally, when God tells Abraham that Sarah will have a child in a year, Sarah laughs behind the tent flap (see Genesis 18). She closes the gap by giving up on hope. A year later when Isaac is born, she realizes that God has transformed her cynicism into joy. She mocks her cynicism by giving her son a name that means "laughter" (see Genesis 21).

Life in the Desert

The hardest part of being in the desert is that there is no way out. You don't know when it will end. There is no relief in sight.

A desert can be almost anything. It can be a child who has gone astray, a difficult boss, or even your own sin or foolishness. Maybe you married your desert.

God customizes deserts for each of us. Joseph's desert is being betrayed and forgotten in an Egyptian jail. Moses lives in the Midian desert as an outcast for forty years. The Israelites live in the desert for forty years. David runs from Saul in the desert. All of them hold on to the hope of God's Word yet face the reality of their situations.

The theme of the desert is so strong in Scripture that Jesus reenacts the desert journey at the beginning of his ministry by fasting for forty days in a desert while facing Satan's temptation. His desert is living with the hope of the resurrection yet facing the reality of his Father's face turned against him at the cross.

The Father turning his face against you is the heart of the desert experience. Life has ended. It no longer has any point. You might not want to commit suicide, but death would be a relief. It's very tempting to survive the desert by taking the bread of bitterness offered by Satan—to maintain a wry, cynical detachment from life, finding a perverse enjoyment in mocking those who still hope.

Thriving in the Desert
God takes everyone he loves through a desert. It is his cure for our wandering hearts, restlessly searching for a new Eden. Here's how it works.

The first thing that happens is we slowly give up the fight. Our wills are broken by the reality of our circumstances. The things that brought us life gradually die. Our idols die for lack of food. That is what happened to Emily in Guatemala. That is what happened to Jill with Kim.

The still, dry air of the desert brings the sense of helplessness that is so crucial to the spirit of prayer. You come face-to-face with your inability to live, to have joy, to do anything of lasting worth. Life is crushing you.

Suffering burns away the false selves created by cynicism or pride or lust. You stop caring about what people think of you. The desert is God's best hope for the creation of an authentic self.

Desert life sanctifies you. You have no idea you are changing. You simply notice after you've been in the desert awhile that you are different. Things that used to be important no longer matter. For instance, before Kim was born, we used to have one of the kids comb the fringes of the living-room rug so it was perfect. Now we are lucky to find a comb for our own hair.

After a while you notice your real thirsts. While in the desert David writes,

> O God, you are my God; earnestly I seek you;
>   my soul thirsts for you;
> my flesh faints for you,
>   as in a dry and weary land where there is no water.
>
> PSALM 63:1

The desert becomes a window to the heart of God. He finally gets your attention because he's the only game in town.

You cry out to God so long and so often that a channel begins to open up between you and God. When driving, you turn off the radio just to be with God. At night you drift in and out of prayer when you are sleeping. Without realizing it, you have learned to pray continuously. The clear, fresh water of God's presence that you discover in the desert becomes a well inside your own heart.

The best gift of the desert is God's presence. We see this in Psalm 23. In the beginning of the psalm, the Shepherd is in front of me—"he leads me beside still waters" (verse 2); at the end he is behind me—"goodness and faithful love will pursue me" (verse 6, HCSB); but in the middle, as I go through "the valley of the shadow of death," he is next to me—"I will fear no evil, for you are with me" (verse 4). The protective love of the Shepherd gives me the courage to face the interior journey.

YOU CRY OUT TO GOD SO LONG AND SO OFTEN THAT A CHANNEL BEGINS TO OPEN UP BETWEEN YOU AND GOD.

The Desert Blossoms

Very early on, Jill and I were aware that because of Kim, God was humbling us, making us more like his Son. Kim saved our family, beginning with me. God used Kim to wake me up spiritually. I'd been thinking about leaving the inner-city school where I was a teaching principal to expand our tax business. I'd opened up another office, and I realized I could make money. Nothing wrong with that, but at the same time my heart was bending away from God. After Kim was born that all evaporated, and six months later, I prayed I could work with my dad and help him organize his missions work. In the fall he called Jill, asking her to help him. I volunteered, and in the winter of 1983 we started World Harvest Mission together. It would not exist without the gift of Kim.

The pressure of a child with Kim's version of autism, pervasive developmental disorder, is at times overwhelming. That pressure combined with other frustrations led Jill, in 1991, to challenge me if I loved her. That was the beginning of my journey into the life of Jesus that led to the book *Love Walked Among Us, The Person of Jesus* study, and the ministry of seeJesus.net.

Kim is the reason Jill and our daughter Ashley became special-ed teachers. We now spend our summer vacations at Joni and Friends Camps, retreats for adults with disabilities. Jesus was drawing us down low, where he lived.

Kept from Harm

Remember Kim's seasonal breathing problem? Ten years later when we sold our house, we discovered that our gas furnace had been improperly installed. Kim's weakened condition had made her particularly susceptible to the effects of carbon-monoxide gas that was filling our house. She was like one of those canaries the miners used to detect dangerous fumes. Kim kept us from harm.

Years later when Kim was about twenty, I was sitting at the

dining-room table writing a Bible study on Psalm 121 that I was going to teach to our small group. I had forgotten about Jill's Psalm 121 prayer.

I looked up from the table and said, "Jill, God did it. He kept us from all harm. He did Psalm 121." We had thought the harm was a daughter with disabilities, but this was nothing compared to the danger of two proud and willful parents. Because Kim was mute, Jill and I learned to listen. Her helplessness taught us to become helpless too.

Kim brought Jesus into our home. Jill and I could no longer do life on our own. We needed Jesus to get from one end of the day to the other. We'd asked for a loaf of bread, and instead of giving us a stone, our Father had spread a feast for us in the wilderness. *Thank you, Jesus, for Kim.*

When we don't receive what we pray for or desire, it doesn't mean that God isn't acting on our behalf. Rather, he's weaving his story. Paul tells us to "continue steadfastly in prayer, being watchful in it with thanksgiving" (Colossians 4:2). Thanksgiving helps us to be grace-centered, seeing all of life as a gift. It looks at how God's past blessings impact our lives. Watchfulness alerts us to the unfolding drama in the present. It looks for God's present working as it unfolds into future grace.[1]

Watch for the story God is weaving in your life. Don't leave the desert. Corrie ten Boom's father often reminded her, "The best is yet to come."[2]

CHAPTER 22

HEBREW LAMENTS

Relearning Desert Praying

WHEN OUR CHURCH was going through a particularly hard time, I showed the congregation some prayers in a special evening service. I set them up a bit by saying, "I got these out of an edgy book of prayers. Do you have any concerns about them?"

Please, GOD, no more yelling,
    no more trips to the woodshed.
Treat me nice for a change;
    I'm so starved for affection.

Can't you see I'm black-and-blue,
    beat up badly in bones and soul?
GOD, how long will it take
    for you to let up?

GOD, are you avoiding me?
    Where are you when I need you?

Long enough, GOD—
　　you've ignored me long enough.
I've looked at the back of your head
　　long enough.

They bit nicely. "Disrespectful." "Inappropriate." "You shouldn't talk to God that way." Then I told them these were from *The Message* translation of Psalm 6, 10, and 13. I showed them the same psalms in a more literal translation.

LORD, do not rebuke me in your anger
　　or discipline me in your wrath.
Have mercy on me, LORD, for I am faint;
　　heal me, LORD, for my bones are in agony.
My soul is in deep anguish.
　　How long, LORD, how long?
PSALM 6:1-3, NIV

Why, LORD, do you stand far off?
　　Why do you hide yourself in times of trouble?
PSALM 10:1, NIV

How long, LORD? Will you forget me forever?
　　How long will you hide your face from me?
PSALM 13:1, NIV

I explained that these were Hebrew laments, a long-forgotten but deeply biblical way of praying. Their initial negative reaction makes sense: Laments do feel disrespectful. We feel uncomfortable praying this way to God. We read these prayers in the Psalms, but we don't actually pray them. Let's dig deeper and explain what lament praying is, how it works, and even why we are allergic to laments.

Understanding Laments

My first experience with a lament made me very uncomfortable, partly because it was a lament for me! In our first year of marriage (Jill was eighteen and I was nineteen!), I shared with Jill that I wasn't sure I was a Christian. I'd grown up in a home filled with faith, and yet sometimes I felt as though I were looking at Christianity from the outside. One night, lying in bed, Jill poured out her heart in prayer for me.

Every part of me recoiled from Jill's prayer. It was invasive, demanding, even offensive. I didn't want any part of it. In my Presbyterian heritage, everything was balanced—our emotions, our reactions, and our theology. Jill's lament was anything but balanced. It was raw and uneven.

Jill was simply recoiling from my deadness. Recall the hope-reality charts we introduced in the last chapter. Jill's prayer expressed, in a heart of agony, the gap between the reality of my cold heart and her hope for me. Her lament connected my spiritual deadness with her desire for me to walk with God. That's what makes laments so messy. They bring together two things (reality and promise) that recoil from one another. A lament connects two "hot" wires—God's promise and the problem. When that happens, sparks fly.

We saw in the last chapter that the gap between hope and reality is a desert. The very emptiness of the desert drives the power of a lament. A lament doesn't flee the desert; it fights the desert. It takes it on. In fact, the bleakness of the desert emboldens the lament. My weak faith was a desert for Jill. That gave energy and passion to her lament for me.

Laments might *seem* disrespectful, but in fact they are filled with faith—a raw, pure form of faith that simply takes God at his word. Every child is a professional lamenter, as in, "Mom, you said you'd take me to the pool this week! Why haven't you? I want to go today." The child is bringing together promise and hope ("Mom, you said . . .") with reality ("Why haven't you?")

There is no such thing as a lament-free life. In fact, if your life is lament-free, you aren't loving well. To love is to lament, to let your heart be broken by something.

LAMENTS MIGHT SEEM DISRESPECTFUL, BUT IN FACT THEY ARE FILLED WITH A RAW, PURE FORM OF FAITH THAT SIMPLY TAKES GOD AT HIS WORD.

If you *don't* lament over the broken things in your world, then your heart shuts down. Your living, vital relationship with God dies a slow death because you open the door to unseen doubt and become quietly cynical. Cynicism moves you away from God; laments push you into his presence. So, oddly enough, *not lamenting* leads to unbelief. Reality wins, and hope dies. Put another way, the reality of a broken world triumphs over the new reality of a redeemed world. You miss resurrection and get stuck in death.

One of the sure signs that the Israelites have wandered from God is that they've stopped lamenting. Listen to God's indictment of Israel through the prophet Jeremiah. The italics indicate the lament that the Israelites are *not* praying.

Thus says the LORD:

> "What wrong did your fathers find in me
>   that they went far from me,
> and went after worthlessness, and became worthless?
> They did not say, '*Where is the LORD*
>   *who brought us up from the land of Egypt,*
> *who led us in the wilderness,*
>   *in a land of deserts and pits,*
> *in a land of drought and deep darkness,*
>   *in a land that none passes through,*
> *where no man dwells?*'

And I brought you into a plentiful land
   to enjoy its fruits and its good things.
But when you came in, you defiled my land
   and made my heritage an abomination.
The priests did not say, *'Where is the LORD?'*"

JEREMIAH 2:5-8, EMPHASIS ADDED

God rebukes his people and his priests because "they did not say, 'Where is the LORD?'" A sure sign of their wandering hearts is that no one is in God's face. No one takes hold of God and pulls. This idea is so strange to our ears that I must repeat it: God is upset with Israel because they are *not* lamenting. We think laments are disrespectful. God says the opposite. Lamenting shows you are engaged with God in a vibrant, living faith.

We live in a deeply broken world. If the pieces of our world aren't breaking your heart and you aren't in God's face about them, then you're becoming quietly cynical. You've thrown in the towel.

Nuclear Praying

One of the misconceptions about laments comes from the word itself. To lament means to grieve. So we naturally think of lament prayers in the same category as funeral dirges—a form of grieving with no expectation that anything will change. Recently a friend lost a young son in a tragic accident. We have no expectation this son will rise from the dead—at least not until Jesus returns. So we lament with our friend. That's how David laments when Saul and Jonathan are killed in battle (2 Samuel 1:17-27). They will not come back.

This is a small subcategory of Hebrew lamenting, but by far most laments are not prayers of surrender, grieving what cannot be changed, but a call to arms. They are the spiritual warfare equivalent of "going nuclear": You have no other option, so you reach for your most powerful weapon—your ability to cry out to the living God for help. Let me explain.

Seventeen years after Jill's lament of me, it was my turn to lament about the state of our family. The camping trip I mentioned in the introduction, where my daughter Ashley lost her contact lens, was a turning point for our family—and for me.

After we discovered Ashley's contact sitting on a leaf, the camping trip slowly disintegrated. The five kids with me (aged three to sixteen) fought constantly. I put up a hammock so they could have fun together. They fought over that. I built a fire so they could burn sticks. They fought over that. Andrew (age six) starting chopping up Park Service property for firewood. Because a friend forgot to return a crucial piece of our propane stove, I had to cook spaghetti over the open fire. They whined about the burnt spaghetti. They whined about the shish kebab I made the second evening. We actually have a random photo of Emily (age three!) standing by the fire holding a hatchet. (Mom wasn't there.) I was running around barking orders, trying to keep us from descending into chaos.

The second night, chaos arrived. We'd camped at the bottom of the mountain in what must have been a dry streambed. That night it poured and it poured. We had an old canvas tent—the kind that water comes through if you touch the sides, which the kids found irresistible since it allowed them to write their names on the inside of the tent. About 2 a.m., I crawled outside and, holding a flashlight under my chin, dug a ditch around our tent with a camping shovel to divert the water that was pouring in the tent because the door zipper was broken. The only thing I could find to tie the tent door closed was the kids' shoe laces, but I was too tired to take the laces off the shoes, so they dangled from the tent door. During the night, our six sleeping bags slid to the bottom of the tent in a sodden mass of humanity. When the sun came up, we unpeeled from one another, ducked our heads underneath the shoes, and stumbled outside.

I was worried. I knew if I didn't dry the kids, they'd get sick. The only dry thing left was our Dodge Minivan. So after breakfast we piled in and headed off for a long drive. It was a beautiful Pennsylvania morning with fog shrouding the valleys. We drove down into the little hamlets and then up into the sunshine. As the kids slowly drifted off to sleep, they looked so sweet and peaceful. It was hard to believe they'd been so selfish and mean.

In the quiet, I began to extrapolate from their selfishness into the future. The pressure of camping brought to the surface a new level of meanness in them. It scared me. But it wasn't just the kids. It was me, too—snapping, super-efficient, always busy. We were headed for trouble. For the first time in my life I saw two things clearly: Our family was headed toward ruin, and I was powerless to stop it.

So I prayed with some desperation, "God, you have got to save our family. We are headed for trouble. We need Jesus." I was surprised with how insistent my prayer was, but when I was finished I knew something had happened in the heavenlies.

God answered my lament in ways that I never expected, in ways far larger than I ever anticipated. I was mainly concerned for my kids. He was concerned for me. Six months later when I'd long forgotten about my lament, I burned out from drinking a Diet Coke (a reaction to NutraSweet) and overwork. That began a decadelong cascade of relentless humbling in every area of my life. His work on me was so deep, so powerful, so complex that I have trouble describing it. During this time, I learned how to pray. I learned how to pray for my family. It became like breathing. God saved our family. He still is.

UNDERSTANDING HOW
LAMENTS WORK

GIVEN THAT LAMENTATIONS, one-third of the Psalms, and large sections of Job, Isaiah, Jeremiah, and the Minor Prophets are laments, why do laments feel so strange? Even more startling, the ancient Israelites didn't just pray laments, they sang them. Songs of lament were front and center in their hymnbook. So why don't we hear them prayed from the pulpit? Why are they so rare?

The answer goes back two thousand years. After the destruction of the temple in AD 70, when Judaism separated from Christianity, the church lost its ability to lament. We lost some of our Jewish DNA and took on some Greek ways of thinking. Here's how it happened.

Ancient people would not have been snookered by Disney's message to "Have faith in yourself." Both the Greeks and the Jews knew the world was a dangerous, chaotic place. Neither were naive about how treacherous and fragile life was. But the similarities end there. The Greeks accepted the chaos. The Jews brought the chaos to God in their lamenting.

Why such a radically different response? The Greeks, like all pagans, assumed that chaos and evil were part of the original order of creation. You can't change it—so you cope. You accept your lot in life, getting through as quietly as possible—trying not to make waves. The only escape was the life of the mind, the disembodied life. The ideal life for the Greeks was that of the philosopher—calm and well-ordered, with long discussions with like-minded, intelligent friends.

The Greeks called this ideal "Stoicism" (see chapter 14). A Stoic would never make a whip to clear out a temple or wail over Jerusalem's coming destruction. Corruption and war were simply accepted. The early church rejected Stoicism, but the church breathed its air for centuries, affecting how we still think and feel today. A Stoic would consider a lament inappropriate: too emotional, too aggressive.

The Israelites lamented because they longed for a better world, the way the world is supposed to be. They believed in a covenant-keeping God, one who keeps his word. That's what makes laments so passionate, so in-your-face.

When you lament, you live simultaneously in the past, present, and future. A lament connects God's *past* promise with my *present* chaos, hoping for a better *future*. So on the cross Jesus cries out, "My God, my God, why have you forsaken me?" (Matthew 27:46). He connects the utter chaos of his life with the love of his Father. That connection is nuclear.

Jesus' lament of God-forsakenness is answered with the Resurrection. His Father acts on his prayer and raises him from the dead, creating a new, deathless body for Jesus, a foretaste of the coming new creation that will utterly transform all of us who believe in him. Laments work.

Jesus is not a Stoic, gritting his teeth until the Resurrection; nor is he a determinist, saying, "I know God is going to raise me from the dead. I just have to get through this." He is fully alive to both his situation and his Father's love for him.

A Template for Laments

Let's examine a lament in some detail to see how this works. Isaiah's lament in Isaiah 63–64 over the destruction of Jerusalem is a classic lament. Many laments begin with an emotional dump, not unlike the beginnings of an argument between a husband and a wife when one of them has been bottling things up. So Isaiah begins, upset with God over Israel's captivity, implying that, because God is sovereign, it is God's fault.

> O Lord, why do you make us wander from your ways
>   and harden our heart, so that we fear you not?
> Return for the sake of your servants,
>   the tribes of your heritage.
>
> ISAIAH 63:17

Because Isaiah believes so deeply in God's sovereignty, he blames God. Many laments begin in a similar fashion: "God, why aren't you listening?" The lamenter shares his messy heart.

After this initial, passionate overflow, Isaiah connects the reality of Israel's desolate state with the hope of God's power. He believes not in a distant God, but in a God who incarnates, who acts in time and space. This is the heart of a lament:

> Oh that you would rend the heavens and come down.
>
> ISAIAH 64:1

Isaiah remembers how God delivered the Israelites under Moses and how God met them at Mount Sinai. Isaiah is in God's face because God has rent the heavens in the past. He pleads, "Do it again, God!"

> When you did awesome things that we did not look for,
>   you came down, the mountains quaked at your presence.
>
> ISAIAH 64:3

Then Isaiah's voice softens as he reflects on what is driving his prayer:

> From of old no one has heard
>   or perceived by the ear,
> no eye has seen a God besides you,
>   who acts for those who wait for him.
>
> ISAIAH 64:4

Isaiah has just given us a perfect description of prayer. This is why I pray for parking spaces, why I lament for the state of the church, why I pray seemingly impossible prayers. Isaiah and I both know a God "who acts for those who wait for him." In a lament we tell God, "Your word has not become flesh."

Now the tone shifts from passionate asking to quiet repentance. In effect Isaiah says, "We're the problem. We've blown it."

> Behold, you were angry, and we sinned;
>   in our sins we have been a long time, and shall we
>   be saved?
>
> ISAIAH 64:5

In quick succession, Isaiah lists five word pictures that describe Israel's desolation (64:6-7):

- Our righteous deeds are like a polluted garment.
- We all fade like a leaf.
- Our iniquities, like the wind, take us away.
- You have hidden your face from us.
- [You] have made us melt in the hand of our iniquities.

In the middle of this, Isaiah answers his own prayer by lamenting. He laments that no one is lamenting!

> There is no one who calls upon your name,
>> who rouses himself to take hold of you.
>
> ISAIAH 64:7

Isaiah's grief over the absence of laments gives us a perfect description of lamenting. A lamenter "rouses himself to take hold of" God. That's what a lament does: It takes hold of God.

Now Isaiah's voice becomes hushed. He submits, calling God his Father, the potter who makes Israel—but that is also a plea for his Father, the potter to act, to create anew.

> But now, O LORD, you are our Father;
>> we are the clay, and you are our potter;
>> we are all the work of your hand.
>
> ISAIAH 64:8

Submitting doesn't mean the prophet loses his voice. In fact, Isaiah's voice becomes clearer as he paints Israel's desperate condition. You can feel his quiet desperation as he pleads,

> Behold, please look, we are all your people.
> Your holy cities have become a wilderness;
>> Zion has become a wilderness,
>> Jerusalem a desolation.
> Our holy and beautiful house,
>> where our fathers praised you,
> has been burned by fire,
>> and all our pleasant places have become ruins.
> Will you restrain yourself at these things, O LORD?
>> Will you keep silent, and afflict us so terribly?
>
> ISAIAH 64:9-12

You can feel Isaiah's broken heart; thousands of years later it still jumps off the page. He begins the lament naked before God, pouring out his heart. Then he reinterprets those feelings in the reality of God. He gradually opens up his heart to God. In a kind of a pilgrimage, he begins feisty, in God's face, then he slowly reveals his faith and his heart.

Isaiah's faith drives this lament. He believes three things about God: First, God is sovereign. He can do something. Second, God is love. He is for me. He wants to do something. And finally, God is a covenant-keeping God. He is bound by his own word. He will do something. Isaiah's faith feeds off the character of God.

Look how different Isaiah's pilgrimage is from the five stages of grief. Instead of withdrawing (Stage 1: Denial), Isaiah boldly moves into God's presence, asking for help. Instead lashing out at God (Stage 2: Anger), he unashamedly holds God to his word. Instead of manipulating (Stage 3: Bargaining), he tells God directly what he wants and why he wants it. Instead of getting lost in his sorrow (Stage 4: Depression), he expresses his sorrow freely to God. And finally, instead of resignation (Stage 5: Acceptance), he tirelessly brings his request to God. The prophet never stops asking because he never stops believing. His asking changes tone, and his reasons change, but he doesn't let go of God. Like Jacob, he wrestles with God. He takes hold of God and pulls. This lack of acceptance of the status quo is what makes laments so fierce.

If you compare Isaiah's lament with other laments, you'll notice that no two laments are the same. You can't reduce lamenting to the "five stages of lamenting," because two people are grappling—Jacob and the angel, one human and one divine. As soon as you reduce a person to "stages," personhood dies, and you become trapped in your stage.

So how did God respond to Isaiah's lament? Jesus. It's that simple. He gave his Son, who created a new Jerusalem, his body. He rent the heavens and came down as a little baby. God became flesh.

Thinking a Lament

When you first read laments, you notice their passion, but most laments are also closely reasoned arguments, where the lamenter argues with God. When you argue, you make a case, using both passion and reason. The closest thing in my life to a lament are my occasional intensive discussions (arguments!) with Jill.

Look at the arguments Isaiah marshals. He begins by making a case that God is all-powerful. (I've reworded each prayer to highlight Isaiah's reasoning.)

> God, if you are sovereign, if you really control everything, why are you permitting this to happen to Jerusalem? (63:17)

Then Isaiah argues, based on God's past deliverance of Israel.

> God, in the past, you've delivered Israel from impossible situations. You delivered them from Egypt. You rent the heavens and came down. That's what you do! It's who you are! It's what we have all experienced from you. Can you do it again? (64:1-4)

Then Isaiah moves to confession. He knows from Deuteronomy (30:1-10) that if Israel repents, God will turn and forgive and deliver them. So even in Isaiah's repentance, he's making a case for deliverance.

> God, this is our fault. We are a mess. We are the problem.
> We repent in dust and ashes. We do not deserve your grace.
> We know we deserve your anger, but we know that you love our brokenness. (64:9)

Finally, he identifies God's honor with the desolation of Jerusalem:

> God, look, this is your city, called by your name! Look how awful it is! (64:10-12)

Isaiah thinks his way through this lament with a closely reasoned argument.

Are Laments Disrespectful?

Still, we wonder: Are laments disrespectful? Isn't it wrong for Isaiah to say, "O LORD, why do you make us wander from your ways and harden our heart?" (63:17). My answer: That's the wrong question. The question is, "What is on your heart?"

Let's reflect on Scottish reformer John Knox's famous lament to God, "Give me Scotland, or I die." Some might critique Knox's lament, saying that he was being demanding. "What do you mean, Knox—if God doesn't give you Scotland, you are going to give up and die? Are you trying to control God?"

No, we are simply watching the overflow of Knox's heart, his deep love for Scotland. Knox so wanted Scotland to know Christ that, if it didn't happen, his life meant nothing to him. "Give me Scotland, or I die" is faith at its finest, its purest. Notice how close it is to the apostle Paul's lament in Romans 9:1-5: Paul wishes that he could be accursed for the sake of the Jewish people. Paul so inhabited the gospel that he wanted to *be* the gospel for his fellow Jews.

Not long after the depression that followed our camping trip, my mission gave me a sabbatical. I burrowed myself into the Gospels and studied how Jesus loved. I was riveted by how much Jesus looked at people, how he entered their world, drawing them out. I learned to love Jill in new ways by listening to her laments about the kids, me, or whatever. Instead of chiding her when she said things that were incorrect or imbalanced, I let her pour out her heart. Instead of making sure the expression of her frustration was correct, I became more concerned that my sense of the state of her heart was correct. I couldn't care for her soul if I didn't feel it.

GOD DELIGHTS IN WELCOMING MESSY, BROKEN HEARTS.

What is so striking about biblical laments is that God almost never critiques them.[1] He delights in hearing our messy hearts. At the end of the book of Job, God honors feisty Job with his demanding laments and rebukes the three friends who've made critiquing Job's laments into a profession. God delights in welcoming messy, broken hearts.

Cautions with Counterfeit Laments

Let me offer a caution with laments. Be careful you don't slip into complaining like the Israelites in the desert.

What's the difference between a complaint and a lament? Three differences stand out.

First, a lament is directed toward God. In Numbers 20, the Israelites complained not to God but to Moses. A lament is faith. A complaint is rebellion.

Second, a lament submits. Notice the difference between "O God, save us; we have no water!" and the Israelites' demand, "Moses, take us back to Egypt. This whole plan was wrong from the beginning!" In the book of Ruth, Naomi angrily accuses God, "You've abandoned me!" (see Ruth 1:20-21). But as she says it, she is returning from Moab to the Promised Land. Her heart is breaking, but her feet are obeying.

Finally, laments almost always circle back to faith. As we saw in Isaiah's lament, a lament is a journey through different moods and arguments that usually settles on a quiet faith. The only exception is Psalm 88, the darkest of all the laments. But even Psalm 88 begins on a note of faith: "O LORD, God of my salvation" (verse 1). In years of darkness, when God in his wisdom took away my future, Psalm 88 was a close friend, a mirror for my soul.

To summarize: Good lamenting is appropriate; it goes somewhere; it is simple and honest. Bad lamenting is magnified, endless; it is complicated by bitterness, self-pity, escapes, and denial.[2]

What Does It Feel Like to Pray a Lament?

The rhythm of lament has shaped my marriage. We began in the early 1970s with Jill's lament for me. Then in the late 1970s I began to lament for her, that she would have the grace to give up control.

God answered with the gift of Kim in the early 1980s—giving us both a situation we could not control. In the 1980s it was Jill's turn to lament, for Kim and then later for me, that I would know how to love Jill with tenderness and compassion. God answered Jill's lament for me, and my lament for our kids, with my burnout and the sabbatical where I studied the person of Jesus.

Now we lament together. Each morning we come to God with what is breaking our hearts. With six children (five with spouses), twelve grandchildren, assorted relatives, my work, Kim's dog-walking business, our church, and a nation in crisis, there is almost always something to lament.

As Jill prays, her anxiety and fear come to the surface. I no longer feel the old pull to shut down—I want to know her heart. I listen carefully to her anxiety. I know that anxiety fuels good lamenting. I watch her grope toward a living God who hears and acts. But she wavers. Will he hear her? Will he act? So I pray for Jill's faith—and mine, too. We battle together to believe.

Still her anxiety comes in waves that swamp her soul. Sometimes it swamps my soul. My faith wavers too. Together, we take hold of God and pull. Jill feels her way through her prayer. I think my way through the prayer. Her feelings help me to think well. She's teaching this old Presbyterian to pray.

Together we turn to the Psalms and pray through them, word by word, personalizing them for what is on our heart. In the dry, empty place, the Word comes alive. It shapes our lament.

Praying this way challenges me at the deepest part of my being. It strips my soul of all supports, because my whole heart and mind bend toward God.

As we finish lamenting, we are quiet. There is nothing more to say or do. Like Mary at the feet of Jesus, we've done what we could (Mark 14:8). We follow in the footsteps of our Lord, who prayed through the great lament psalms of Israel as he slowly died:

- "My God, my God, why have you forsaken me?" (Psalm 22:1)
- "I thirst." (see Psalm 42:2)
- "Into your hand I commit my spirit." (Psalm 31:5)

Like Isaiah, Jesus believes his Father can act, wants to act, and will act. But now he waits. Now, as death approaches, Jesus says, "It is finished" (John 19:30). It's completed. It's done. There's nothing more to do but wait.

CHAPTER 24

HOW GOD PLACES HIMSELF
IN THE STORY

WHEN WE ARE IN THE MIDDLE of the desert, we feel like God is absent. We long for God to show himself clearly, to make sense of the mess. Like Job, we say to God, "Why do you hide your face?" (13:24). To answer, let's watch how Jesus positioned himself with three different women, all of whom were suffering in what seemed like a meaningless story.

The Canaanite Woman and Her Needy Daughter

The Gospel of Matthew tells the story of a Gentile woman, a Canaanite, who is pestering Jesus and the disciples relentlessly because her daughter is possessed by a demon and needs help. Initially, Jesus is silent, neither driving the woman away nor accepting her. He is deliberately ambiguous. He just listens.

The disciples feel the awkwardness of the situation and ask Jesus to resolve it: "Send her away, for she is crying out after us" (15:23). They are likely aware that another Canaanite woman, Jezebel, introduced demon worship to Israel. She got what was coming to her.

Jesus ignores his disciples. Instead of sending her away, he continues the confusion by simultaneously addressing her yet putting up a wall by referring to the ethnic barrier between them. He says, "I was sent only to the lost sheep of the house of Israel" (15:24).

Sensing an opening, the woman throws herself at his feet and pleads, "Lord, help me" (15:25). She overlooks the content of what Jesus says and focuses on the fact that he is finally acknowledging her. His actions have spoken louder than his words.

Jesus' response is maddening. He continues his ambiguity, putting up still another barrier: "It is not right to take the children's bread and throw it to the dogs" (15:26). Yet at the same time, he takes another step closer to the woman by conversing with her. She ignores his bluff and goes for the win: "Yes, Lord, yet even the dogs eat the crumbs that fall from their masters' table" (15:27). She has a royal flush. She has him now. She knows it. He knows it. How can Jesus, with his welcoming heart, resist her complete weakness? Jesus marvels at her faith and gives her his Great Faith Oscar—"O woman, great is your faith! Be it done for you as you desire" (15:28).

If Jesus were a magic prayer machine, he'd have healed this woman's daughter instantly, and we would not have discovered her feisty, creative spirit. Likewise, Jesus' ambiguity with us creates the space not only for him to emerge but us as well. If the miracle comes too quickly, there is no room for discovery, for relationship. With both this woman and us, Jesus is engaged in a divine romance, wooing us to himself.

The waiting that is the essence of faith provides the context for relationship. Faith and relationship are interwoven in dance. Everyone talks now about how prayer is relationship, but often what people mean is having warm fuzzies with God. Nothing wrong with warm fuzzies, but relationships are far richer and more complex.

Another Woman and Her Needy Daughter

I saw Jesus do the same thing with another woman and her needy daughter. Over a twenty-five-year period, Jill wrestled with God for

Kim. Week after week during our family prayer time Jill would pray for strength and faith—strength to get from one end of the day to the next and faith not to throw in the towel. Soon the rest of the family didn't even have to ask Jill what her prayer request was. We already knew.

Here's a glimpse of what was behind Jill's prayer for faith. She wrote this journal entry right after she discovered that she was pregnant with our sixth child, Emily. Kim was five years old.

> I'm now 32—oh dear! I wonder what this year will bring. Maybe Kim talking? It has been very hard for me not seeing much progress in Kim. We are in the middle of her being evaluated again at Children's Hospital of Philadelphia. It's so hard to tell what she can't do or just won't do. All of this is so hard . . . hard to see and still believe Jesus loves her and me and hears me beg for her continual healing. It really is faith that is at stake—the suffering is really a side issue. Just to tell Jesus what I need and leave it with him is such a struggle— especially as I see Kim struggle daily. It really breaks my heart.

Two days later after the visit to Children's Hospital, Jill wrote, "Give me the faith to leave this with you. Please help her to talk." Then the journal goes silent. It would be ten years before Jill would have the faith and the energy to write another entry in her prayer journal. It would be twenty years before Kim would begin to speak, at age twenty-five. God left Jill in confusion in order to grow her faith, her ability to connect with him. To become like a child, Jill had to become weak again.

Jesus' ambiguous interaction with both Jill and the Canaanite woman is a minicourse on prayer. God permitted a difficult situation in both of their lives, and then he lingered at the edge. Not in the center, at the edge. If he were at the center, if they had had regular visions of him, they would not have developed the faith to have a real relationship with him. God would have been a magic prayer machine, not a friend and lover.

WHEN YOU PERSIST IN A SPIRITUAL VACUUM, WHEN YOU HANG IN THERE DURING AMBIGUITY, YOU GET TO KNOW GOD.

When God seems silent and our prayers go unanswered, the overwhelming temptation is to leave the story—to walk out of the desert and attempt to create a normal life. But when we persist in a spiritual vacuum, when we hang in there during ambiguity, we get to know God. In fact, that is how intimacy grows in all close relationships.

Mary Magdalene in a Minidesert

Jesus treats Mary Magdalene in a similar way when he meets her on Easter morning. When he first greets her outside the tomb, he deliberately conceals his identity; then he draws her out with a question: "Woman, why are you weeping? Whom are you seeking?" (John 20:15). It is classic Jesus, a genuine question mixed with a tender rebuke. She doesn't need to cry because he is alive. Jesus stands at the edge of the story, unwilling to overwhelm her so that a richer, fuller Mary could emerge. He allows her pain to continue for just a moment so Jesus the person could meet Mary the person.

Mary responds, thinking he is the gardener, "Sir, if you have carried him away, tell me where you have laid him, and I will take him away" (20:15). Of course, she can't "take him away" because she is too small. Her words imply that she has servants or access to people who do. She knows how to get things done. She has wealth, access, and chutzpah. Luke tells us that she, along with several other women, "provided for [Jesus and the disciples] out of their means" (Luke 8:2-3). If Jesus had disclosed himself immediately, we'd never have discovered Mary, the manager. This new Adam is a gentle gardener.

Jesus announces his presence by just saying her name: "Mary." In other words, "Mary, stop your rushing, your planning. I was always here, at the edge of the story. I am all you need." It is so like him to identify himself so simply, so subtly. It is pure poetry.

Many of us wish God were more visible. We think that if we could see him better or know what is going on, then faith would come more easily. But if Jesus dominated the space and overwhelmed our vision, we would not be able to relate to him. Everyone who had a clear-eyed vision of God in the Bible fell down as if he were dead. It's hard to relate to pure light.

Listen to this description of Jesus' resurrection from the false *Gospel of Peter*, written a hundred years after the event.

[The soldiers guarding the tomb] saw three men come out of the tomb, two of them sustaining the other one, and a cross following after them. The heads of the two they saw had heads that reached up to heaven, but the head of [Jesus] that was led by them went beyond heaven.[1]

You can tell this is one of the false Gnostic gospels because it is so "otherworldly." As we saw earlier, the Greek mind didn't like the physical. So it tried to create an ethereal Jesus. In this story Jesus' head is literally in the clouds. He is so big he needs a couple of angels to prop him up. That immensity doesn't leave any room for relationship. We can't relate to him. This vision of Jesus doesn't leave any room for faith.

When we suffer, we long for God to speak clearly, to tell us the end of the story and, most of all, to show himself. But if he showed himself fully and immediately, if he answered all the questions, we'd never grow; we'd never emerge from our chrysalis because we'd be forever dependent. Jill was profoundly changed in her twenty-year wait. If God had instantly explained everything to her and healed Kim, that change would not have taken place. No one works like he does. He is such a lover of souls.

PRAYING WITHOUT A STORY

WHAT HAPPENS WHEN YOU don't have a sense of your life as a story being told by your Father? Listen to this story from Joanne as related by Philip Yancey.

If you had asked me as a young Christian whether I believed in prayer, I would have quickly said yes. I would have told you about the time I spun out in the snow and didn't get hurt, or the time I dropped a house key somewhere in my '74 Dodge Dart and couldn't find it for hours, until I prayed. Maybe God takes care of neophyte believers, I don't know. He doesn't seem to take care of old-timers, though.

I could list probably a hundred prayers that haven't been answered. I'm not speaking of selfish prayers, but important prayers: *God, keep my kids safe, keep them away from the wrong crowd.* All three ended up in trouble with the law, abusing drugs and alcohol.

I've got to say, Jesus' story of the persistent widow who keeps pestering the judge *sours.* Thousands of people pray for a Christian leader who has cancer, and he dies. What did Jesus mean by that parable—that we keep beating our heads against a wall?

I've been living at the edge of the abyss for several years now. Yes, I have had close times, have felt the presence of God, and these memories alone are what keep me from checking out. Two times, maybe three, I have heard from God. Once the voice almost seemed audible. I was driving to the hospital as a young woman just out of college, having learned that I had leukemia, when these words from Isaiah came sharply to mind, "Do not be dismayed, for I am your God. I will strengthen you and help you; I will uphold you with my righteous right hand." I cling to those few memories, and get nothing else, no new sign that God is listening.

I'd guess maybe 20 percent of my prayers get anything like the answer I want. Over time, I give up. I pray for those things I believe will happen. Or I just don't pray. I review my journal and see God doing less and less. I get mad. Like a child, I stop talking. I'm passive-aggressive with God. I put him off. Maybe later.

I went to a mentor and poured out my soul, describing in detail all I've been through in the past few years with my health and especially with my kids. "What do I do?" I asked.

He sat there for the longest time and said, "I don't know, Joanne." He sighed. I waited for words of wisdom. None came. That's how it is with prayer too.[1]

My heart breaks for Joanne. She's had a lot coming at her. Leukemia while in college, struggles with her three children, and deep disappointment with God. Many of the psalms give voice to Joanne's heart cry: "My God, my God, why have you forsaken me?" (Psalm 22:1). On the cross Jesus himself echoes Joanne's agony.

I have some sense of what it feels like to be deserted by God.

During one year in particular I was in agony. A week didn't go by where I didn't burst into tears. Toward the end of that year I began to wonder if I had God wrong. Was my view of his gracious heart skewed? Had I overestimated his grace?

We don't like the messiness of unanswered prayer—or answers that are different from what we requested. A distraught heart, like Joanne's, makes us uneasy. Joanne's story helps us see the fuzziness of prayer.

Reflecting on the Story

If I were Joanne's mentor, I would first want to know her story. I suspect she's given us just the tip of the iceberg. How was she sinned against? Did the church or her husband neglect her? Was she left to fend for herself? Is she a single parent? Conversely, how was Joanne a sinner? Did she make choices that contributed to her kids struggling? How did she deal with her kids when she saw early signs of trouble? I don't mean to imply that if you parent right, then God will protect your kids. God himself struggles with his children. But Joanne's story tells only one side. I hear "sinned against" but not "sinner." The way she tells it, God is the only bad guy.

If Joanne were open to questions, I'd ask her how she views prayer. She talks about it the way many Christians do, separating it from the rest of her life, as if prayer exists in a vacuum, like a satellite orbiting the earth. I don't hear any story thread of how Joanne's praying is interacting with the other pieces of her life. The praying life is inseparable from obeying, loving, waiting, and suffering.

Joanne has some sweet memories of prayer. She said, "I . . . have felt the presence of God, and these memories alone are what keep me from checking out." Memories like that can encourage us, but if the experience becomes an end in itself, then God becomes an object for my pleasure. No wonder God's only at 20 percent.

The most difficult part to raise with Joanne is her bitterness.

Despair mixed with cynicism comes through in almost every paragraph. I wonder if she was set up for bitterness by bad teaching on prayer that disconnected it from life. Did Joanne's bitterness contribute to her children's struggle? She talked about her children's distance from God and then acknowledged her own.

It could be that Joanne is a modern-day Job, enduring meaningless suffering of which she is innocent. But Job never shuts down his heart. His robust faith expresses itself in a resounding declaration of his own innocence. It takes faith to maintain your innocence when your three best friends think you are wrong. Job repeatedly calls for God to justify himself. Job is in God's face. Joanne, as she acknowledged, has pulled away. The one is pure faith; the other is not. One trusts that God is weaving a larger story; the other does not.

If we don't get passionate with God in the face of disappointment, like the Canaanite woman, then cynicism slips in, and our hearts begin to harden. We begin a living death.

This chart summarizes two approaches to a praying life.

No Story	Story
Bitter	Waiting
Angry	Watching
Aimless	Wondering
Cynical	Praying
Controlling	Submitting
Hopeless	Hoping
Thankless	Thankful
Blaming	Repenting

Another Story of God's Weaving

I'd love to tell Joanne the story of God's twenty-five-year answer to our prayers that Kim speak. I'd describe for her the dance between our prayers and Kim slowly developing one form of communication after the other. It was work, prayer, mistakes, frustration, more work, more prayer, breakthrough, work, prayer, and so on. Again and again, often at the last moment, we saw God provide. And he never did it without humbling us.

In 1993 Jill secured a grant through our school to get Kim a speech computer. After the initial enthusiasm wore off, the speech computer sat on a shelf. We, along with Kim, were overwhelmed with learning the computer's 128-key-icon, 3,000-word language. Even if Kim learned the language, she didn't have the ability to put together a coherent sentence. We didn't know if she ever would.

In the spring of 1996 Kim was functioning well with a sign-language interpreter at school. I wanted to begin writing a book in my spare time about the person of Jesus and how he loves. As I was praying about this, the thought came to me, *Paul, how can you speak about me when Kim doesn't speak?* This simple challenge to my integrity had the ring of God about it. God was determined that my hidden life with my family match my open life of ministry. He didn't want a robust public ministry focused on love (the book) and an unfinished private ministry (Kim's not speaking). He didn't want the outer life to look bigger than the inner. He didn't want a split self.

So I set aside plans to write the book and began to think about ways to get Kim speaking on her speech computer. Soon after that prayer time, we received a newsletter that mentioned a speech-computer camp, run by one of the pioneers in the field. Kim and I spent a week together at the camp, immersing ourselves in using the speech computer. Seeing the other kids using their computers took away some of the oddity of having an electronic voice. Then when school started in the fall, we asked the administrator to reopen Kim's Individualized Education Plan so we could have a special class for learning the speech computer's language.

We gave Kim every opportunity to speak with her computer, such as praying for a meal. At times, we'd be out to eat and forget that the volume on her electronic voice was set too high. Her computer would belt out, "JESUS, THANK YOU FOR THIS FOOD." When this happened, our teenagers tried in vain to make themselves inconspicuous by slinking down in their seats. Our son Andrew pulled Emily aside once and told her, "You might as well give up. You just can't look cool with Kim around."

Slowly but surely, Kim's sentences became clearer and clearer. She began to "speak" with an electronic voice—which was fun to manipulate because we could switch her voice to other personas, such as Huge Harry or Rough Rita.

A year after I set aside plans to write, a friend of ours, Linda, who had no idea of my desire, called unexpectedly and said, "Paul, I have a friend, a gifted writer, who would like to teach a class on writing. Are you interested?"

One seeming coincidence followed another. While visiting a pastor whose wife was struggling with depression, I discovered he had a personal connection with a major evangelical publisher. While speaking at a retreat, I made friends with an Oxford-trained writer from India. I agreed to disciple her if she would agree to edit the book I wanted to write. Then the door opened for me to go to seminary, where I began writing about the life of Jesus. Three years after God stopped me from writing, I had a contract to write what became *Love Walked Among Us*. Six months later, a generous gift from good friends enabled me to devote myself full time to writing.

In my case, seeking God's kingdom first meant *not* writing publicly about Jesus but doing a hidden work of love. Almost every door that opened up before I wrote the book had little tests of integrity to it. The Father deliberately delayed a book about the beauty of his Son for the sake of Kim being able to speak more clearly. He put Kim ahead of his Son's own honor. I do not understand that kind of love. I guess that is what the cross is all about.

Do you see the difference between making an isolated prayer

request and praying in context of the story that God is weaving? God answered our prayer for Kim to speak, but the answer was inseparable from repenting, serving, managing, and waiting. Most of our prayers are answered in the context of the larger story that God is weaving.

Living in Our Father's Story

Living in our Father's story means living in tension. (Will the book get written? How can Kim speak if she can't do sentence structure?) After all, tension and overwhelming obstacles make for a good story! How boring life would be if prayer worked like magic. There'd be no relationship with God, no victory over little pockets of evil.

To live in our Father's story, remember these three things:

1. Don't demand that the story go your way. (In other words, surrender completely.)
2. Look for the Storyteller. Look for his hand, and then pray in light of what you are seeing. (In other words, develop an eye for Jesus.)
3. Stay in the story. Don't shut down when it goes the wrong way.

This last one, staying in the story, can be particularly difficult. When the story isn't going your way, ask yourself, *What is God doing?* Be on the lookout for strange gifts. God loves to surprise us with babies in swaddling clothes lying in mangers.

Sometimes when we say, "God is silent," what's really going on is that he hasn't told the story the

> **WHEN THE STORY ISN'T GOING YOUR WAY, ASK YOURSELF, "WHAT IS GOD DOING?" BE ON THE LOOKOUT FOR STRANGE GIFTS.**

way we wanted it told. He will be silent when we want him to fill in the blanks of the story we are creating. But with his own stories, the ones we live in, he is seldom silent.

Here's a ministry that captures what I mean. While I was speaking at a camp for children with disabilities, one of the volunteer workers felt falsely accused by a parent. After listening to her, I brightened up and told her, "Now you can serve Jesus instead of the parents." Having been in similar circumstances, I was genuinely excited for her. Nothing clears out self-righteousness better than serving someone who is critical of you.

To see the Storyteller we need to slow down our interior life and watch. We need to be imbedded in the Word to experience the Storyteller's mind and pick up the cadence of his voice. We need to be alert for the story, for the Storyteller's voice speaking into the details of our lives. The story God weaves is neither weird nor floaty. It always involves bowing before his majesty with the pieces of our lives.

Watching for the Divine Artist

Let me show you what I mean by taking a moment to reflect on the story God was weaving in Joseph's life.

Like Joanne, Joseph's life is characterized by disappointment. His jealous brothers sell him for twenty pieces of silver, strip him of his multicolored coat, and use it as "evidence" that he has died. Just when it looks like his life is making a turn for the better, the wife of his owner tears another coat off his back and uses it as "evidence" that he has tried to rape her. He ends up in prison, alone and forgotten (see Genesis 37; 39–40).

But look at the story God is weaving. Twice Joseph loses his coat as he is being humbled; each time the coat is used as evidence for a betrayal. Twice, as God elevates him, he is given a new coat. You can tell that Joseph realizes God is weaving a story with coats and silver because when his brothers arrive, Joseph gives each of them a coat and silver. He wraps up the story of his life by blessing his brothers with the very items they have stolen from him (see Genesis 41–45). Joseph has not given in to bitterness and cynicism; instead he discovers the gracious heart of his God, grace he extends to those who have harmed him. Forgiveness flowed.

By giving his brothers coats, Joseph has become an artist. He has noticed God's use of themes in his life and extended it. He takes God's brush and finishes the painting. He has learned his heavenly Father's rhythms.

Look at the artistry in the story of Kim learning the computer. The thought *How can you speak about me if Kim doesn't speak?* used two senses of the word *speak* to unmask an area of my heart. (The first *speak* was in terms of writing, declaring. The second *speak* was actual, physical speaking.) It was a line of poetry. Look at the divine artistry in "as I put my energies into God's heart [helping Kim speak], God put his energies into my heart [helping me write a book]." I love to watch how God weaves a story.

We've lost a sense of divine artistry in our lives because the Enlightenment put art, poetry, and literature in the same category as religion. It defined these things as "not real." So poetry isn't allowed in history or biology books. This, of course, is a false separation. Open any biology book, and you are immediately confronted by the work of a spectacular artist and designer.

When confronted with suffering that won't go away or with even a minor problem, we instinctively focus on what is missing, such as the lost coats and the betrayal in Joseph's story, not on the Master's hand. Often when you think everything has gone wrong, it's just that you're in the middle of a story. If you watch the stories God is weaving in your life, you, like Joseph, will begin to see the patterns. You'll become a poet, sensitive to your Father's voice.

HOPE

The End of the Story

HOPE IS A NEW IDEA in history, a uniquely Christian vision. We take it for granted because the mind of Christ is so pervasive in shaping the modern mind, but it wasn't always that way. The ancient Greeks had two kinds of stories: comedy and tragedy. A comedy was fun, but it wasn't real. A tragedy was real but not fun. If you took a hard look at life, it was sad. If you ignored life, then it was funny. Their philosophy mirrored their plays. Stoic philosophers sought to be moral in a meaningless world. Life was a tragedy. They toughed it out. Epicureans just had fun; life was a comedy. They coined the phrase "Eat, drink, and be merry, for tomorrow we die."

The gospel is Good News. Because God broke the power of evil at the cross, we can, along with Sarah, look at our cynicism and laugh. Not surprisingly, Jesus' first miracle was making about 150 gallons of fine wine so a good party could become a great party (see John 2). Tragedy doesn't have the last word. God saves the best for last.

Some writers suggest that God focuses simply on us knowing him. That is just another version of the despair chart (see chapter 21). He is also concerned about our situation. He is concerned that Kim is mute. Ashley's brokenhearted prayer that Kim would speak touches his heart. He is for Kim in the details of her life. He wants Kim to thrive. He is, after all, the God of hope.

These writers give up hope by spiritualizing it. But Abraham and Sarah had a son. Joseph's brothers bowed before him. David got the kingdom, and Jesus rose from the dead. And last but not least, Kim learned to talk on her speech computer and is now beginning to actually use her voice. The infinite God touches us personally. Paul alludes to this when he says, "Now to him who is able to do far more abundantly than all that we ask or think, according to the power at work within us" (Ephesians 3:20). We can dream big because God is big.

Dreaming Big for Kim

Let me share with you a story of hope, of Kim getting a job. It is a tragedy that became a comedy.[1]

When Kim was sixteen, Jill and I started a low-level panic over what she would do when she graduated from high school at age twenty-two. With so many overlapping disabilities, how could she find work? We began to pray daily that God would provide Kim a job.

We tried everything. Kim got a volunteer job at a nursing home. She loved feeding the rabbit but hated setting the tables. Even with the help of her aide, she found the organization overwhelming. Jill tried to teach Kim how to set tables by using a magic marker on placemats to outline where the plate, cup, and utensils went, but the table still looked like a small hurricane hit it when Kim set it.

Since Kim loved books, she volunteered at the library as a page. However, this was a bit like asking an alcoholic to stock the shelves of a liquor store. Kim would put two books away and read one. Getting the books ready for shelving by putting them in alphabetical order was especially challenging for her. On top of that, Kim can be stubborn. One day she was pushing her aide around, acting dumb, and the aide called Jill in tears. Jill hates it when Kim manipulates with her disability. She drove to the library and asked how many books she could take out on her library card. Fifty. She borrowed three other cards and checked out two hundred books. She borrowed two library carts, stuffed everything in the car, and brought Kim home. Jill made Kim put all two hundred books in order. Then Jill would mix them up, and Kim would put them back in order again. This went on for two days. In other words, "Kim, if you don't listen to your aide, your life is going to be library-cart hell." After that Kim did not hassle her aide anymore.

Kim got her first paying job at a video store, shelving movies. Again, it was like an alcoholic working in a bar since Kim absolutely loves movies. One day the bus dropped off Kim at the video store, but her aide didn't show up. When you are autistic, you need the structure a schedule provides. When that is disrupted, panic can set in. Kim used to panic on the days when school had a two-hour snow delay. So when the aide didn't show up, she had a major hissy fit. We're used to them; Blockbuster was not. In a couple of days Kim was out job hunting again.

She loves dogs, so we looked for a job at vets and kennels. We found some volunteer jobs but nothing permanent. We took her to some sheltered workshops, as this was our backup plan, but Kim didn't like them. Five months before graduation, we'd still not found her a job. With the job situation looking bleak, we toured another sheltered workshop with Kim. Jill and I liked it, but just minutes into the tour, tears welled up in Kim's eyes. She didn't want to be there. Jill and I looked at one another, stepped outside, and compared notes. We decided that no matter what, we'd pay for the cost of an aide to allow Kim to get a regular job. But still we had to find an employer who would hire an adult with disabilities.

Jill was unabashed about asking strangers to pray that Kim would get a job. She made the persistent widow look like a wallflower.

In late April, with six weeks to graduation, we still had nothing. Jill happened to stop at our printer, who asked, "Did you find a job for Kim yet?" When Jill said no, the printer called a friend who owned a kennel. The friend said he would hire Kim as a dog walker as long as she had an aide. When we visited the kennel, Kim found it charming that her current aide, Skip, a six-foot, 250-pound former navy man, was nervous about going into the cages with the dogs. Kim was absolutely fearless.

Kim had found a job, but Jill and I needed to find a way to pay for the aide. The county had turned us down, but then two weeks before graduation, Kim's social worker called. "Paul, the state came in this month for an audit and told us, 'You have to get more creative with what you are doing.' I suggested that we fund an aide for Kim, and they approved it. We'll pay for Kim's aide."

Everything went well for the first couple of weeks until a new aide came late and Kim had a meltdown in the parking lot. I got the dreaded call: "We don't think this will work out." I pleaded. I begged. I promised. I stopped just short of selling my soul, and the kennel gave Kim another shot.

Kim's been walking dogs since 2003 and loves her work. She does about 75 percent of the job; the aide does the other 25 percent. Even on the bitterest winter days or the hottest summer days, she is out there walking. Every winter she saves up her money and goes to FL (her name for Florida on her speech computer) to worship at the shrine of Disney.

Occasionally we can't get an aide, so Jill or I will go in and help Kim. I have prayed for humility, and it dawned on me that God was answering my prayer. I would have preferred humility to come over me like magic. Instead, God teaches humility in humble places. He keeps me sane by letting me pick up dog manure after I've spoken at a conference. What I thought was a stone was really a loaf of bread.

God created a wonder with Kim finding work. I suspect that the jobless rate among adults who have Kim's level of disability is close to 99 percent. When we were praying for Kim to get a job, sometimes we felt like we were praying for the sky to turn from blue to pink. But as the angel told Mary, "Nothing will be impossible with God" (Luke 1:37).

Our prayers didn't float above life. Our family was focused on both the reality line and the hope line. Praying was inseparable from working, planning, and good old-fashioned begging.

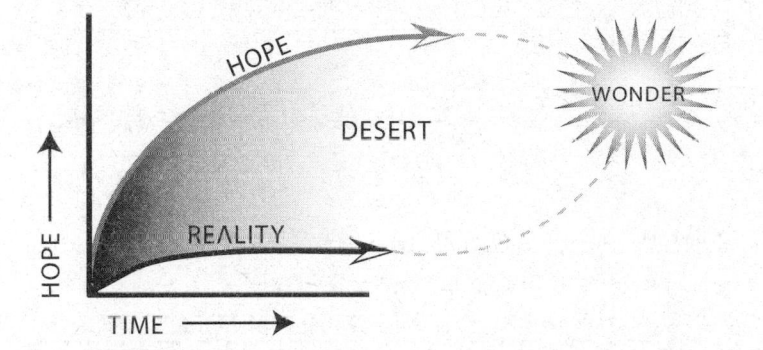

The Willingness to Be Enchanted

As we wait and pray, God weaves his story and creates a wonder. Instead of drifting between comedy (denial) and tragedy (reality), we have a relationship with the living God, who is intimately involved with the details of our worlds. We are learning to watch for the story to unfold, to wait for the wonder.

When the kids were little, we would sometimes take a cheap vacation by speaking at a Christian camp for a week. At one camp I remember carrying our four-year-old daughter Courtney in my arms, walking outside into the pitch-black night, and showing her the sky. I showed her Orion, Cassiopeia, and the Big Dipper. I showed her the different colors of the stars and the Milky Way. She was wonder-struck by God's creation. If you wait, your heavenly Father will pick you up, carry you out into the night, and make your life sparkle. He wants to dazzle you with the wonder of his love.

> **IF YOU WAIT, YOUR HEAVENLY FATHER WILL PICK YOU UP, CARRY YOU OUT INTO THE NIGHT, AND MAKE YOUR LIFE SPARKLE. HE WANTS TO DAZZLE YOU WITH THE WONDER OF HIS LOVE.**

To see the marvel of the stories that our Father is telling, we need to become like little children. That was the secret of C. S. Lewis's storytelling. Ruth Pitter, a good friend of Lewis, said this about him: "His whole life was oriented and motivated by an almost uniquely-persisting child's sense of glory and of nightmare."[2] Alan Jacobs, author of *The Narnian*, said this about Lewis:

Lewis's mind was above all characterized by a willingness to be enchanted, and it was this openness to enchantment that held together the various strands of his life—his delight in laughter, his willingness to accept a world made by a good and loving God, and (in some ways above all) his willingness to submit to the charms of a wonderful story.[3]

I am enchanted by the stories that God weaves around Kim's life.

Not Just a Job, a Calling

In the middle of our frustrating job search, Jill and I began to pray even bigger prayers for Kim. We started praying not just for a job, but for a calling—that Kim would feel God's pleasure in her work and minister to others. Our thinking was, *What the heck! Since we're still at ground zero, we might as well ask for the sky!*

What will God do with Kim's calling? I'm not sure, but it is fun to watch and pray. In the last year Kim has spoken several times at conferences or seminars. I usually interview her about some incident in her life. One of the stories we've told is in the next chapter, the story of the first time Kim accompanied me to a seminar. When we told the story together at a Joni and Friends conference, Kim smacked her head every time she thought something was funny. She had the audience rolling in the aisles. The tragedy had become a comedy.

CHAPTER 27

LIVING IN GOSPEL STORIES

In the spring of 2001, Jill and I attended a day of prayer hosted by L'Arche, a community for the disabled where Henri Nouwen had been a pastor. I happened to sit next to Bill, a disabled adult who had been Nouwen's traveling companion. Meeting Bill gave me an idea: Why not take Kim with me to my next seminar? It would give Jill a much-needed break, and besides, I love spending time with Kim.

One Friday in May, Kim and I headed to Florida. While waiting for the shuttle bus at the Philadelphia airport, Kim discovered that Jill hadn't packed a book for the plane ride. As I stood there holding our two suitcases and a large cardboard box with *seeJesus* written on it in large red letters, Kim began a low-pitched, fingernails-on-the-chalkboard whine as a crowd of travelers looked on. I could have throttled her. I briefly considered turning the box so I could hide its lettering.

Kim finally stopped whining, but only because I was yelling at the bus driver—he was closing the rear door on me as I helped Kim navigate the step. We rushed into the terminal to discover that the baggage line stretched forever. Our flight left in thirty minutes, so I lugged my increasingly conspicuous box upstairs to the metal detectors. As soon as we got in line, they closed one of the two metal detectors and combined the lines. Kim began to whine again.

When we got to the scanner, Kim refused to put her speech computer on the belt and started arguing with the security officer, typing, "This is my voice." I yanked it out of her hand and guided her through the scanner. Of course, my Jesus box wouldn't fit. It required a separate scan by a particularly scrupulous guard.

With only twenty minutes to get to our gate, I discovered that we needed to be one terminal over. I contemplated running with Kim while carrying our baggage, but then I saw an electric cart and begged for a ride. As we whizzed off for our gate, Kim broke into a smile. It was like having our own personal roller coaster. The tension was just starting to leave my shoulders when we got stuck behind a guy on his cell phone, oblivious to the beeping of our cart. Kim thought it was funny. I didn't. We arrived at the gate with minutes to spare.

Kim had just settled into her seat on the plane, listening to a CD, when the pilot's voice came over the intercom: "Please turn off all electronic devices." Kim had to turn off not only her CD player but also her speech computer. When she lost an argument with the flight attendant, it started again—that same low-pitched whine. Ten minutes later when the pilot told us we were twelfth in line for takeoff, all Kim's hot buttons went off: schedule change, no book, and waiting. The whine turned into a meltdown.[1]

As I sat there on the plane, frazzled, with Kim melting down next to me, I thought, *This was a mistake. I will never do this again.* What I didn't realize was that the kingdom had come. It is always that way with the kingdom. It is so strange, so low; it is seldom recognized. It looks like a mistake.

Later as I reflected on the weekend and on the ways of God, I realized that I was in the middle of one of God's stories. On Saturday, I spoke in front of a crowd who listened to my every word and respected me. When you speak, no matter how hard you try, you are at the center. Even if you are talking about Jesus and how he loves people, as I was, it's tempting to take credit for your speaking.

However, on Friday I was in front of three different crowds (at the bus stop, in the security line, and on the plane), helpless and embarrassed. I looked inadequate, I felt inadequate, and I was inadequate. God was reminding me of what I am really like. He was preparing my heart on Friday, so I'd not be confused by people's praise on Saturday. I wanted success; he wanted authenticity.

The Father was taking me on the same downward journey he took his Son. Paul invited the Philippian church to join Jesus, "who, though he was in the form of God, did not count equality with God a thing to be grasped, but made himself nothing, taking the form of a servant, being born in the likeness of men" (Philippians 2:6-7). The downward journey is a gospel story. Our lives repeatedly reenact the dying and rising of Jesus. I call it the J-Curve, because, like the letter "J," Jesus' life first goes *down* into death, then *up* into resurrection.

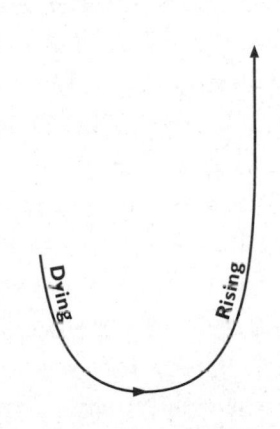

The pattern of Jesus' life is the pattern of our lives—of our everyday moments. We think everything has gone wrong. No, the apostle Paul says, the J-Curve is the shape of the normal Christian life. Our lives mirror his.

Gospel Stories

The gospel, the Father's gift of his Son, is so breathtaking that since Jesus' death, no one has been able to tell a better story. If you want to tell a really good story, you have to tell a gospel story.

In Yann Martel's bestseller *The Life of Pi*, a Hindu boy named Pi meets a Catholic priest, Father Martin, who tells Pi the story of the gospel. Pi asks for more:

I asked for another story, one that I might find more satisfying. Surely this religion had more than one story in its bag— religions abound with stories. But Father Martin made me understand that . . . their religion had one Story, and to it they came back again and again, over and over. It was story enough for them.[2]

My trip with Kim was a J-Curve. I gave up a piece of my life for Jill. On Sunday when Kim and I were waiting at the Nairobi Train Station at Busch Gardens (she was whining again because we missed the train!), I called home. Ashley picked up. She and Jill were at a Mother's Day dinner. She said, "Every fifteen minutes Mom says, 'It's just so nice. I can't believe how calm it is.'" In the gospel, Jesus took my sin, and I got his righteousness. That is how gospel stories work. Jill gets a restful weekend, and I get a stressful one. Whenever you love, you reenact Jesus' death.

Consequently, gospel stories always have suffering in them. American Christianity is allergic to this part of the gospel. We love to hear about God's love

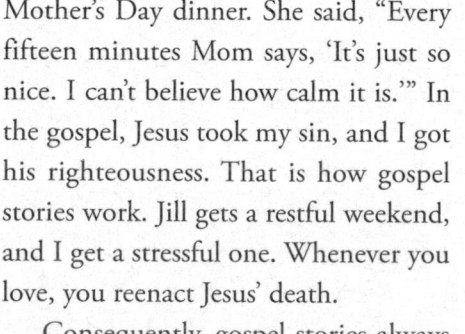

for us, but suffering doesn't mesh with "the pursuit of happiness." So we pray to escape a gospel story, when that is the best gift the Father can give us. When I was sitting on the plane thinking, *Everything has gone wrong*, that was when everything was going right. That's how love works. I'd forgotten my location: I was at the bottom of the J-Curve!

The Father wants to draw us into the story of his Son. He doesn't have a better story to tell, so he keeps retelling it in our lives. As we reenact the gospel, we are drawn into a strange kind of fellowship. The taste of Christ is so good that the apostle Paul told the Philippians that he wanted to know "the fellowship of sharing in [Jesus'] sufferings" (Philippians 3:10, NIV). It was Paul's prayer.

Living in a gospel story exposes our idols, our false sources of love. Look at what showed up in my life that Friday. As I went on the downward path of the J-Curve, my idols of people's approval, efficiency, and order were all uncovered as I tried to love my wife and my daughter. When our idols are exposed, we often give up in despair—overwhelmed by both the other person's sin and our own. But by simply staying in the story, continuing to show up for life, even if it seems pointless, the kingdom comes. Poverty of spirit is no longer a belief. We own it. It describes us.

Repentance is refreshing. In C. S. Lewis's *Voyage of the Dawn Treader*, after Eustace is overcome with greed, he turns into a dragon. When Aslan rips off his dragon skin with a stroke of his huge paw, Eustace compares it to the childhood joy of picking a scab: "It hurts like billy-oh, but it *is* such fun to see it coming away."[3] When we remove our false selves, it creates integrity. We return to the real source of love—our heavenly Father. We become authentic.

If we stop fighting and embrace the gospel story God is weaving in our lives, we discover joy—the resurrection side of the J-Curve. Paul bubbles over with joy as he writes the book of Philippians, chained between two Roman soldiers. He even prays with joy: "Always in every prayer of mine for you all making my prayer with joy" (Philippians 1:4). If we pursue joy directly, it slips from our grasp. But if we begin with Jesus and learn to love, we end up with joy.

You should have seen Kim smile when we went through the Congo River Rapids or when she was feeding the giraffes at the zoo. When you bind yourself to someone who at times can be difficult, you are in a place where you can discover God and then joy.

How does this change how I view taking Kim to Florida? I don't *have to* take Kim. I *get to* take her. It is my privilege. It is my joy.

Gospel Stories Give Meaning to Suffering

Few have grappled more with suffering than Abraham Lincoln. In his second inaugural address just six weeks before his assassination, Lincoln raised the conundrum of two competing sides both praying they will win. He said about the war, "Both read the same Bible, and pray to the same God; and each invokes his aid against the other." Lincoln was no relativist: "The prayers of both could not be answered; that of neither could be answered fully." He suggested God was weaving a larger story—in fact, a gospel story—bringing redemption through blood where "every drop of blood drawn with the lash shall be paid by another drawn with the sword."[4]

Joseph had that same sense of redemptive history, of God bringing grace through suffering. The betrayal he experienced from his brothers reversed the gospel. Joseph's brothers gave up his life for their freedom, freedom from their father's favoritism. Twenty years later his brother Judah told Joseph that he would substitute his life for his brother Benjamin's, whom Joseph had threatened to take captive. Judah's willingness to give up his freedom for Benjamin was a gospel story that reversed the earlier betrayal.

Underneath both Joseph's and Lincoln's sense of gospel story lies an awareness of the sovereignty of God, that God is the weaver of stories. In his second inaugural address Lincoln said, "The Almighty has His own purposes." Reflecting on the speech Lincoln wrote to a friend, "Men are not flattered by being shown that there has been a difference of purpose between the Almighty and them."[5] Joseph said something similar. When his brothers came to him, fearful that Joseph would pursue revenge, he told them, "Do not fear, for am I in the place of God? As for you, you meant evil against me, but God meant it for good, to bring it about that many people should be kept alive, as they are today. So do not fear" (Genesis 50:19-21). Seeing God's design in our lives brings meaning and hope.

Watching for Unseen Connections

To see a gospel story, we need to reflect on how seemingly disparate pieces are connected. The best place to pick up the unseen connections of our designer God is in disappointment and tension—such as my plane trip with Kim. We saw the hidden connection between the humbling of a plane trip and the potential pride in front of an audience. We saw the connection between my pressure and Jill's relief. In chapter 25 when Kim was learning to speak on her speech computer, we saw an unseen connection between repentance ("Paul, how can you speak about me when Kim doesn't speak?") and grace ("Paul, would you like to take a course on writing?"). By *unseen* I mean that there are no visible, causal links. As we bring God's mind to our stories, we can see his hand crafting connections behind the scenes. The J-Curve gives us a map for the Christian life that protects us from seeing our life through a victim narrative. It kills bitterness.

Nothing in the modern mind encourages us to see the invisible links binding together all of life. We have no sense that we live in the presence of a loving Father and are accountable for all we do. The marketing slogan—"What happens in Vegas stays in Vegas"—describes how our secular world views life. You can come to Vegas, have sex anonymously, and return home to your spouse as if nothing happened. There is no link between Vegas and the rest of your life. You have unlimited freedom to pursue feeling good about yourself.

Baloney. This is my Father's world. Everything you do in Vegas is connected to the rest of your life. Everything you do is connected to who you are as a person and, in turn, creates the person you are becoming. Everything you do affects those you love. All of life is covenant.

Imbedded in the idea of prayer is a richly textured view of life, organized around invisible bonds or covenants that knit us together. Instead of a fixed world, we live in our Father's world, a world built for divine relationships between people where, because of the Good News, tragedies become comedies and hope is born.

PART 5

PRAYING IN REAL LIFE

USING PRAYER TOOLS

When I do a prayer seminar, I ask for a show of hands of how many people keep their calendars electronically. Typically, one-third will raise their hands. Then I ask how many use a small pocket calendar, a wall calendar, or any other kind of written calendar. By that point almost everyone, about 95 percent, has raised his or her hand—only a couple of people are still stuck in the nineteenth century without a calendar. A few men use their wives as their calendars! Then I ask how many regularly use a written prayer system. Just a few hands go up, usually about 5 percent.

When I ask why 95 percent write their schedules down but only 5 percent write their prayer requests, someone usually answers, "If you forget an appointment, you pay for it." The obvious implication is if you forget to pray, then you don't "pay for it." If you don't do it, no one notices! My favorite response was, "Our calendar involves people. That's why we write it down." So prayer doesn't involve people? We're back to the influence of the Enlightenment on our modern world. Prayer is in the category of values and opinions. It doesn't connect with life.

The bottom line is we don't write down our prayer requests because we don't take prayer seriously. We don't think it works.

It is clear from Paul's description of his prayer life in his letters that he regularly prayed for an enormous number of people. James Dunn, the New Testament scholar, wrote, "Paul must have had an extensive prayer list and presumably spent some time each day naming before God all his churches, colleagues, and supporters. This would help maintain and strengthen the sense of a faith shared with 'all the saints.'"[1]

It is clear from the love that pours out of Paul in letters such as 1 Thessalonians that Paul has been praying for them. With the Thessalonians, he assumes that Satan is attacking; he fears that faith is eroding. He bubbles over with thanksgiving when he hears reports about their faith. They are on his heart.

I am not naturally a people person, but when I regularly pray for people using some kind of written system, my heart tunes in to them. I am bolder about asking them how things are going because they are already on my heart.

Disabled by the Fall

Remember that we are not normal children learning how to pray. Like Kim, we are disabled by the Fall. We have a disorder that mars our ability to talk with God. As Kim needs a speech computer in order to communicate, so we need written aides in order to communicate with God.

Deep within the American psyche is the 1960s' Romantic idea, originally from Emerson and Rousseau, that if something doesn't feel natural, it isn't real. We think spiritual things—if done right—should just flow. But if you have a disability, nothing flows, especially in the beginning.

One morning when Kim was six months old, Jill called me into the living room, where Kim was lying on her stomach, struggling to turn over. Kim would bring one shoulder as high as she could; then she would twist her little hips to give herself a boost. She would almost reach the tipping point only to collapse again. With Jill and me hovering over her, she tried again and again.

We couldn't help Kim. If we did, then she would never learn. She knew the general idea; she just needed to make it work. Finally, after half an hour and hundreds of attempts, she got her little shoulders high enough and flipped over.

Just as Kim had to work at turning over, we will need to persist when prayer doesn't feel natural, especially during the learning stage when we can't quite tip over.

There are many different prayer tools, but in this final part of the book we'll look at just two: prayer journals and prayer cards. But first a cautionary note about tools and systems used in prayer.

Be Careful of Systems

One prayer system many people have found helpful is ACTS (Adoration, Confession, Thanksgiving, and Supplication). But systems can become rote, desensitizing us to God as a person. We can become wooden or mindless as we pray. When I come home, I don't first adore Jill for a couple of minutes, confess my failure to take out the trash, thank her for making dinner, and then give her my list. Jill is a Philadelphian. Philadelphians boo their *own* sports teams. I could probably have an ACTS-conversation entrance once, and then Jill would roll her eyes and ask me if I had a touch of autism. And rightly so. When you are autistic, you have trouble picking up social clues from the other person. You are so lost in your own world that you miss people. None of us wants to be treated like robots—including God. He is, after all, a person.

Many people are so aware of this caution that they are suspicious of all systems. They feel it kills the Spirit. Systems seem to fly in the face of what we learned about childlike praying. But all of us create

REMEMBER, LIFE IS BOTH
HOLDING HANDS AND
SCRUBBING FLOORS. IT IS
BOTH BEING AND DOING.

systems with things that are important to us. Remember, life is both holding hands and scrubbing floors. It is both being and doing. Prayer journals or prayer cards are on the "scrubbing floors" side of life. Praying like a child is on the "holding hands" side of life. We need both.

KEEPING TRACK OF THE STORY

Using Prayer Cards

THE IDEA OF USING PRAYER CARDS instead of a prayer list came to me one day when I was sitting on our living-room sofa, trying to pray. Life over the past few months had become almost unbearable. I was frozen on the inside.

While sitting like this, spiritually numb, a thought suddenly came to me: *Put the Word to work.* I got some three-by-five cards, and on each one wrote the name of a family member, along with a Scripture that I could use to shape my prayers for that person. I began developing a stack of prayer cards that allowed me to pray through my life—for loved ones and friends, for non-Christians I'm building relationships with, for my church and its leaders, for missionaries, for my work and my co-workers, for character change in my own life, and for my dreams.

Here are the overall guidelines I use when creating a prayer card.

1. The card functions like a prayer snapshot of a person's life, so I use short phrases to describe what I want.

2. When praying, I usually don't linger over a card for more than a few seconds. I just pick out one or two key areas and pray for them.

3. I put the Word to work by writing a Scripture verse on the card that expresses my desire for that particular person or situation.

4. The card doesn't change much. Maybe once a year I will add another line. These are just the ongoing areas in a person's life that I am praying for.

5. I usually don't write down answers. They are obvious to me since I see the card almost every day.

6. I will sometimes date a prayer request by putting the month/year, as in 8/07.

A prayer card has several advantages over a list. A list is often a series of scattered prayer requests, while a prayer card focuses on one person or area of your life. It allows you to look at the person or situation from multiple perspectives. Over time, it helps you reflect on what God does in response to your prayers. You begin to see patterns, and slowly a story unfolds that you find yourself drawn into. A list tends to be more mechanical. We can get overwhelmed with the number of things to pray for. Because items on a list are so disconnected, it is hard to maintain the discipline to pray. When I pray, I have only one card in front of me at a time, which helps me concentrate on that person or need.

Prayer Cards for Family Members

You've already seen my card for Emily. Here's my son Andrew's card.

Notice that each phrase represents some area of my son's life I'm praying for. The order is not important. I'm praying through his friendships, his character, his relationships, his heart, and his mind—nothing is too mundane. When Andrew was in eighth

> *6/02:* Be a kingdom influencer
>
> *Andrew*
>
> With Emily—"Accept one another, then, just as Christ accepted you, in order to bring praise to God." Romans 15:7
> How do I disciple him?
> Math + Reading + Science + S.S. + Bible!
> Honesty "put away all deceit"—enjoy reading
> basketball, track, ping-pong
> friends—good friends that love Jesus
> Psalm 51:6 "You desire truth in the inward parts."
> Know and walk with Jesus   1/03 Ephesians 4:2 "Be completely humble"

grade, working on finding a sports niche, I wrote down a couple of sports—basketball and track—to help me pray. He ended up loving track.

I put the Word to work by writing down Scripture. Jill and I saw God repeatedly answer my prayer that Andrew "desire truth in [his] inward parts" (Psalm 51:6, NKJV). As I was watching this prayer request unfold in his life, one thing led to another, and my son and I ended up going to counseling together. That created a lasting friendship between us. God dragged me into my own prayer request.

Over time, almost every phrase on that card became a mini-story with twists and turns on the way to an answer. I showed Jill the card several years after I'd first created it, and her only response was "Wow."

Kim's card follows the same general pattern as Andrew's, has the same haphazard look to it. Hidden in Kim's prayer card is a way of praying that I learned from J. O. Fraser, a China Inland Mission missionary to the Lisu in southwestern China about one hundred years ago. Faced with the impossible task of converting the resistant

---

Kimberly

Galatians 5:22-23 "The fruit of the Spirit is . . . self-control."
Ephesians 6:1 "Children, obey your parents in the Lord."

"And the God of all grace, who called you to his eternal glory in Christ, after you have suffered a little while, will himself restore you and make you strong, firm and steadfast." 1 Peter 5:10

"Be patient." Ephesians 4:2

"Dear friend, I pray that you may enjoy good health and that all may go well with you, even as your soul is getting along well." 3 John 2

—computer mouse   —Liberator better   —clean up   —wonderful aide
—software   —get breakfast   —public manners   —horse
Job: announcer, library, data entry—a calling, a way to help

Lisu, he learned two kinds of prayers: big and small.[1] If you think back to the Hope–Reality chart (see chapter 21), the big prayers focus on the hope line and the little prayers focus on the reality line. We need both kinds of prayers.

My big prayers for Kim are reflected in the passages from 1 Peter, Ephesians, and 3 John. Kim's life has been hard, so I'm praying for blessing. I often pray, "The God of all grace, . . . after you have suffered a little while, will himself restore you" (1 Peter 5:10, NIV).

At the bottom of Kim's card, I have listed nitty-gritty, daily-life prayers for the small issues in her life. Finding a computer mouse bedeviled us for a couple of years. Finally, we found a large trackball that Kim is able to manipulate easily. "Liberator better" is a prayer for her speech computer. I wrote that request the summer she went off to speech-computer camp. I wrote down "horse" because Kim has always wanted a horse. Lately that has shifted to wanting a cow. Now that her brother Andrew is marrying the daughter of a Lancaster dairy farmer, we might be able to work something out.

The big prayers were the huge, impossible prayers, such as the ones that Kimberly would be "strong, firm and steadfast" (1 Peter 5:10,

NIV). I remember when I first wrote that, it felt strange, like I was opening a door that I didn't know existed. We'd been so preoccupied with survival that it was hard to imagine Kim prospering. Big prayers help you dream impossible dreams. They help you to think big.

Now eleven years after writing those big prayer requests, I'm slowly seeing God answer them. Take a simple thing like "steadfast." When I wrote this card, Kim was anything but steadfast, especially physically, but as a dog walker she has to step over hoses, bend down in cages, and manage a dog on a trail. She has literally become more steadfast.

A Prayer Card for People in Suffering

The church prays well for people who suffer if the person has a clear diagnosis with an end in sight. But if the diagnosis isn't clear or if it is endless, the church tends to get overwhelmed. In other words, when it becomes real suffering, we don't pray!

"I'll keep you in my prayers" is the easiest way to back away politely. Roughly translated it means, "I have every intention of praying for you, but because I've not written it down, it is likely I will

---

David Gray Jr., both struggling, Rodney & Sarah Lee

Bob & Annette Winter

Mom/Sue/Charlene

John

Isaiah 61:1a, 2b, 3a

Cancer
Jenny
Roberta

"The Spirit of the sovereign LORD is on me, because the LORD has annointed me . . . to comfort all who mourn, and provide for those who grieve in Zion—to bestow on them a crown of beauty instead of ashes, the oil of gladness instead of mourning, and a garment of praise instead of a spirit of despair."

Single women who want to get married
Carol
Jane

Struggling Marriages
Roberta & George Carter

never pray for it. But I say it because at this moment I do care, and it feels awkward to say nothing." It is the twenty-first-century version of "Be warmed and filled" (James 2:16).

A prayer card devoted to people in pain enables you to take suffering seriously because you are able to watch what God does over time. Surrounding this passage from Isaiah, I have written the names of people who are struggling with a difficult situation or illness. By praying regularly for them, my heart tunes in to their struggles. I am bolder about asking others how things are going because those people are already on my heart. I don't feel like a phony.

A Prayer Card for Non-Christians
I've had several cards for non-Christians. My first card was for people in an evangelistic Bible study I used to lead. Before I'd written out this card, the study was going okay, but my message wasn't penetrating people's hearts. After six months, I decided to write up a prayer card and start praying for each person daily. Almost immediately, things began to happen in all of their lives. Jane's three children all began to

---

Bible Study

Brad, "I'm on my way to becoming a Christian!"
Jane, "Where should we go to church?"
 1. Jane—submit and believe that Jesus is the only way.
    Wisdom for me to know how and when to address it.
 2. Brad & Jane—continue to believe—deepen their faith.
 3. Go to a good church. Wisdom to know what to say.
 4. Tom & Sandra—God's Word would guide them.

---

struggle. Her husband, Brad, quit the study, telling his wife it was for weaklings. Later he rejoined the study for several months, but then quit again, telling her the same thing. God obliged him and made him weak by permitting cancer in his life. Although still young in his faith, Brad now professes faith in Christ.

A Prayer Card for Friends

I would not have started praying regularly for other men in my life unless I had a prayer card for them. We usually don't pray for things that function like wallpaper in our lives. We only pray when the wallpaper starts peeling.

Men

Sam—Not be passive, want intimacy/closeness with X X X, not comfort and privacy.

"Am I now trying to win the approval of men, or of God? Or am I trying to please man? If I were still trying to please men, I would not be a servant of Christ." Galatians 1:10

Robert—heart, eyes

Ralph—forgiveness for X X X, X X X

James—X X X oneness of X X X + X X X, writing, health

Doug—filled w/ Jesus, very profitable with business

Building a Sample Deck

Here is an outline of a sample deck of prayer cards that will allow you to pray through your entire life. Some cards I pray through every day; others I rotate through, using one or two cards a day. How many cards you use for a particular area depends on the shape of your life. It is completely up to you.

- 4–10 family cards (one for each person)
- 1–3 people-in-suffering cards
- 1 friends card
- 1 non-Christian card
- 1 church's leadership card
- 1 small-group card
- 1 missionary, ministries card
- 1–3 world- or cultural-issues cards
- 3 work cards
- 1 co-workers card
- 3–5 repentance cards (things I need to repent of)
- 3–5 hope or big-dream cards

If you can't find time to write out these cards, then use your prayer time to write them out. One morning a week, instead of praying, write out a card for one of these areas. You can begin with just a partial card. That's how all my cards started. For example, just write out one Scripture and the names of a couple of people in suffering on a card and leave it at that.

IF YOU TRY TO SEIZE THE DAY, THE DAY WILL EVENTUALLY BREAK YOU. SEIZE THE CORNER OF HIS GARMENT AND DON'T LET GO UNTIL HE BLESSES YOU. HE WILL RESHAPE THE DAY.

The hard part of writing out prayer cards isn't the time. It is our unbelief. We seldom feel unbelief directly—it lurks behind the feelings that will surface if we start to write out prayer cards, feelings like "This is so corny" or "I feel straightjacketed" or "What good will it do?" The old red herring of legalism may come to mind. You might fear that it will take away the spontaneity of childlike praying.

Get Dirty

Prayer is asking God to incarnate, to get dirty in your life. Yes, the eternal God scrubs floors. For sure we know he washes feet. So take Jesus at his word. Ask him. Tell him what you want. Get dirty. Write out your prayer requests; don't mindlessly drift through life on the American narcotic of busyness. If you try to seize the day, the day will eventually break you. Seize the corner of his garment and don't let go until he blesses you. He will reshape the day.

PRAYER WORK

BOB DIDN'T PARTICULARLY LIKE ME—he hadn't for quite a few years. He didn't like the way I looked, dressed, or talked. And that was just for openers. Every couple of years his anger would flare out at me, but generally he just treated me like a servant. Over time, the mellowing and acceptance that often occur in relationships didn't happen. In fact, Bob got more irritated with me.

Then it dawned on me that I'd tolerated and even loved Bob, but I had not prayed regularly for him. I had assumed that his attitude toward me was like the blue sky, part of the backdrop of life that doesn't change. I am constantly discovering areas of my life like this. So I wrote up a prayer card for Bob and scribbled 1 Peter 3:4 on it, and I began to pray daily that God would gentle his critical spirit. Then I waited.

Within a year, Bob went through suffering, and I was able to serve him. Several years later, he went through even more suffering, and I had the opportunity to serve him again. This time, his suffering was so severe that he couldn't help but feel my love and care for him. For the first time in our relationship, his attitude toward me softened significantly.

Bob

"a gentle & quiet spirit" 1 Peter 3:4

—he will know God in the face of Jesus Christ.

—complete healing

When I begin praying Christ into someone's life, God often permits suffering in that person's life. If Satan's basic game plan is pride, seeking to draw us into his life of arrogance, then God's basic game plan is humility, drawing us into the life of his Son. The Father can't think of anything better to give us than his Son. Suffering invites us to join his Son's life, death, and resurrection. Once you see that, suffering is no longer strange. Peter writes, "Beloved, do not be surprised at the fiery trial when it comes upon you to test you, as though something strange were happening to you. But rejoice insofar as you share Christ's sufferings" (1 Peter 4:12-13).

Working Your Prayers
My prayer for Bob had a familiar threefold pattern. First, I wrote the prayer down. Then I watched for God to work while I prayed. Finally, God provided an opportunity where I "worked" the prayer request. By *worked* I mean that God involved me in my own prayers, often in a physical and humbling way.

Look at how similar this pattern is to Jesus' description of how the kingdom works:

The kingdom of God is as if a man should scatter seed on the ground. He sleeps and rises night and day, and the seed sprouts and grows; he knows not how. The earth produces by itself, first the blade, then the ear, then the full grain in the ear. But when the grain is ripe, at once he puts in the sickle, because the harvest has come.   MARK 4:26-29

Notice the three-step pattern: planting, waiting, and then working again at the harvest. Jesus' description of how the kingdom works is alien from how many of us pray. First, it seldom occurs to us to plant the seed of thoughtful praying because we think people like Bob don't change. Or, prayer just feels too easy, almost like a cop-out.

Second, if we do pray, we don't watch and wait. We want the answer now. We grumble right at the point when God is about to do his biggest work. When Bob suffers, we think that karma has finally kicked in. Bob is just getting what he had coming. We'd likely not admit it, but we are tempted to enjoy his suffering. And people like Bob don't suffer quietly.

> IF SATAN'S BASIC GAME PLAN IS PRIDE, SEEKING TO DRAW US INTO HIS LIFE OF ARROGANCE, THEN GOD'S BASIC GAME PLAN IS HUMILITY, DRAWING US INTO THE LIFE OF HIS SON.

Finally, we don't recognize the harvest when it comes. We are so cut off from an agrarian society that we forget that Jesus' image of reaping is hard work. We reverse the kingdom pattern of ask (seed), watch (growth), and work (harvest). Instead of working in partnership with God, we attack the problem. We tell Bob what a pain in the neck he is. Then we watch the relationship disintegrate. Finally, when nothing is working, we might pray. But by that time we've concluded that Bob is hopeless and God is powerless. We decide that prayer doesn't work.

But what really doesn't work is us. For starters, we only prayed after we'd mucked up the situation. Then, by praying at the end, we didn't allow any time for God to weave his story. Secretly we want him to answer our prayer by doing a magic trick on the other person's soul. Our "prayer doesn't work" often means "you didn't do my will, in my way, in my time."

Bob Again

Only by watching do we realize the bizarre connections God makes in the kingdom. God answered my prayer for gentleness in Bob's life by my serving Bob while he went through a lengthy time of suffering. Bob's sufferings flowed over into my life. According to Paul, that is the essence of ministry: "For as we share abundantly in Christ's sufferings, so through Christ we share abundantly in comfort too" (2 Corinthians 1:5). Suffering opens the door to love. Suffering reaps a harvest of real change.

Bob is still Bob, but he is gentler in how he relates to me. Also, I have a new love for him. When you care for someone who is suffering, you bond with that person. Here's a snippet of a recent conversation we had:

"Paul, have you ever taken speech lessons?"

"Yes, in seminary."

"Are you speaking a lot?"

"Yes."

"You say *uh* a lot when you are talking to me. Do you know that you say *uh* a lot?"

"Yes, that is one of my bad habits."

"It sounds bad."

"Yes, you are right. It does sound bad. I need to work on it."

"You just need to be quiet instead of saying *uh*."

"You are right. Would you be willing to help remind me every time I say *uh* by pointing it out?"

"Yes, I would."

Bob is sincerely trying to help by pointing out a need in my life. It helps me to know that Bob relates by criticizing. For folks like him, it's satisfying to restore moral order to the universe.

As I've thought about Bob and his life, I've been struck by how the two of us have some of the same sin patterns. We both need Jesus. Seeing how I can be like Bob is probably the best kingdom harvest of all.

LISTENING TO GOD

A NUMBER OF YEARS AGO I took a retreat day in December to pray through my goals for the coming year. During longer times of prayer such as this, I meditate and pray through passages of Scripture. Sometimes I am simply still before God, slowing down so I can become more aware of the direction of my life and my heart. I'll ask, *How is God speaking into my life? What is God doing?*

As I thought about the coming year, I wrote in my prayer

What do you want me to focus on?	
How do you want me to focus?	
1.	*Waiting and prayer*
2.	*Listening; patience with people*
3.	*Relaxing with people*
4.	*Cultivate humility*
5.	*Quiet heart before you*
6.	*Prudence; dignity*
7.	*Witness—unashamed of Jesus*

journal, *What do you want me to focus on? How do you want me to focus?* The thought came to me as clear as the words on this page: *I don't want you to have any goals this year. I'm going to work on your character.* Surprised, I asked, *What character issues?* Again, a clear thought came to me, *You know.* And I did. Almost immediately seven items came to mind, and I wrote each of them down in my prayer journal.

Was God speaking to me during that day of prayer, or was I just recording my own thoughts in my prayer journal? To answer that question, let me tell you the rest of the story; then we'll reflect on both the benefits and dangers in listening to God.

If I'd used that day to record my goals instead of praying, it would have been an exercise in futility. God did nothing that year but work on my character. Each of those seven areas became a little story shaped by God through suffering. Let me explain by looking at the last of those seven items: Witness—unashamed of Jesus.

Shortly before my prayer retreat, I asked my boss (who was also my father) how he'd like me to improve in my work. Dad replied, "I'd like you to have more of a burden for the lost." Inwardly, I bristled. For thirteen years he and I had worked side by side growing our mission to ninety missionaries. Few had done more in reaching the lost than I. But I knew that wasn't what Dad was talking about. He wanted me *personally* to have more of a concern for people who didn't know Jesus. But that intimidated me. Growing up in a Christian home and having attended Christian schools, I was not used to non-Christians. I thought, *Paul, you are just too proud to admit that your dad is correct.* So I began to pray that God would help me to love and enjoy non-Christians.

Four months later in April, I was praying again while walking along the Mediterranean in Spain. My heart was heavy. Dad had had open-heart surgery and was not recovering from it. He was dying. As I walked along the wharf, numb, I thought again of my dad's love for non-Christians, and I prayed that God would give me my dad's heart and multiply it.

After Dad's funeral, a friend called me, asking if I wanted to postpone the start of an evangelistic Bible study we had been planning. I said, "No, Dad would have wanted me to do it." In early June, I nervously began my first *Person of Jesus* Bible study with a group of people from a variety of backgrounds. That little seed began to multiply, and now years later, I regularly get e-mails from all over the world from people who are introducing seekers to Jesus using *The Person of Jesus* study.

Was God Speaking?

So, was God speaking? Did the Spirit prompt me, or was it just my intuition? I believe God was hands-on, working on me, speaking to me during that day of prayer. Here's why.

First, my question and the subsequent answer were immersed in reflections on God's Word. It was just one stage in an unfolding, biblically informed story of repentance. Psalm 25:14 says, "The friendship of the LORD is for those who fear him, and he makes known to them his covenant." It was the opposite of human intuition gone amok. In fact, my intuition was being mastered by God.

Second, the answer surprised me. I'm almost obsessive about goals, yet I'd never had a thought like that one before. In the Bible, we see the same surprising quality to God's intervention. Who would have guessed the incarnation, the cross, and the resurrection? The thought that I was too proud sounded like God. It was distinctively his *voice*. It matched Scripture. He writes his Word on our hearts.

Finally, it came true. God did nothing but work on my character that year. There was no point in having goals. The kingdom came. God's will was done. Scripture tells us we can discern a false prophet if his prophecy does not come true (see Deuteronomy 18:21-22).

Where Christians Go Wrong

Let's explore two common ways Christians go wrong when it comes to hearing God's voice in their lives and how we can correctly discern when God is speaking to us.

1. "Word Only"—Going Wrong by Not Listening

If we focus exclusively on God's written Word when looking for God's activity in our lives but don't watch and pray, we'll miss the unfolding story of his work. We'll miss the patterns of the Divine Artist etching the character of his Son on our hearts. Our lives will lack the sparkle and immediacy of God's presence.

When the Spirit convicted me, he was personalizing the Word to my heart. "Humble yourselves, therefore, under the mighty hand of God" (1 Peter 5:6). If I hadn't taken the time that December morning to pray and put my questions before God, the following year would have lacked some of the rich meaning God intended. I would have missed the drama.

The thought—*Paul, I'm going to work on your character*—had a similar impact on me as Jesus' words—"You will deny me three times" (Matthew 26:34)—had on Peter. After his fall, reflecting back on Jesus' warning would have brought Peter to a deeper repentance. It also gave Peter hope, possibly saving him from suicide. He could say, "Jesus knew this about me ahead of time, yet he loved me and prayed for me that I wouldn't despair." In my life, when suffering came the following year, that unexpected thought gave the suffering meaning and purpose. It gave me hope.

If we believe Scripture only applies to people in general, then we can miss how God intimately personalizes his counsel to us as individuals. We can become deists, removing God from our lives. But everywhere in Scripture we see God speaking to us with a personal touch, prompting us to obey and love.

Look at the variety of places that the Spirit was personalizing the Word to my life: (1) when I asked Dad how I could improve, (2) when Dad encouraged me to have more of a burden for the lost, (3) when I realized, *Paul, you are just proud*, (4) when I prayed in Spain, and (5) when I started the Bible study. Each qualifies as "low-level divine communication."

Seeing the finger of God in our circumstances, creation, other Christians, and the Word keeps us from elevating our thoughts to a unique status. God is continually speaking to each of us, but not just through our intuition. Seeing God's activity in the details of our lives enhances the application of God's Word. We actually undermine the impact of God's Word if we define God's speaking too narrowly.

What is at stake here is developing an eye for the Shepherd. I need to tune in to my Father's voice above the noise of my own heart and the surrounding world—what C. S. Lewis called "the Kingdom of Noise." I need to develop a poet's eye that can see the patterns in my Father's good creation. Like a good storyteller, I need to pick up the cadence and heartbeat of the Divine Storyteller.

Jill and I were poets when we slowly realized what a gift Kim is to us, two self-confident people. Almost every story I've told you has poetry in it. "Watch and pray" is Jesus' repeated refrain to his disciples at Gethsemane (Mark 14:38). Don't pray in a fog. Pray with your eyes open. Look for the patterns God is weaving in your life.

2. "Spirit Only"—Going Wrong by Elevating Human Intuition

One morning, I was praying in Emily's room, and I heard a voice—as clear as if you were talking to me now—coming from above: "Paul, this is God speaking. Your wife needs a new kitchen." About a minute later, Jill's smiling face poked through the door. "Paul, did God speak to you in any special way this morning? Did he say anything about a kitchen?"

Jill's goofiness is a window into the problem of people frequently hearing God speak. When people call their own thoughts or feelings

"God's voice," it puts them in control of God and ultimately undermines God's Word by elevating human intuition to the status of divine revelation. Unless Scripture guards and directs our intuitions, we can easily run amok and baptize our selfish desires with religious language ("God told me to marry her . . .").

The first inner-city Christian school I taught at used to write its payroll checks "on faith," believing that God would provide. We teachers cashed the checks on faith, but unfortunately our banker didn't have any faith, and the checks bounced. Not surprisingly the school went bankrupt. Religious language was hiding financial irresponsibility.

If after my December prayer retreat, I had told our staff, "God told me that I wasn't supposed to have any goals this year," I would have elevated my own thoughts to the level of biblical authority. I actually forgot about that prayer time until the year started getting difficult. It was a personal word to me from God that gave meaning and hope during a hard time. It wasn't something to build my life around, just a kind word from my heavenly Father.

The problem is that the Holy Spirit comes in on the same channel as the world, the flesh, the Devil. The Lord does lead—we just need to be careful that we aren't using the Lord as a cover for our own desires. If we frequently interpret random thoughts and desires as "God speaking," we get weird. That's what happened to one couple.

The husband was in the ministry and was struggling with chronic fatigue and several other illnesses. His wife had just discovered that he had become addicted to painkillers, and she was bitter with God. I was visiting them when she told me, "Both my husband and I felt we had a clear word from the Lord that we should get rid of all the yeast. We got rid of all the yeast in the house, but he's still sick." I was so surprised, I blurted out, "That's heresy. You are elevating human intuition to the level of the Word of God." I also shared with them that yeast in Scripture is a metaphor for a small amount of evil that pervades the whole. I suggested that the yeast was the husband's dependence on painkillers. This couple had been wooden in how they interpreted God's voice. They needed to develop a poet's eye.

Sometimes I get premonitions of something bad happening to someone I love. When that happens, I pray *against* my intuitions. I pray for blessing, for safety, for long life. The simplicity and clarity of God's Word—"Beloved, I pray that all may go well with you and that you may be in good health, as it goes well with your soul" (3 John 1:2)—keeps me from getting lost in my feelings. I wonder if the "dark night of the soul" that many mystics experience is just getting lost in the darkness of their hearts.

Paul cautions the Colossians against a person "going on in detail about visions, puffed up without reason by his sensuous mind, and not holding fast to the Head" (Colossians 2:18-19). He links communication from God with the danger of creating a false, elevated spirituality. Paul wants us to keep our eye on the Head, the Good Shepherd, not on the means of communication. In fact, Paul doesn't ever mention God speaking directly to him, except in 2 Corinthians 10–12, when so-called super apostles were boasting about their visions from God and attacking Paul. Even then he can't bring himself to say that he personally saw these visions. He says, "I know a man" (12:2). The same pattern emerges in Acts, where Luke occasionally describes Paul getting specific leading from God, usually in times of crisis, but more frequently Paul just talks about his own desires and plans.

To correctly discern when God is speaking to us, we need to keep the Word and Spirit together.

Keeping the Word and Spirit Together

Spirit Only people, on the right side of the chart, can separate the activity of listening to God from obedience to God's Word. Under the cover of "being led by the Spirit," they can easily do what they want.

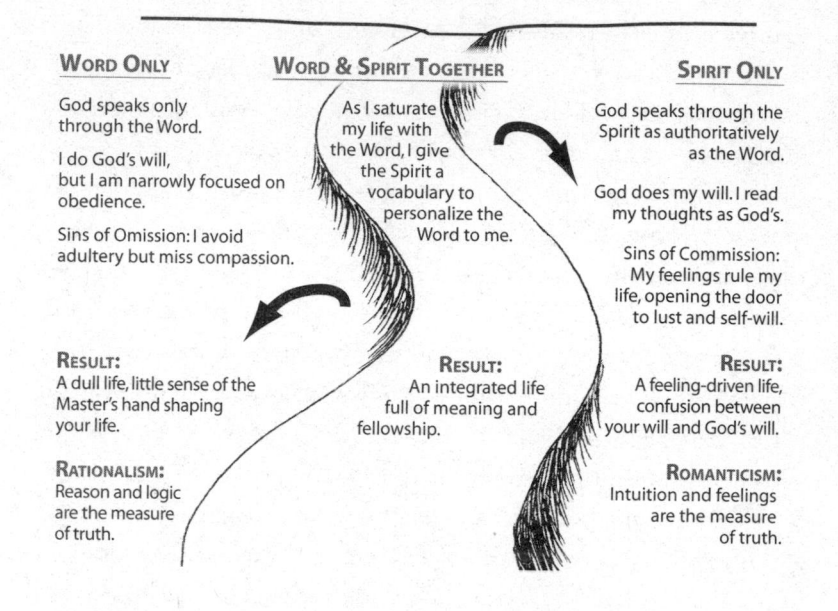

WORD ONLY

God speaks only through the Word.

I do God's will, but I am narrowly focused on obedience.

Sins of Omission: I avoid adultery but miss compassion.

RESULT:
A dull life, little sense of the Master's hand shaping your life.

RATIONALISM:
Reason and logic are the measure of truth.

WORD & SPIRIT TOGETHER

As I saturate my life with the Word, I give the Spirit a vocabulary to personalize the Word to me.

RESULT:
An integrated life full of meaning and fellowship.

SPIRIT ONLY

God speaks through the Spirit as authoritatively as the Word.

God does my will. I read my thoughts as God's.

Sins of Commission: My feelings rule my life, opening the door to lust and self-will.

RESULT:
A feeling-driven life, confusion between your will and God's will.

ROMANTICISM:
Intuition and feelings are the measure of truth.

What they "hear" from God might be masking their self-will. This is emotionalism (a form of Romanticism), which makes feelings absolute.

Word Only people can also separate hearing and obedience by focusing on obedience and ignoring a life of listening and repentance. Listening to and obeying God are so intertwined in biblical thought that in the Hebrew they are one word, *shama'*. Under the cover of being obedient to the Word, Word Only folks can be rigid. We need to guard against rationalism as much as we need to guard against emotionalism.

We need the sharp-edged, absolute character of the Word and the intuitive, personal leading of the Spirit. The Word provides the structure, the vocabulary. The Spirit personalizes it to our life. Keeping the Word and the Spirit together guards us from the danger of God-talk becoming a cover for our own desires and the danger of lives isolated from God.

Cultivate a Listening Heart

There is nothing secret about communion with God. If we live a holy life before God, broken of our pride and self-will, crying out for grace, then we will be in communion with God. It is really that simple.

Listening is just one of the things that happens in the course of my soul connecting with God. You can't listen to God if you are isolated from a life of surrender that draws you into his story for your life. And it must be a gospel story. By that I mean your dying, your weakness is what you bring to the table. God brings to the table his grace, his resurrection.

There is a tendency among Christians to get excited about "listening to God" as if they are discovering a hidden way of communicating with God that will revolutionize their prayer lives. Writers will often couch it correctly ("it must be in obedience to God's Word"), but they make the activity of listening to God front and center. This subtly elevates an experience with God instead of God himself. Without realizing it, we can look *at* the windshield instead of *through* it.

When referring to communication with God, Scripture assumes that I know what God is saying. The problem isn't the activity of listening, but my listening heart. Am I attentive to God? Is my heart soft and teachable? Am I remembering his ways, his commands? Psalm 25:15 says, "My eyes are ever toward the LORD." The means of communication is secondary to a surrendered heart. Our responsibility is to cultivate a listening heart in the midst of the noise from our own hearts and from the world, not to mention the Devil.

The interaction between the divine Spirit and my own spirit is

> **THE PROBLEM ISN'T THE ACTIVITY OF LISTENING, BUT MY LISTENING HEART. AM I ATTENTIVE TO GOD? IS MY HEART SOFT AND TEACHABLE?**

mysterious. David captures this mystery in Psalm 16:7—"I bless the LORD who gives me counsel; in the night also my heart instructs me." The parallel structure of the verse suggests that "the LORD who gives me counsel" is identical to "my heart [literally 'my gut'] instructs me." So what happened? Is David's heart talking to him, or is God giving him counsel? The two are impossible to separate.

Tuning in to your Father's voice has a hard-to-pin-down-but-nevertheless-real quality. We can only experience it and observe some of its characteristics. We don't have the capacity to analyze this interaction. The counsel God gave David is inseparable from David's active pursuit of God: "I have set the LORD always before me" (Psalm 16:8). The counsel from God doesn't function like a fortune-teller; it is inseparable from a humble heart seeking after God.

CHAPTER 32

PRAYER JOURNALING

Becoming Aware of the Interior Journey

THE PRACTICE OF JOURNAL WRITING and the idea that my life is a meaningful story are both rooted in Christianity. Augustine's *Confessions*, an autobiography written around AD 400, describes the interior journey of the soul. It was the first true journal. Augustine was the first person to recognize the inner workings of his heart and write about the meaning he saw laced through his life.

He described how he encountered the living, speaking God when he overheard the voice of a neighborhood child chanting a little song. He had been listening to the preaching of Bishop Ambrose and coming under great conviction of sin, particularly sexual sin. He wrote:

> So was I speaking and weeping in the most bitter contrition of my heart, when, lo! I heard from a neighboring house a voice, as of boy or girl, I know not, chanting, and oft repeating, "Take up and read; Take up and read." Instantly, my countenance altered. . . . I arose; interpreting it to be no other than a command from God to open the book [the New Testament], and read the first chapter I should find. . . . I seized, opened, and in silence read that section on which my eyes first fell: "Not in rioting and

drunkenness, not in chambering and wantonness, not in strife and envying; but put ye on the Lord Jesus Christ, and make not provision for the flesh." . . . Instantly at the end of this sentence, by a light . . . infused into my heart, all the darkness of doubt vanished away.[1]

The Spirit, speaking through a child, brought the Word to life in Augustine's heart. When God touched Augustine's soul, he came alive, his life rich with meaning.

When life makes sense, it becomes a journey, a spiritual adventure. Writing down the adventure as it happens gives us a feel for our place in the story God is weaving in our lives. Journaling helps us to become aware of the journey.

The idea that we are on a spiritual journey is imbedded deep in the psyche of Christianity. Look at all the hints of a journey in Psalm 23. The Good Shepherd "*leads me* beside still waters. . . . He *leads* me in *paths* of righteousness. . . . Even though I *walk through the valley* of the shadow of death . . . [he is] with me. . . . Goodness and mercy shall *follow me all the days of my life*" (emphasis added).

Dangers lurk on the journey. On the outside "the valley of the shadow of death" and "the presence of my enemies" threaten. On the inside I battle a restless soul. Just like a character in a good novel, I have choices to make. Will I run from the presence of my enemies, or will I wait for the Lord to provide a table for me? Will I try to fill it with stuff, or will I let the Shepherd make "me lie down in green pastures"? Life becomes an adventure.

This awareness of the soul's interior journey has continued throughout the history of Christianity. However, the journal writing of sixteenth- and seventeenth-century English Puritans took it to a new level. They wanted to keep a record of what God was doing in their lives. It was a small step from Puritan journal writing to John Bunyan's *The Pilgrim's Progress* and Daniel Defoe's *Robinson Crusoe*.

Both are interior adventure stories that paved the way for character development in the novel. Edward Said, a leading Palestinian scholar, pointed out that "the novel is a specifically Christian form of writing. It presupposes a world that is incomplete, that is yearning for salvation, and moving toward it. By contrast . . . the world of Islam is a closed and complete world."[2]

The stories I've told in this book are miniadventures. Will Ashley find her contact? Will Kim speak? Will Kim find a job? Walking with God is anything but boring.

Many of us rush around without much conscious knowledge of the pilgrimage God is carving out for us. When tragedy strikes, we've not learned the ways of God, so we have no frame of reference from which to respond. So, we slog through life, missing the divine touches.

Writing in a prayer journal helps us take stock of our location on the journey. We can become poets, artists with our souls. When we keep a prayer journal, we can reflect on what God is doing, on the patterns of our Father's care instead of reacting to life.

> IF WE SEE OUR LIVES AS A PILGRIMAGE, THEN IT BECOMES AN INTEGRATED WHOLE. IT MAKES SENSE.

If we see our lives as a pilgrimage, then it becomes an integrated whole. It makes sense. When we understand the story, it quiets our souls. It's okay to have a busy life. It's crazy to have a busy soul.

Becoming Aware of Self on the Journey

As we walk with the Shepherd, we become aware of our true selves. In his autobiography, Augustine recalled when he was a boy stealing unripe pears from his neighbor's orchard even though he had ripe pears on his side.[3] Because Augustine had encountered the living God, he was able to see the irrational bent in his heart toward evil.

We have seen how personal Psalm 23 is, with *me* or *my* or *I* appearing seventeen times. When we discover the Shepherd, the self is liberated. David is aware of self because he is aware of God's love. The light of God lets us see the interior journey.

The modern quest for self-fulfillment is a secularized version of Christianity's discovery of the self. Without the Shepherd guiding us to see our true selves in relationship to him, we can lose our way and become obsessed with self. Instead of seeing our bent toward evil, we can become increasingly touchy, supersensitive to self but insensitive to others. We no longer see ourselves clearly.

The spiritual pilgrimage is the opposite. The discovery of self in relationship to God leads to a lifestyle of repentance. For example, we are seldom aware of our impatience. What we feel is everyone else's slowness. Because we are naturally the center of our own universes, we don't feel irritable. We just notice everyone getting in our way. Here's where a prayer journal can help.

Communion or conversation with God breaks down into two questions:

1. How am I doing? What is coming at me? Am I happy, sad, thankful, discouraged, angry, frustrated?
2. What is God saying to me? What does the Word say?

When I reflect on these two questions in my prayer journal, the Living God removes the fog, and I see my true self. This leads to repentance. Not surprisingly, repentance has a prominent place in the Lord's Prayer. As we've seen, "Your kingdom come, your will be done" (Matthew 6:10) strikes at the heart of our kingdoms and our self-will; "lead us not into temptation" (6:13) tries to keep us from sinning; and "forgive us our debts" (6:12) picks up the pieces.

You can't walk with the Shepherd and not begin to change. His presence allows us to take an honest, interior look. Let me show you from two different perspectives what this looks like in my life. The first is using a journal over the course of a year; the second is using my journal during a day of prayer.

Using a Journal over the Course of a Year

The year following my December prayer retreat was an interior journey. In February when things started getting difficult, I wrote in my journal, *Help me not to shrink from any cup of suffering you might have prepared for me.* I remembered the list of seven character qualities I'd written in my journal two months before, and decided to turn each of them into a prayer. I was keenly aware that God wanted to develop my character through suffering.

In late March I wrote the following reflection about myself:

When I think I am right, I tend to be quick to defend and slow to incarnate [understand]. I can be intense, judgmental, and proud. Jesus, make me quiet, prudent, and humble, and until you do—help me to shut up!

In December God had shown me parts of my character that I needed to submit to him; now my prayer journal allowed me to track what he was doing in the larger story of his determination to make me like his Son. Month by month he worked on me.

By June, I realized that God didn't seem particularly interested in saving me from the difficult situation. He just wanted to change me. I wrote, "For the first time in the last four months the idea of primarily focusing on my repentance is appealing to me." It was a relief to realize God had boxed me in. It took off some of the pressure. I stopped hunting for ways to improve my situation and focused on my own repentance.

Later that month I realized God wanted to teach me how to listen to those who had a problem with me. Here's what I wrote in my journal about what I was learning:

- Be sensitive to how hard it is for the other person to share. Ask, "Do you want me to respond or to just think about it?"
- Even if it doesn't seem true, try to find something I've done wrong.
- Don't be truth-focused. The truth is that I need to love the other person.
- Repeat back what the other person says.
- Ask questions about the person.
- Wait on explaining yourself.
- Really wait in telling the other person what he or she did wrong.

The following month I felt I hadn't made much progress. I wrote this about a recent situation: *I wasn't slow to anger. I wasn't quick to listen. I wasn't slow to speech.* But by the end of the year I was writing entries like this one: *I am a different person than I was before all this started. I pray that will last. Give me an obedient heart.*

When we keep our eyes on the Shepherd, we become aware of ourselves. The valley of the shadow of death becomes a valley of vision. As you can see, journaling allows us to discover the story that God is writing in our lives. Instead of rushing through life, it allows us to pause and reflect.

Using a Journal during a Morning Prayer Time
Writing in a prayer journal helps us to articulate the state of our hearts. Follow me as I take you through a morning prayer time when some hard things were going on in my life.

As soon as I slowed down to pray and reflected on how I was doing, I realized I was upset. The first word I wrote down was *anger*. I wrote about why I was angry, and I prayed for grace. Then I reflected on what God might be saying to me. I paged through the Psalms until I found one that reflected the state of my heart: Psalm 102.

- I am like a lonely sparrow on the housetop. (verse 7)
- You have taken me up and thrown me down. (verse 10)
- My days are like an evening shadow; I wither away like grass. (verse 11)
- Take me not away in the midst of my days. (verse 24)

In a strange way, it was comforting to meditate on Scripture that reflected the state of my life. I told God, *I am not confident of your deliverance. I feel like I am drowning.* I prayed that he would save me, and as an afterthought, I wrote, *Until you do save me, give me the faith to wait.*

Then I reflected on the state of my soul: *My inability to wait on you comes from thinking salvation comes from me.* That got me thinking about all the suffering in the book of Revelation, so I turned there and looked up the passages on patient endurance (emphasis added).

- I, John, your brother and partner in the tribulation and the kingdom and the *patient endurance* that are in Jesus. (1:9)
- They were . . . told *to rest a little longer.* (6:11)
- Here is a call for the *endurance and faith* of the saints. (13:10)
- Here is a call for the *endurance* of the saints. (14:12)

Then I remembered three recent situations where I'd not waited. I jotted them down. Toward the end of my prayer time I turned to Isaiah 30:15, where God tells Israel that their salvation came from "repentance and rest" and "quietness and trust" (NIV), as opposed to running around and trying to save themselves.

My prayer time began with me feeling angry and overwhelmed, and it ended with the Spirit personalizing Scripture to the state of my heart. Without realizing it, my prayer time had shifted from "Paul as victim" to "Paul as sinner." By the end I had a clear plan: Do nothing. Wait on God.

The key was being honest about what I was feeling and then letting Scripture speak to my heart. By being honest, the real me was talking. I wasn't trying to be good. When we look at our life through the lens of Scripture, we seldom lose our way. We can be real, but we don't get lost in our feelings.

If I hadn't written down my reflections, I wouldn't have known what God was teaching me. By the time I was finished, I knew my part in God's play. It was offstage in a corner, waiting. Not particularly glamorous but crystal clear. Opening my heart up for God to speak to me through his Word opened the door to repentance. My prayer time itself was a journey, a mininovel.

You don't have to write well to keep a prayer journal, nor do you have to be consistent. It is just a written version of childlike praying, except more organized. Begin with what's on your heart, what's bugging you, what you are thankful for. If you are real before God, then everything else flows.

The act of writing out your worries, joys, and prayers helps you focus and keeps your mind from wandering. But the best part is that over time you will begin to see patterns of what God is doing, to pick up the threads of a story.

CHAPTER 33

REAL-LIFE PRAYING

PRAYER IS WHERE I do my best work as a husband, dad, worker, and friend. I'm aware of the weeds of unbelief in me and the struggles in others' lives. The Holy Spirit puts his finger on issues that only he can solve.

I'm actually managing my life through my daily prayer time. I'm shaping my heart, my work, my family—in fact, everything that is dear to me—through prayer in fellowship with my heavenly Father. I'm doing that because I don't have control over my heart and life or the hearts and lives of those around me. But God does.

The following morning prayer time is a small window into how all of this works.

A Morning Prayer Time

The day I wrote this summary of a morning prayer time, my alarm went off at five forty. I slept through it for five minutes, crawled out of bed, got dressed, and sat down in a living-room chair to pray. Jill was already downstairs praying. No sooner had I sat down than Kim began to pace. I told her to get back in bed. (This was before it had occurred to me to pray that she wouldn't pace.)

Now to my morning prayer time. I began with childlike praying, reflecting on the previous day and thanking God for specific ways I'd seen his shepherding care for our family. The day before we'd had a wonderful phone call from our nineteen-year-old daughter Emily in Guatemala, saying she was willing to go to the college we wanted. Just a couple of days prior, we'd been discussing colleges with her on the phone, and there had been some tension. When we hung up, Jill and I prayed about it. We decided that we should support Emily's choice. Then Emily called again to say she had been praying and also reading the book of Esther, and God had impressed on her that she should follow our lead the way Esther followed Mordecai. My heart was bubbling over with thanksgiving. Ten years before, I'd written out this verse on a prayer card for Emily: "Children, obey your parents in the Lord, for this is right" (Ephesians 6:1). I had prayed many times that God would bring about this verse in her life. But Emily's willingness to go where we wanted her to go for college was secondary to me; more important was the heart change reflected in her new attitude toward us on the phone. I dated my prayer journal and wrote out a brief prayer of thanksgiving.

In the middle of this I began to think about an online news blog I frequented. Yesterday it occurred to me that visiting several times a day gave me a nice break, but it might feed unbelief in my life. Just last week I'd prayed that my Father would show me what feeds a lack of faith in me. I was beginning to see that too much media was subtly framing how I viewed the world. I wrote that out, not so much as a prayer but just some thoughts.

Kim started pacing again. I told her to get back in bed. She quieted down. I began to slowly pray through my cards. One of the first was a new card I'd written a couple of months ago called "Jill's Pressures." It listed areas in her life where she was feeling pressure. It had started with just four areas but was now up to eight.

I prayed the Scripture I'd written on the card, that Jill would be

Jill's Pressures

Philippians 2:14-16

Do all things without grumbling or questioning, that you may be blameless and innocent, children of God without blemish in the midst of a crooked and twisted generation, among whom you shine as lights in the world, holding fast to the word of life, so that in the day of Christ I may be proud that I did not run in vain or labor in vain."

—XXXXXXX   —XXXXXXX
—XXXXXXX   —XXXXXXX
—XXXXXXX   —XXXXXXX
—XXXXXXX   —XXXXXXX

"blameless and innocent, [a child] of God without blemish in the midst of a crooked and twisted generation, among whom you shine as lights in the world" (Philippians 2:15).

Just after six o'clock, I heard the pitter-patter of feet again. Yelling wasn't working, so I stopped praying, went upstairs, and told Kim to stay in bed. This made her so angry that she bit her arm. I told her that meant no movies today. She bit her arm again. I sighed. Taking away her privilege of viewing movies would make my day more complicated. Kim was sick with double pneumonia, and I'd promised Jill I'd work at home since Jill had taken off a couple of days already. Kim calmed down, and I went back to praying.

I continued to pray through the rest of the family, using the prayer cards, sometimes thanking, sometimes asking. My son-in-law Ian needed a job; my son John had grown spiritually; my son Andrew was starting student teaching. When I came to the prayer card called "Kim's Housing," I paused to thank God for the clarity he'd given us recently in our two-year quest to get a duplex so that Kim could live separately but close to us. I continued to flip through my prayer cards, praying for my friends, my church, my work—every area of my life. Somewhere in the middle of that Jill came upstairs and started chatting with me while she made the bed. I switched back and forth between God and Jill, praying when Jill wasn't talking. I stopped at six fifteen.

Reflections on a Morning Prayer Time

Kim's interruptions give that prayer time a real-life feel. As I pray, I'm dealing not with surface stuff, but with the state of my heart and of the people for whom I am praying. My prayer time is anything but boring. I am thanking, repenting, protecting, and caring. My prayer time is alive with God.

Except for yelling at Kim, that prayer time is a window to what a praying life looks like. It is both being and doing. I'm with God. I sense his presence. He is speaking into my life. But our relationship doesn't float. I'm not hunting for an experience with God; I'm inviting God into my life experience. He is in me, and I am in him. As I bring to him my real life with my real needs, he acts in amazing ways. He is at work touching my life, doing what I can't do. The result? Thanksgiving. You don't have to work at worship when God is so alive.

Learned helplessness lurks just underneath the surface of that prayer time. I simply can't do life on my own. Without God's intervention, I am completely helpless. I need Jesus.

I woke up in the middle of the night recently with this rather odd question on my mind: *How would you love someone without prayer?* I mean, what would it look like if you loved someone but couldn't pray for that person? It was a puzzle to me. I couldn't figure out what it would look like. Love without being able to pray feels depressing and frustrating, like trying to tie a knot with gloves on. I would be powerless to do the other person any real good. People are far too complicated; the world is far too evil; and my own heart is too off center to be able to love adequately without praying. I need Jesus.

I can't emphasize enough that *things are happening because I pray.*

Emily's attitude dramatically changed. She is cheerfully going to the college we wanted. We have new clarity on our house search for Kim. Not long after I prayed that Jill would "shine as [a light] in the world," someone came up to her at work and said, "You light up this whole place." God is touching the lives of people I love with a poetry all his own.

God's activity takes the familiar shape of stories. My rejoicing over Emily was the climax of a ten-year-old story. I could rejoice because I'd been so aware of the story that God was weaving.

My thanksgiving for clarity on our search for a duplex was the middle of a story. The clarity had

> I WOKE UP IN THE MIDDLE OF THE NIGHT RECENTLY WITH THIS RATHER ODD QUESTION ON MY MIND: *HOW WOULD YOU LOVE SOMEONE WITHOUT PRAYER?*

come from Jill. She had said, "Paul, with the housing market so bad we should sell our house first. We don't know what it is worth, and in a buyer's market it would give us lots of leverage." I thought we'd get stuck without a house, but Jill was right. Three months after this prayer, we sold our house. We were ready to purchase a lot and build (a bad idea in retrospect), and we decided to wait and pray one more day. The next morning a house came on the market that was perfect for turning into a duplex.

Some stories, such as Kim's pacing, hadn't even started yet. It had yet to occur to me that my words to her wouldn't work. I needed to direct my words to God.

We don't need a praying life because that is our duty. That would wear thin quickly. We need time to be with our Father every day because every day our hearts and the hearts of those around us are overgrown with weeds. We need to reflect on our lives and engage God with the condition of our souls and the souls he has entrusted to our care or put in our paths. In a fallen world, these things do not come automatically.

CHAPTER 34

UNFINISHED STORIES

IN THE STORIES I'VE TOLD in this book, we can see God weaving a tapestry. In my experience, as we abide in him, he usually shows us what he is doing. But sometimes he doesn't. Job is the most famous example. Job never knew why he suffered. In this chapter I want to deal with a particularly difficult set of stories: the unfinished, the ones with sad endings, the seeming tragedies. We live in many overlapping stories, most of which are larger than us. Each of us will die with unfinished stories. We can never forget that God is God. Ultimately it is his story, not ours.

Sometimes the participants in the story don't get to see the end. This was the case for the children of Israel after the Babylonian invasion in 586 BC.

Israel's Agony
Israel was in agony. "By the waters of Babylon, there we sat down and wept, when we remembered Zion" (Psalm 137:1). The Babylonians had destroyed the city of Jerusalem, tearing down the walls and leveling Solomon's temple. They killed the sons of the king in front of his eyes, blinded him, and led him away in shackles. The young

men—such as Daniel and his friends, the future of the kingdom— became eunuchs in the service of the Babylonian king. Even their names were changed. The kingdom of Israel was gone; their king was gone; and the kingship was gone. For all practical purposes, Israel *ceased* to exist. So, by the rivers of Babylon they sat and wept.

The return from captivity didn't help. In 520 BC at the dedication ceremony for the makeshift temple they'd thrown together, the older people wept when they remembered the magnificent structure that Solomon had built. Haggai the prophet told Zerubbabel, "Who is left among you who saw this house in its former glory? How do you see it now? Is it not as nothing in your eyes?" (Haggai 2:3).

The Israelites' only hope was a few words from the prophets. At the same dedication Haggai prophesied,

> In a little while, I will shake the heavens and the earth and the sea and the dry land. And I will shake all nations, so that the treasures of all nations shall come in, and I will fill this house with glory. . . . The latter glory of this house shall be greater than the former. HAGGAI 2:6-7, 9

Every person who heard these words died without seeing anything happen. In fact, their children and grandchildren died. For five hundred and fifty long years, nothing happened. God was present but silent.

Nevertheless, the children of Israel didn't stop hoping and praying. The opening scene in the Gospel of Luke is a prayer meeting. When Zechariah went into the temple to burn incense, "the whole multitude of the people were praying outside" (1:10). What was God doing? How had he answered their prayers?

The Weaving of God

Let's join the weeping poets by the rivers of Babylon praying for God to restore the glory of Israel.

God's answer to their prayer for the restoration of the temple and Israel is mind-boggling. What happened to the nation of Israel? He created a new Israel, one that included the Gentiles as the people of God. What about the temple? He sent his only Son to be the temple. Look how God used the captivity, this seemingly unfinished story, to prepare for the coming of his Son and the birth of the church:

1. God used the destruction of the temple and the removal of the Israelites to Babylon to create the synagogue structure, a precursor to the local church. If temple worship had continued uninterrupted, the early church would not have had a model for local congregations. They learned to worship God without a temple.

2. The Old Testament canon was organized during this time. Severed from their land in a virtual spiritual desert, the Israelites clung to their scrolls. That gave the early church the category of Old Testament, which in turn created the New Testament.

3. God purified Israel of mixing with other religions.

4. The dispersion of the Jewish people provided a base from which Paul and others could easily spread the gospel.

5. Israel was forever purified of outward idolatry. Never again would the Jewish people worship idols. Monotheism became permanently central to Israel. This is the foundation of Christian thought and Western civilization.

6. Because the Jews became devout monotheists, they got upset when Jesus claimed to be God. When Jesus claimed to be the unique Son of God, the high priest tore his robe and delivered Jesus up to be crucified.

God was weaving a spectacular tapestry through the suffering of Israel. Without the Babylonian captivity there would be no Israel, no cross, no Christianity, and no Western civilization. Haggai was right. The glory of the new temple was greater than Solomon's.

But the Jewish poet who wept by the rivers of Babylon never saw the end of the story. Like all the heroes of faith in Hebrews 11, he lived with the story unfinished in his lifetime. He lived by faith.

Not Your Story

In part 4, Joanne mentioned another kind of unfinished story when she said, "Thousands of people pray for a Christian leader who has cancer, and he dies." I've come to realize that the more distant I am from a story, the less I know what God is doing. God will help me with my story but not someone else's.

While walking near the Sea of Galilee just after his resurrection, Jesus tells Peter that one day he will die for Jesus. Peter responds by turning to John, who is right behind them, and asking Jesus what will happen to John. Jesus tells Peter, "If it is my will that he remain until I come, what is that to you? You follow me!" (John 21:22). In effect, Jesus is saying, "Peter, I will help you with your story but not John's. Frankly, John's story is none of your business." Jesus' answer had a little snap to it because Peter has moved to a godlike stance.

There are times when I can see what God is doing in another person's life, but telling that person would crush his or her spirit. I suspect God is at times silent about stories because we just can't handle it.

"God Know What He Be Doing"

A friend of mine overheard a grandmother and her daughter in the supermarket. The grandmother told her daughter, whose son had been murdered just three days before, "Well, izz hard, but, you know, God know what he be doing." My friend, of course, interrupted them to tell them that he, too, knew that life was hard, but God knew what he was doing.

Tony Snow, a news commentator and White House press secretary, described what it felt like to awaken in a hospital bed after surgery with a lingering cloud of anesthesia, only to be told that he had cancer, possibly terminal. After the initial shock wore off, Tony's natural reaction was to turn to God, hoping that God would become a "cosmic Santa," healing him.

But Tony knew that in a mysterious way God was permitting the cancer, using it to draw Tony closer to himself, closer to those he loved, and to show him what really matters in life.

One of Tony's first discoveries in the valley of the shadow of death was that Christianity is far from mushy. In fact, suffering draws us "into a world shorn of fearful caution." We discover that life has gone from a predictable canal to a class 5 rapids, totally out of our control but filled with adventure. Tony came to see that "through such trials, God bids us to choose: Do we believe, or do we not? Will we be bold enough to love, daring enough to serve, humble enough to submit, and strong enough to acknowledge our limitations? Can we surrender our concern in things that don't matter so that we might devote our remaining days to things that do?"

> WELL, IZZ HARD, BUT, YOU KNOW, GOD KNOW WHAT HE BE DOING.

A friend of Tony's, also dying of cancer, told him, "I'm going to try to beat it, but if I don't, I'll see you on the other side."[1] A year later, Tony met his friend on the other side. Like the Israelites and the young mother in the supermarket, he didn't know why. "Izz hard, but God know what he be doing."

Come Quickly, Lord Jesus

The first time I took Kim with me on a speaking retreat, a little girl came up to her as we were finishing dinner and asked, "Why don't you speak?" Kim leaned over her speech computer, which was propped on the table, and typed, "I will have a beautiful voice in heaven." We walked away with tears in our eyes.

Some stories aren't tied up until heaven. Because of Kim, Jill longs for heaven. This desire permeates her conversation. Jill doesn't say, "It's a beautiful day outside." She says, "This would be a good day for Jesus to come back. Everyone can see him." Jill wants to go home.

Living in unfinished stories draws us into God's final act, the return of Jesus. While we wait for his return, it is easy to predict the pattern of the last days. The book of Revelation pictures a suffering church, dying as creation itself is unraveling. Through suffering God will finally make his church beautiful and reveal his glory. In the desert you see his glory. In the last days the bride will be made beautiful, pure, waiting for her lover. Come quickly, Lord Jesus.

Appendix

Getting Started with Your Prayer Cards

KEEP IT SIMPLE. Don't overthink it! Use tools that help you, and ignore those that don't.

Prayer cards are merely a snapshot of what you are asking of God, and of what Scriptures you are applying to particular people, circumstances, or concerns. As you interact with these prayer cards over time, stories will emerge, shaping how you observe life and showing how the Holy Spirit is leading you toward loving, repenting, believing, obeying, and living.

Depending on whether you want to create physical or digital prayer cards, any or all of these resources may be useful:

- Download the *A Praying Life*—Prayer Cards app at either the iTunes or Google Play store
- Join our 30-day Vimeo prayer course at https://vimeo.com/122355206
- Access other free resources at seeJesus.net/prayercards

The following suggestions will help you develop your use of prayer cards to organize and focus your prayers:

How to Create a Prayer Card

There's no wrong way to create a prayer card. But here's one method that works well for me:

1. Label the card with a person's name. Take a moment to see that person in your mind's eye and think about various areas in his or her life. Sometimes I go for a month or two with just a name on the card as I consider how to pray.

2. Jot down phrases that capture your concerns or what you want to ask for. The order of the phrases is not important. Think beyond the person's immediate need (such as that a surgery would go well) to consider the big picture of his or her influence, character, calling, faith, and so on. Be specific about what you want to see. I like to write down the date so I know when I started praying about a specific item. Some helpful questions to ask yourself might be:

   - What is this person facing? What is it like to be him or her?
   - How do I feel about this person in general and in this particular situation?
   - What would I like to see the Spirit do in his or her heart and character?

   These questions help you to slow down and actually look at the person for whom you are praying. Like Jesus, you are incarnating into their world.

3. Put the Word to work by considering what particular Scripture you want to see working in that person's life. You can find a sample compilation of Scriptures by category and topic at

www.seeJesus.net/prayercards. Or, if you are using our prayer app, you will find a built-in selector tool to help you choose.

4. Slip into prayer for the person as you jot down short phrases to help you remember what you are asking.

That's it! It doesn't have to be complicated. Now watch what the Father does in the person's life over time.

Start with Three to Four Daily Cards

Begin by creating three to four cards that you pray through every day. Depending on your life situation, these cards might be for a spouse, a child, or a health need. One might be for a project at work that is causing you anxiety, or anything in life that is always on your mind. I call these daily cards, because I pray the same cards every day. I suggest praying about a minute over each card.

Slowly Add In Weekly Cards

Once praying a few cards has become a regular habit (say, after a month), then gradually add two to three weekly cards to each day of the week. I don't recommend adding more than a card or two a week at the most.

Here are some suggested categories for weekly cards:

- *Family cards.* One for each person in your family not featured in your daily cards.
- *People in suffering card.* Keep it general; even a list of names works. It's easy to get bogged down in medical details.
- *Friends card.* List friends on one card, or create a card for each close friend.
- *Non-Christians card.* Again, feel free to simply list them unless you want to create cards for individuals.

- *Church leadership card.* Your pastors, elders, deacons, staff, lay leaders, and so on.
- *Small group card.* Friends in your small group at church, if you are part of one.
- *Missionaries card.* Missionaries' names, locations, and what they are facing.
- *World issues card.* Terrorism, abortion, military conflicts, your country and its leaders—anything that burdens you.
- *Coworkers card.* Colleagues who are not necessarily close friends outside of your office.
- *Work card.* Key projects, major decisions, or difficult relationships at work.
- *Repentance card.* Sins that keep cropping up that you want help with.
- *Stewardship card.* Use of time, talent, and treasure.
- *Thanking God card.* Blessings you notice that you do not want to forget.
- *Worship card.* Scriptures or quotes that help you honor your Father.

I begin a prayer time with my daily cards, and then I add a few weekly cards to each day of the week. Our app will allow you to easily distinguish between daily and weekly cards and to set them on a rotation.

Regularly Create Cards for Yourself

Many of my prayer cards for myself emerge from my failures or weaknesses. That's when I get desperate and ask God for help! I call these my repentance cards, and I add new ones with some regularity. As God helps me in a particular area, I retire them.

Sometimes, Scripture will spark unexpected prayer cards. For example, maybe you are reading Matthew 17 and are struck by the account of the little boy with a demon, whose father begs Jesus for help. Jesus loves the man by delivering his son. The disciples privately ask Jesus why they could not deliver the boy. Jesus says, "Because of your little faith" (verse 20). He then says that with greater faith they will be able to do seemingly impossible things, such as moving mountains.

Your prayer card might be labeled "Myself—the need for mountain-moving faith." Simply record the Scripture, date the card, ask for that kind of faith, and watch. Almost always, I see God weave a prayer story.

Feel the Freedom

Remember, the whole idea of cards is for you to track what God is doing in each of your prayer stories. Don't worry that you might be "doing it wrong." Modify the system in any way that suits you.

As you create these cards, you may experience feelings of unbelief. Don't be surprised. You are seizing the corner of his garment. Don't let go.

For more resources, see www.seeJesus.net/prayercards.

Acknowledgments

WITHOUT OUR FAMILY STORIES, this book would be something of an empty shell. My family's willingness to share their stories makes praying nitty-gritty, accessible. I'm especially thankful to Jill, Kim, and Emily for opening up pieces of their lives.

A good book is a group process. As the author, you get too close to the book and need the honesty of good friends for perspective. These friends especially took the time to read and comment on the manuscript: Bob Allums, Gena Cobb, Boyd Clarke, Patricia Clarke, Julie Courtney, Lindy Davidson, Cathie Martin, Emily Miller, Jill Miller, Courtney Sneed, David Powlison, Glenn Urquhart, David Rice, and Annie Wald.

I am very thankful for Liz Heaney's careful editing—our second book together. She didn't just edit; she was a friend of the book, thinking through every piece, making sure it all fit together.

Carol Smith did the hard work of converting my scratchy drawings into all the charts that you see in the book.

The board of seeJesus, including Keith Albritton, Lynette Hull, Jeff Owen, Michael Simone, Tim Strawbridge, Doug Wallace, and Justin Wilson, continue to bless me with their wisdom, support, and encouragement.

Don Simpson's enthusiasm for the book, along with that of the entire NavPress staff, has made it possible to be published.

Notes

CHAPTER 1: "WHAT GOOD DOES IT DO?"
1. C. S. Lewis, *The Screwtape Letters* (New York: HarperCollins, 2001), 171.

CHAPTER 2: WHERE WE ARE HEADED
1. To speak the word *lasagna* Kim first selects the "Apple" icon for food groups. Then she selects the "Truck" icon, which narrows it down to Italian foods. Then she selects the third icon, "Rainbow." The layers of a rainbow are like the layers of lasagna. When she touches the third icon, the computer speaks.
2. Anthony Bloom, *Beginning to Pray* (New York: Paulist Press, 1970), 66.

CHAPTER 3: BECOME LIKE A LITTLE CHILD
1. The French Enlightenment thinker Jean-Jacques Rousseau taught that children were born good but were corrupted by people. Not surprisingly, Rousseau had five children, all of whom he abandoned to an orphanage. Leo Damrosch, *Jean-Jacques Rousseau: Restless Genius* (New York: Houghton Mifflin, 2005), 202.

CHAPTER 5: SPENDING TIME WITH YOUR FATHER
1. R. Scott Rodin, *Stewards in the Kingdom* (Downers Grove, IL: InterVarsity Press, 2000), 99.
2. Jesus is also fully God, but in his earthly life his divinity was veiled. Theologians debate what Paul meant in Philippians 2:6-7 (NASB) by "He . . . emptied himself" (ἐκένωσεν). We do not know how or to what extent Jesus' divinity was veiled. It is a mystery. We get a glimpse of his unveiled divinity at the Mount of Transfiguration.
3. Marjorie J. Thompson, foreword, in Martin Luther, *A Simple Way to Pray* (London: Westminster John Knox Press, 2000), 11.

CHAPTER 6: LEARNING TO BE HELPLESS
1. Ole Hallesby, *Prayer* (Minneapolis: Augsburg, 1994), 18–28.
2. Thomas Merton, quoted in Mark E. Thibodeaux, S.J., *Armchair Mystic* (Cincinnati, OH: St. Anthony Messenger, 2001), ix.
3. John of Landsburg, *A Letter from Jesus Christ* (New York: Crossroad, 1981), 58–59.

CHAPTER 7: CRYING "ABBA"—CONTINUOUSLY
1. St. Augustine, *Confessions* (New York: Oxford University Press, 1998), 3.
2. *The Philokalia: The Complete Text*, vol. 4, compiled by St. Nikodimos and St. Makarios, trans. and ed. G. E. H. Palmer, Philip Sherrard, and Kallistos Ware (London: Faber and Faber, 1999), 206.

CHAPTER 8: BENDING YOUR HEART TO YOUR FATHER

1. David Powlison, "'Peace Be Still': Learning Psalm 131 by Heart," *Journal of Biblical Counseling* 18, no. 3 (Spring 2000): 2.
2. This passage includes my adaptations to the English Standard Version translation. The Hebrew preposition in Psalm 131:2 reads "on its mother" and not "with its mother."
3. Archibald A. Hodge, *The Life of Charles Hodge* (Manchester, NH: Ayer, 1979), 13.

CHAPTER 9: UNDERSTANDING CYNICISM

1. R. R. Reno, "Postmodern Irony and Petronian Humanism," *Mars Hill Audio Resource Essay*, vol. 67 (March/April 2004): 7.
2. Yoani Sánchez, quoted in Joseph Contreras, "Island of Failed Promises," *Time*, March 3, 2008, 31.

CHAPTER 10: FOLLOWING JESUS OUT OF CYNICISM

1. Alan Jacobs, *The Narnian: The Life and Imagination of C. S. Lewis* (San Francisco: HarperSanFrancisco, 2005), xxv.
2. C. S. Lewis, *The Abolition of Man* (New York: Macmillan, 1978), 81.
3. Jacobs, *The Narnian*, 158.

CHAPTER 12: WHY ASKING IS SO HARD

1. N. T. Wright, *The Crown and the Fire* (Grand Rapids, MI: Eerdmans, 1992), 42.
2. For an example of a non-Western culture, the Japanese emperor prays publicly at shrines to the spirits of Japanese soldiers killed in World War II.
3. Nancy Pearcey, *Total Truth* (Wheaton, IL: Crossway, 2004), 101–106.
4. Pearcey, *Total Truth*, 106.
5. C. S. Lewis, *Surprised by Joy* (New York: Harcourt, 1955), 170.
6. Walter Hooper, *C. S. Lewis: A Complete Guide to His Life & Works* (New York: HarperOne, 1998), 583.
7. This quote is ubiquitously attributed to Johannes Kepler, but the source is unknown.
8. "Interview with Peter Jennings," Beliefnet.com, http://www.beliefnet.com/Faiths/2000/06/Interview-With-Peter-Jennings.aspx (accessed October 4, 2016).
9. Charles Malik, *The Wonder of Being* (Waco, TX: Word, 1974), 94.
10. Robertson McQuilkin, "Muriel's Blessing," *Christianity Today*, February 5, 1996, 33.
11. Dana Tierney, "Coveting Luke's Faith," *New York Times Magazine*, January 11, 2004.
12. Malik, *The Wonder of Being*, 69.
13. Albert Einstein, "Einstein to Phyllis Wright," January 24, 1936, AEA 52-337, quoted in Walter Isaacson, *Einstein: His Life and Universe* (New York: Simon & Schuster, 2007), 551.

CHAPTER 13: WHY WE CAN ASK

1. Albert Einstein, "Einstein to Phyllis Wright," January 24, 1936, AEA 52-337, quoted in Walter Isaacson, *Einstein: His Life and Universe* (New York: Simon & Schuster, 2007), 388.
2. Isaacson, *Einstein*, 389.
3. Albert Einstein, "Einstein to Herbert S. Goldstein," April 25, 1929, AEA 33-272, quoted in Walter Isaacson, *Einstein: His Life and Universe* (New York: Simon & Schuster, 2007), 551.

CHAPTER 14: HOW PERSONAL IS GOD?

1. John Westerhoff, *Spiritual Life: The Foundation for Preaching and Teaching* (Louisville, KY: Westminster John Knox, 1994), 63.
2. Augustine, quoted in Donald G. Bloesch, *The Struggle of Prayer* (Colorado Springs: Helmers and Howard, 1988), 75. Another possible version of this is "God is loved gratis; one asks for no other gift. Whoever seeks another gift from God, makes what he desires to have a more precious gift than God himself. God's gift is himself" (Augustine, *Expositions on the Psalms*, in Psalm 72, 32; Migne *Patrologia Latina* 36.923).
3. James Houston, *The Transforming Power of Prayer* (Colorado Springs: NavPress, 1996), 27, 37.
4. Bowen Matthews, quoted in C. Jack Orr, "A First-Time Visit to an Old-Time Place," *DreamSeeker Magazine* 2, no. 4 (Autumn 2002): 9.
5. Reinhold Niebuhr, *Human Nature* (New York: Scribner, 1964), 201.
6. *The Village*, dir. M. Night Shyamalan (Burbank, CA: Touchstone Pictures/Buena Vista Home Entertainment, 2004).
7. Philip Lawler, "A Life of Purity," *Wall Street Journal*, Monday, September 8, 1997, A18.

CHAPTER 15: WHAT DO WE DO WITH JESUS' EXTRAVAGANT PROMISES ABOUT PRAYER?

1. Dr. Bob Burrelli, "Questions & Answers," *Songtime Newsletter*, November 1998.
2. Vern Poythress, "Keep on Praying," *Decision*, October 1998, 33.
3. Thomas Merton, *No Man Is an Island* (New York: Shambhala, 2005), 124.

CHAPTER 16: WHAT WE DON'T ASK FOR: "OUR DAILY BREAD"

1. For a more careful discussion of this, see J. D. G. Dunn, "Prayer," in *Dictionary of Jesus and the Gospels*, ed. Joel Green, Scot McKnight, and I. Howard Marshall (Downers Grove, IL: InterVarsity Press, 1992), 622.
2. Albert Einstein, quoted in George Viereck, "What Life Means to Einstein," *Saturday Evening Post*, October 26, 1929, 117.

CHAPTER 20: A FATHER'S LOVE

1. David Powlison, *The Journal of Biblical Counseling* 12, no. 1 (Fall 1993): 2–6.

CHAPTER 21: UNANSWERED PRAYER: UNDERSTANDING THE PATTERNS OF STORY

1. "Future grace" is John Piper's language.
2. Corrie ten Boom, *In My Father's House* (Grand Rapids, MI: Revell, 2000), 79.

CHAPTER 23: UNDERSTANDING HOW LAMENTS WORK

1. The only exception to this is God's response to Job in Job 38–39, but even then the whole weight of the book of Job critiques Job's three friends, who don't like Job's laments. Eliphaz finds Job's laments impatient (4:2), unbelieving (4:4-5), and vexing (5:2).
2. Insight from David Powlison, director of Christian Counseling and Educational Foundation.

CHAPTER 24: HOW GOD PLACES HIMSELF IN THE STORY

1. *Gospel of Peter* 10:2-3.

CHAPTER 25: PRAYING WITHOUT A STORY
1. Philip Yancey, *Prayer: Does It Make Any Difference?* (Grand Rapids, MI: Zondervan, 2006), 64–65.

CHAPTER 26: HOPE: THE END OF THE STORY
1. I've taken this image from Frederick Buechner, *Telling the Truth: The Gospel as Tragedy, Comedy, and Fairy Tale* (New York: HarperCollins, 1977).
2. Ruth Pitter, quoted in Alan Jacobs, *The Narnian: The Life and Imagination of C. S. Lewis* (San Francisco: HarperSanFrancisco, 2005), xxv.
3. Jacobs, *The Narnian*, xxiii.

CHAPTER 27: LIVING IN GOSPEL STORIES
1. This story first appeared as an article, "Loving Kim," in *Discipleship Journal*, September/October 2002.
2. Yann Martel, *The Life of Pi* (New York: Harcourt, 2001), 53.
3. C. S. Lewis, *Voyage of the Dawn Treader* (New York: Macmillian, 1967), 89.
4. Carl Sandburg, *Abraham Lincoln: The Prairie Years and the War Years* (New York: Harcourt, 1954), 664.
5. Sandburg, *Abraham Lincoln*, 665.

CHAPTER 28: USING PRAYER TOOLS
1. James D. G. Dunn, *The Epistles to the Colossians and to Philemon* (Grand Rapids, MI: Eerdmans, 1996), 316.

CHAPTER 29: KEEPING TRACK OF THE STORY: USING PRAYER CARDS
1. Geraldine Taylor, *Behind the Ranges* (Chicago: Moody, 1964), 140–158. Fraser's story was retold by his daughter in Eileen Fraser Crossman, *Mountain Rain* (Littleton, CO: OMF International, 1982).

CHAPTER 32: PRAYER JOURNALING: BECOMING AWARE OF THE INTERIOR JOURNEY
1. St. Augustine, *Confessions* VIII.12.29.
2. Peter J. Leithart, summarizing Edward Said in "Bunyan, Defoe, and the Novel," *First Things*, November 5, 2005, https://www.firstthings.com/blogs/leithart/2005/11/bunyan-defoe-and-the-novel.
3. St. Augustine, *The Confessions of St. Augustine* (Grand Rapids, MI: Revell, 2008), 11.

CHAPTER 34: UNFINISHED STORIES
1. Tony Snow, "Cancer's Unexpected Blessings," *Christianity Today*, July 2007, http://www.christianitytoday.com/ct/2007/july/25.30.html (accessed October 4, 2016).

About the Author

PAUL E. MILLER is executive director of seeJesus, the global discipling mission he founded in 1999 to help Christians and non-Christians alike "see Jesus." Today, seeJesus works in over 30 countries and has books and interactive Bible study materials translated into at least a dozen languages.

Paul is the author of more than a dozen interactive Bible studies and books, including the bestselling *A Praying Life* and *J-Curve*. If you read any of Paul's writing, you'll quickly see that he loves to tell stories—most of which start with his own failures and mishaps and end with God's faithfulness. Paul is married to Jill, who is known for her sense of humor and faith. They have six children and a growing number of grandchildren and live in the Philadelphia area. Follow @_PaulEMiller on Twitter, listen to the *Seeing Jesus with Paul Miller* podcast, and learn more at seeJesus.net.

Grab a Discussion Guide

A Praying Life Discussion Guide leads readers step by step through the pages of the expanded second edition of the best-selling book. Includes a Leader's Guide and 18-week reading schedule.

Available at
seeJesus.net

Go Deeper with a Seminar or Cohort

A PRAYING LIFE

· In Person or Online ·

Learn to pray by praying! Join the thousands who have experienced an *A Praying Life*® seminar or cohort. Browse upcoming 10-week cohorts or schedule a seminar at your church today.

seminars@seeJesus.net
seeJesus.net/events

Power Up

"*A winsome and utterly compelling rallying cry to step out of the smiling unbelief infecting our churches.*"
— **Dane Ortlund**

Discover how the Holy Spirit uniquely powers the church, and how praying together is the spark that ignites the world's mightiest spiritual force—the everyday saints around us.

Available at
seeJesus.net/APrayingChurch

Enter the J-Curve®

"Take time with this book. You will become a deeper, wiser, truer person. You will become more humble, more joyous, more purposeful. And you will walk more steadily in the light."
— **David Powlison**

The *J-Curve* is so encouraging, so liberating, that once you see it, you can't unsee it! You'll find yourself joyfully dying and rising with Jesus in everyday life.

Available at
seeJesus.net/J-Curve

About

seeJesus is a global discipling mission passionate about equipping the worldwide church to reflect all the beauty of Jesus.

✉ **Subscribe at seeJesus.net/joinus**

🎙 **Listen at seeJesus.net/podcast**

f **Facebook.com/seeJesus.net**

📷 **Instagram.com/SeeingJesus**

Scan to learn more about us.